W9-BIK-460

TAKEOFF!

TAKEOFF!

The Story of America's First Woman Pilot for a Major Airline

by BONNIE TIBURZI

An Eleanor Friede Book

CROWN PUBLISHERS, INC.

NEW YORK

Grateful acknowledgment is made to
Academy Chicago Publishers for permission
to reprint material from *The Fun of It*
by Amelia Earhart
and to *Harper's Bazaar* for permission to reprint
excerpted material from the article entitled
"Bonnie Tiburzi: In Control"
copyright © 1973 by The Hearst Corporation.

Published by Crown Publishers, Inc.,
One Park Avenue, New York, New York 10016, and
published simultaneously in Canada
by General Publishing Company Limited
Manufactured in the United States of America
Library of Congress Cataloging in Publication Data
Tiburzi, Bonnie
Takeoff!
"An Eleanor Friede Book."
1. Tiburzi, Bonnie. 2. Women air pilots—United States—Biography. I. Title.
TL540.T52A33 1984 629.13'092'4 [B] 83-18909
ISBN 0-517-55263-9
Book design by Camilla Filancia
10 9 8 7 6 5 4 3 2 1
First Edition

PUBLISHER'S NOTE: This book is autobiographical. However, some names and other identifying details have been changed to protect the privacy of the individuals involved.

To Mother and Daddy

Valerie Moolman has unscrambled my notes,
transcribed my tapes and patiently listened to my tales.
Without her endless energy and strong friendship,
Takeoff! *would still be just part of my dreams.*

Contents

Acknowledgments

Both this book and my career hinge on a single event.

In 1973 American Airlines hired me as a pilot when no other major airline seemed willing to take that chance. For the sense of fundamental fairness they displayed, American's top management and flight department deserve special recognition.

I wish to thank Captain "Bud" Ehmann, Vice-President–Flight, for his encouragement and his efforts to provide opportunities for women in aviation.

My warm thanks go to all my friends and colleagues who appear in the following pages, and who gave me invaluable help by lending their time, sharing their experiences and giving their expertise. Thanks, too, to fellow crew members Captain Greg Gaudet and First Officer Dick Baum, who do not appear in the book, but whose cooperation and technical advice are greatly appreciated.

To my editor, Eleanor Friede, aviation authority Robert Buck and writer Doug Terman, my special thanks for their continuing belief that I had a story to tell and should tell it in a book.

TAKEOFF!

1

In a Place Called the Cockpit

It was just another night flight, not much more than an air taxi ride from La Guardia to Buffalo, the sort of bid you draw when you're a young flight officer with only a few weeks on the line and no seniority. Thunderstorms had threatened all day, but so far the weather had held in a glowering sort of way.

In the darkness of the leaden summer night I did my preflight check. The only slight irregularity was that one generator bore a placard reading INOPERATIVE. But that presented no problem. It had no effect on the operation of the three engines of the Boeing 727, all of which were running flawlessly. All I would have to do would be to download some of the less vital electrical functions, such as galley power when not needed and the fans used to draw air into the plane during takeoff while the flaps are down.

We taxied and lifted off into the murk, Captain Roger Norton in the left seat, Copilot Larry Fuller on his right, and myself at the flight engineer's desk behind them. The flaps were up, pressure controls set, and my after-takeoff check list was done. Everything was normal if a little bumpy as we cruised at 20,000 feet. Number One Flight Attendant Jessie Knowles sat in the cockpit talking to us, her preliminary duties taken care of and everything in the cabin under control. In a moment we would be climbing sedately through 24,000 feet on the way to our cruising altitude.

I glanced at my panel again, automatically double-checking the compact array of lights and gauges. Fuel tanks 1 and 3 were turned off, fuel tank 2 was on, cabin maintaining the correct air pressure. I had set the cabin altitude to climb at 500 feet per minute, much more slowly than the aircraft's rate of climb, so that at a height of 24,000 feet the cabin pressure would correspond to a comfortable altitude of no more than 1,000 to 1,500 feet.

Outside, the sky was heavy with unspent rain. Cumulonimbus clouds drifted around us. The air was unstable, perhaps turbulent enough to compel some attention from nervous passengers but nothing to cause alarm. Just some little potholes in the sky.

With heart-stopping suddenness there was a sucking of air through the cockpit. My ears popped. Blood pounded in my head and everything went black for one split second. Swift, simultaneous actions appeared as if on slow-motion film, playing out in stately, measured steps the reflex movements that in fact took place in a flash of time.

With the first rush of air I knew the cabin pressure had plummeted. It was as if the plane had become a balloon losing its air in one whooshing gust. Still in that first instant, reaching for my oxygen mask, I looked at my pressure controls and saw that the cabin altitude was shooting up at a rate of two thousand feet a minute. I pulled on my mask and turned to the flight attendant to tell her—but she was already up and out, in one instinctive swift move to be with her passengers. Admiration flooded one part of my mind as another part realized that the captain had leveled off at twenty thousand feet, preparing to descend if necessary, wisely not making any drastic moves.

In that same moment I reached automatically for the toggle switch marked PASSENGER OXYGEN. And stopped. I had a sudden memory of being in the training simulator: the same darkness in the cockpit, broken by the glimmering gold and silver of the instruments, and outside the silhouette of clouds against the moonshine, a lurching loss of pressure and a voice reminding me, "Don't pull that switch too soon. You don't know that you need it. Wait. Evaluate."

I left the switch untouched, thinking of that great orange grove of oxygen masks dropping down and enveloping the passengers. There's no need to scare them—not yet. Don't do anything to aggravate a situation we haven't yet defined.

Intent on my panel, I worked with my pressurization controls. What we had was a rapid depressurization. What we didn't have was a reason for it. When I adjust my pressurization controls as we climb, outflow valves open and shut to suck out little quantities of air. When the cabin suddenly starts to climb at two thousand feet a minute, the indication is that the air is being sucked out in one enormous gulp. One of two things can be wrong: there's a nasty hole in the plane and in seconds we're going to have an explosive decompression with a huge bang as part of the cargo compartment falls out, in which case we have to get down fast before everybody turns blue, or else there's an outflow valve stuck wide open, and it's sucking all the air out.

But there was nothing on my panel to pinpoint the problem, or even to indicate any problem. The panel lights, small gleams of amber, showed normal configuration.

I heard the muffled voice of Captain Norton talking through his oxygen mask. "Turn around and help her," he said to the copilot. Larry turned, an oddly clumsy figure in his mask, saw the lights glowing on my panel and made an instinctive gesture with his hand.

Just as instinctively I said, "Would you please turn around and do your job?"

Like a diver deep under water, he turned clumsily away.

There was no need for his help at my desk, and he knew it.

My ears pounded and the adrenaline pumped as we skimmed through the dark. I wondered whether we had blown a hole somewhere in the baggage compartment. One of us would have to go back and check it out, or we'd have to land at the nearest airfield—or both.

The cabin altitude was climbing. Five thousand feet . . . six thousand feet. I was icy-excited, conscious of being in a very small world of panels and controls, as beloved and familiar as the dashboard of my first car, locked in by silvery darkness and the capricious currents of the air. We three became one with the machine.

There was a change on the panel. The cabin altitude was slowing, reversing, steadying, coming back to normal. There was no big bang, no dramatic resolution. Whatever had happened was over. It might only have been a sticky outflow valve after all.

The captain pushed the throttle forward. The nose of the aircraft pointed up and we started to climb. Masks off, we looked human again. Larry half turned and gave a faint grin. He seemed relieved. Well, so was I, but why that particular look at me?

Now that I had time to think, the answer dawned on me. The captain had been a little apprehensive of the flight officer in the third seat. "Omigod, the girl's done something wrong! Help her!"

Damn them, anyway! But maybe I shouldn't blame them for being unsure of me. Not only was I new to the job but I was the first woman they had flown with. For the first and almost the last time, I was aware that my being a woman in the cockpit, that bastion of masculinity, was more of a problem for the men than it was for me. I was used to male fliers. They weren't used to me.

Airline flying is a macho job, sought after by the guys with the right stuff and a particular kind of cool swagger. But a masculine image is not required in the pilots' seats. It may be reassuring, but coordination, training and a fierce desire to do the job as well as it can be done are far more important than muscles.

Perhaps if I had been bigger, it might have been easier for

all of us. I am 5 feet 6¼ inches tall, weigh in at 120 pounds, and am distinctly lacking in bulging biceps. I go to exercise classes and I jog. My dark hair hangs down almost to my shoulders because both my employers and I like it that way. I wear a frilly blouse and a designer uniform cap.

When I started flying out of Buffalo in 1973, I was an unsophisticated twenty-four-year-old only subliminally conscious of what it might mean to be the first woman to join the flight crew of a major airline. In small ways it became apparent that the men did not know how to treat me. Were they supposed to open doors for me and carry my bags? Should they compliment me on the cut of my uniform or pretend they didn't notice? Was I going to be their kid sister or a stiff-necked prude getting uptight about their sexist jokes? Does one pilot ask another pilot for a date?

And now the bigger questions had come up. Would I panic in a crisis? Did I really know my stuff? Well, doggone. I hoped they knew the answers now. I thought they did. After that one instant when I'd said indignantly that I would do my own work, the two men had left me to it. We had become a smoothly functioning team. Something had happened. It was *our* world up there. We knew what we were there for, and nothing else existed for us but our jobs. So one flight crew member wore lipstick, and now and then tossed her hair. So what?

Jessie Knowles brought coffee and went away. I felt something ease inside me, and it was not simply a sense of relief. There was something new in the atmosphere of the cockpit.

We flew on through the bumpy clouds, more aware than usual of the eerie beauty of the night and the throbbing of the 727's powerful engines. Old-timers, I reflected, think there's no longer any romance in flying. If you're not in an old biplane with the wind singing in the baling wires and tearing at your goggles, you're not flying. Many famous fliers have written about the joy and the wonder of flight in days long gone. Charles and Anne Lindbergh, Antoine de Saint-Exupéry, Amelia Earhart—these people lived, breathed and spoke the language of flying and knew the blessed immensity of the sky before it was mapped by jet trails. Nothing can match what they experienced.

Don't let anybody kid you. Flying is still magic. Flying jets is exhilarating. It may not be as much of a thrill in the passenger seat, but up front, where the action is, the airplane is a marvelous man-made bird soaring through an element that man started to explore only in this century.

All-night flights are drudgery. And yet they're not. Sitting them out with eyes bloodshot and muscles stiffening, you see the sun set, the moon rise, and the sun rise again, doing things to the clouds that make your heart lift. It's worth the weariness. You forget that there's dirt and smoke down below, and junkyards and mean streets and poverty and despair. The sky is clean and radiant, a great living ocean of buoyant eddies and currents, sometimes violent with storm but never petty with malice, a world above a world—and you are in it, in a tiny little capsule called the cockpit, looking out and down at miracles. There is the aurora borealis; there are the great, bejeweled spectral shapes that are our stars and galaxies. Down below, ahead, is a tiny glint of light that becomes a brilliant sparkle, then a glittering carpet and then a welcoming city.

I was warm in the glow of that cockpit, feeling humble and exalted at the same time. It seemed as though there was nobody up there but the three of us, three people in a closed-in intimacy that has nothing to do with sex. Or hardly anything. . . .

Voices murmured. We began our descent. The magic glow below turned into Buffalo. Not the city of my dreams, but my temporary base. I had my first airline job and I loved it.

There was a small party later that night at the copilot's house. We talked very little about the evening flight, because in fact it had not been eventful. Some kind of reserve had dropped away from the men. I had shared something with them, and now we were comrades. It was as if they had seen me with new eyes and said to themselves, "Well, yeah, she *is* our flight engineer. She managed to do her job okay." That's it, and no point talking about it.

For a moment I was alone, relaxing with a glass of wine and trying not to overdo the potato chips and dip. A young man who had come in with one of the flight attendants stopped beside me, shoveled up some chips, and said tentatively, "I didn't get what it is that you do with the airlines. . . ."

"I'm a flight officer."

Eyebrows rose. "What does that mean? You schedule flights?"

"No, I'm a pilot, currently flying as flight engineer." I tried to look modest while feeling very proud.

Recognition dawned. "Oh, you're Bonnie! *That* Bonnie!" He grinned cheerfully. "You'll fly me, right?"

This was not a line of conversation that entertained me greatly.

"Yeah, that Bonnie. What do you do?"

"No, listen. I want to know—how did you get into this business? What made you want to do it?"

Always the same questions. Funny, how men ask them in that curiously resentful way. Or was he thinking, oh, isn't she cute. It was sometimes hard to tell.

"It's just an idea I grew up with," I said vaguely. "Actually, I don't know how to do anything else."

And then Larry's wife joined us and we began to talk about the political happenings of the day.

2

How I Got into This Line of Work

My first job in the aviation business was as a sideshow barker at the Danbury Fair. "Step right up!" I'd bellow seductively into the mike, fourteen years old, pigtailed and with no shame at all. Ordinarily I was very shy, but for some reason the microphone transformed me. "Two dollars and fifty cents for the ride of your life! See Danbury as you've never seen it before!" Shy families and bare-chested teenage boys dragging their girlfriends stepped up and handed me their money.

I'd give them their tickets and their change.

"You gonna fly us?"

"No, but I could."

"Oh, yeah, sure!"

"Opportunity of a lifetime, folks. Get your cheap rides here. It's fun, it's safe. We never lost a passenger in our lives. Get a bird's-eye view of the fair with Tiburzi Airways. Tiburzi flies the fair!"

Tiburzi Airways was trying to develop a commuter service between the Danbury area and New York, a pioneer venture in the early sixties and a difficult proposition. While my parents were working on it I'd been getting my first flying lessons at my father's knee—either sitting on his lap or in the front seat with him. By the time I was eleven or twelve I was already familiar with the instrument panels of half a dozen types of planes. I also knew how to fly them, theoretically if not in practice. Flying was a family occupation that involved all five of us, except that my mother and sister showed no interest in taking the controls. My brother did, and so did I.

My father, Gus Tiburzi, had been an airline pilot until he struck out on his own with an FBO in Danbury. An FBO is a fixed base operation. In the case of Tiburzi Airways it meant a flight training school, charter flights, sightseeing trips and pleasure rides for whoever wanted them. I used to hang around the airport after school and on weekends. To me, the hangars and the airstrip were an extension of our house. The mechanics and the flight instructors were my best friends. I got used to being around planes. There were little Cessnas, a twin-engine Cessna 310, a twin Apache and an enormous Lockheed Lodestar that carried as many as twenty people for our bigger charter parties. They were like a fleet of private cabs. Other people jumped into cars for trips, but whenever we went anywhere we all piled into one of the planes.

Flying permeated our lives. Many of the family friends were old-time fliers—Gill Robb Wilson, one of the World War I Lafayette Escadrille; Earroll Boyd, the first Canadian to fly the Atlantic; and Duke Krantz, a daring wing walker for Gates Flying Circus.

With them, and with the mechanics and pilots, I was absolutely at home. These blunt-spoken roughnecks and adventurers were my friends. I had school friends too, but school itself was a nuisance, and short of being with the planes there was nothing I liked better than to listen to the old-timers share their memories and tell their hair-raising tales with broad grins that made me wonder if they weren't laying it on a little thick.

They shared a sort of gutsy camaraderie that, it seemed to me, could be possible only in the world of flying. They were free and easy and everything they did was fun. I liked them better than everyone else I knew.

The only drawback to a great life was that I was not yet

actually flying. I got to wash and polish the airplanes and to fuel them, and I knew how to fly them, but I was too young to take the controls alone and get my license.

I have a very vivid memory of my brother Allan soloing at that time, right in the midst of the raucous activity of the fair. It was his sixteenth birthday and my father wanted him to solo on that day. I could hardly stand it. I knew I wasn't old enough, but I was also sure that I could fly those things as well as anyone.

And Allan was really cool. My mother got weak at the knees and had to sit down, but my father was very proud of his textbook performance and I was green with envy. In two years I, too, would be sixteen and be able to solo. But two years was a long time and I found it tough to wait my turn.

The wait was longer than any of us anticipated. The family dream of building a commuter airline service between Danbury and the New York airports was ahead of its time. Suddenly Tiburzi Airways was grounded and we were out of the aviation business. My brother and sister, both older than I, went off to private schools, and my parents took me down to Florida.

All our airplanes were gone, and so were the free flying lessons.

"Bonnie! You're going to grow up to be nothing! Don't you ever study?"

Of course I studied, and Miss Weston, a guidance counselor, knew it. I was at school in Pompano Beach. For a significant part of the year I studied hard and got myself on the honor roll.

"Yes, ma'am. I'm on the honor roll," I pointed out.

"Yes, but only in the tennis season, and we know why that is, don't we?"

We did. It was something I was quite proud of. I was the

only tenth-grader on the varsity tennis team. The other players were all juniors and seniors. A prerequisite to being on the tennis team was a place on the honor roll, so immediately before and during the tennis season I studied hard and with absolute concentration so that I could get my work done quickly. There seemed little point in doing homework at any other time of year.

Generally speaking, I liked living in Florida. I liked being on the tennis team. I liked skipping class and going to the beach. I loved to surf. There was only one thing about hanging out with the sun-and-surf bunch that struck me as a little strange, and that was the delineation of sexual roles. All the boys and girls would go down to the beach together. All the girls but one would sit in their bikinis on the sand. I'd get my surfboard and run down to the water with the rest of the guys and go surfing.

A pattern of some sort was already starting to form, though I was barely conscious of it at the time. There were boyfriends, and then there were boys who were friends. Sports were the breath of life to me, and the boys were more interested in sports than most of the other girls. I had grown up with the men at the Danbury airfield and now I was growing up with the beach boys in Florida. In a way I thought of myself as one of the boys, which is not a thought that pleased me when I recognized it. I was simply doing what I loved to do, with people in whose company I felt most comfortable.

My father's flying buddies still dropped around at our house. Most were members of the order of the Quiet Birdmen, or QBs, a brotherhood of not-so-quiet aviators whose credentials dated back to World War I and those daring young men in their flying machines.

I missed the airplanes. Once or twice a year we'd rent a plane and take a little flight, but it was nothing like the old Danbury days. And yet my life was saturated with the idea of flying. It was what the real people did. It was the only truly important thing in life. People would ask me, "What're you going to do when you grow up?" I'd say, "I'm going to be an airline pilot, just like my father was."

They looked indulgent and slightly amused. Pigtailed Bonnie. Cute kid. She'll grow out of that.

I drifted idly through school, applying myself only when absolutely necessary. Between tennis and surfing I had very little time for study. Classes were no inspiration at all. I tried to sign up for shop and was refused. Home economics was what the girls were supposed to take. So I took it. I knew that shop would have been much more fun. I resented being forced into home ec and at the same time felt slightly guilty about wanting to do what the boys did.

Years later, when need and experience had taught me how to cook and keep house, I read something by Amelia Earhart —one of the most liberated of women.

"It has always seemed to me," she wrote, "that boys and girls are educated very differently. Even from the early grades they take different subjects. For instance, boys are usually put into the woodworking classes and girls into sewing or cooking —willy-nilly. I know many boys who should, I am sure, be making pies and girls who are much better fitted for manual training than domestic science. Too often little attention is paid to individual talent. Instead, education goes on dividing people according to their sex, and putting them in little feminine or masculine pigeonholes."

That was written in 1932. To a large extent it is true even today. As a teenager in the late sixties, I found the traditional pattern still very much in evidence, and it made me uneasily aware that I was going to have to find my own pigeonhole. I was far from ready to commit myself to airline flying as a career, but there was nothing else I was interested in doing.

"Well, that's quite an ambition, Bonnie. But it's not very practical. You know you can't really be an airline pilot. There aren't any women airline pilots."

"But there are plenty of women fliers. Why not on the airlines?"

"Because the airlines don't want to hire them."

I supposed this was true, although I couldn't see why it should be. The impression seeped into me that neither the airlines nor the passengers would trust a woman pilot. It was made clear that if I really believed I could fly for a scheduled airline I was living a pipe dream and I had better sort myself out.

Only gradually did I discover that women can do anything they set their minds to. No honest aspiration should be considered beyond us. We simply have to keep on proving ourselves as we try to go where no woman has gone before. Earhart knew this, and knew why. "From the period when girls were not supposed to be able to do anything comes a natural doubt whenever they attempt new or different activities."

Times change. But not enough, and not fast enough. Every generation is a new generation of prejudices, of misperceptions about women.

In 1967, a fresh and skimpily educated high school graduate, I was only dimly aware of the unfairness of a tradition that barred me from the career I chose. Silly of me, to think that I could do what my father had done and what my brother was preparing to do. Deep down, even I did not believe that I could. Fly the planes, yes. Get the job, no.

It was easy enough to talk about flying that airliner like Daddy used to do. In practical terms, I had no idea what I was going to do with my life. Maybe my guidance counselor had been right. Maybe I never would amount to anything.

Mine are not the kind of parents to sit idly by while a daughter of theirs grows up to be nothing. We had agreed that college was not the next step for me, but neither was I going to hang out and be a beach bum or an airport groupie. If I were to wind up doing anything worthwhile—my parents decided —I must acquire something I could later call a background. My sister, Anita, had gone to Nice to learn French and then moved on to Sweden to be with our grandmother. The least I could do before going to whatever Florida college might eventually accept me was to see something of the world and learn another language.

In September of 1967 I arrived in Tours, eighteen years old and still growing, ready and eager to become well-rounded. As arranged by an exchange agency, I was to attend l'Institut d'Etudes Françaises de Touraine to study French and live with a French family to practice it. The exchange part was that I was a paying room-and-boarder, available to help with cooking and housecleaning.

It didn't take long to find out that life in a French suburb was not for me and that this French family all yearned to speak a foreign language—mine. My French was going nowhere. I hitchhiked to Paris with another young boarder and trotted off to the Sorbonne to see what kind of jobs might be listed on the bulletin board. There were several under the heading of *Au Pair*.

I found the perfect setup in no time. The Polinis, a young couple with three children, lived directly across from the Luxembourg Gardens and near the Sorbonne. We took to each other at once. Within a couple of days I had collected my bags from Tours and settled in Paris.

Now this was more like it, I thought. Here I was in the Latin Quarter, near the Boulevard Saint Michel, within an easy stroll of the famous Sorbonne. The Polinis, in spite of their name, were vociferously French and delighted to share their language. Their apartment was one of twelve in the building, occupying half of the fifth floor. On the seventh floor were twelve small rooms, one per apartment, which the residents used as storage rooms or studies or to lodge their *au pairs*. Up there in my seventh-floor walkup I could look out of my window and see the Eiffel Tower and feel that I was truly in the center of Paris, the very heart of France.

The heart of France did not have an attached bathroom but the communal washroom down the hall was adequate for basic needs. In payment for about fourteen easy hours of work a week I got my room, a breakfast of *café au lait* and bread with the family, $10 a month and one bath a week. My job was to pick up the two little girls and the boy after school and take them to the gardens to play. Then I would shepherd them home, give them their baths, polish their shoes and turn them over—squeaky-clean and shining—to their parents. If I did some extra babysitting of an evening or weekend I was rewarded with either a dinner or an extra bath.

I had not been long at the Polinis when I heard from home that my brother Allan had been hired at Seaboard World Airlines to fly the DC-8-68, which was the largest transport aircraft in existence at that time. Only twenty-one when he was hired, he would be twenty-two when he started to fly copilot—the youngest pilot of his time to fly that giant of an airplane.

I was pleased and proud. He was a superb pilot and, even at that age, an extremely experienced one. He deserved his success.

So Allan was an airline pilot. I was envious.

For the next few weeks, picking up the Polini youngsters and giving occasional English lessons in the gardens or at sidewalk cafés, I thought about what I might do with my life. For a while I had wanted to be a dancer, but that never became a consuming passion. At another time I considered being a veterinarian, but again I shied away. There was only one thing I really wanted to be.

Face it, I told myself, I want to be an airline pilot! A pilot for a major airline. And that is all I want to be.

But I'm not ready for it. I need more time in Europe. This is my kind of finishing school, and I want to stay.

Yes, but I need more formal education for whatever I want to do. I don't know the requirements for an airline pilot. I almost don't want to find out. First requirement: male. Why doesn't my brother tell me how to go about preparing myself? Because I am a woman. I do not meet the first requirement. He does not want me in the Macho Men's Club.

But I understand the mechanics of flying. I am enveloped in the mystique of it. My life is so closely intertwined with flying that I *must* fly. It is not that I want to imitate my father and my brother, or follow in anybody's footsteps. It is that I am acutely aware of flying as an essential part of my life. A passion for it has seeped into me by osmosis. I must learn. Too bad we no longer had our own airplanes. But that is not going to stop me from learning.

With a curious reluctance I wrote home and said that I had finally decided what I wanted to do. I would stay in Europe for another year or so but then I would come home and put my mind to becoming an airline pilot. Undoubtedly the gaps in my scientific and mathematical knowledge were going to cause me some serious problems, but with hard work I was sure I would overcome them. And so on.

Back came a warm letter from Pompano Beach followed by a package from my father. It contained his old, disk-shaped computer in its weather-beaten leather case and his aviator glasses in theirs, both cases initialed *A.R.T.* for August Robert Tiburzi.

I was touched and slightly shaken. The gift seemed to express a confidence I had not yet earned. I had not expected my father to react that way. It had always seemed to me that he thought it was fine for me to fly for fun, but not to try to do a man's job.

No matter. All Paris was still open to me and I was not going home yet. I tucked the computer and the glasses away and went back to the full-time business of living in France.

Paris in the springtime of 1968 was not the idyll it had been for the previous months. Student demonstrations against the de Gaulle government, followed by violent workers' strikes, turned the street scene into a riot. Communications were shattered. There was no telephone service. Airlines and trains stopped running. The only news of home came through American Express, the message center for most Americans in Paris. When I heard they were arranging bus service to get Americans to Geneva, I felt I had better grab the chance. Reducing my belongings to one enormous suitcase, I hopped on the bus before dawn one morning and tried to figure out how I was going to spend a very long evening in Geneva.

As usual, I had hardly any money. Enough for a snack and a bus ride, but that was about all. I did have a railroad ticket from Geneva to Rome, and in Rome I would pick up my airline ticket home. The immediate problem was that the bus was due to arrive in Geneva late that afternoon and the next train to Rome didn't leave until almost four in the morning. What would I do for all those hours?

A woman must be resourceful, I told myself.

We arrived in Geneva before dinner. Hungry yet hopeful, I carried my bulky bag to the railroad station and checked it. Then I strolled over to a pleasant little café and ordered an espresso.

I had no illusions about the way I looked. My clothes were wearing out even as I was outgrowing them, and my hair was an untamed mass that fell well below my shoulders. I had freshened myself up without overdoing it, and looked like a typical American student of the sixties—unkempt, naïve, thinly layered with new learning.

There he was, just as I had known he would be: a total stranger, and a rather nice-looking one, making his way toward me with a hopeful smile on his lips.

It was a lovely evening. His name escapes me, but he charmed me into having another espresso with him, and then dinner. Feeling much stronger, I happily accompanied him to an enchanting outdoor *son et lumière* show, and then, tirelessly, to a disco. We talked and laughed and joked and danced until it seemed to me that the moment of truth must be very near. I excused myself, skulked past the restrooms and slid out into the darkness to the railroad station. By some sort of poetic justice the lovely night turned on a downpour that soaked me to the skin before I reached the train station. I opened my locker feeling like a drowned rat, but a guilty rat deserving of whatever Mother Nature chose to dump on me.

I ran to the train with my heavy bag and got myself a seat. What if this guy came after me? I huddled into my corner. Ridiculous. Trains, planes, buses—he couldn't check them all. There he is! No, he isn't.

He did not find me. He didn't even look. The train left on time and I fell into a pleasant sleep.

Rome. One exhilarating day of sightseeing. I had a plane reservation for the next day but I was not all that anxious to get home. Still, I did not feel like pulling my panhandling trick again and I could not afford to stay.

I was sitting at the Café de Paris on the Via Veneto, enjoying an espresso with a travel acquaintance who had found a job with a cabaret, when a stranger came up to our table.

This time it was a woman. She ignored my companion and pounced upon me.

"Are you an actress?" she demanded, in unmistakable Italian-English.

The answer was quite easy. Everybody in Rome was an actor or an actress.

"Oh, yes," I said. "I am." My friend the cabaret dancer squinted at me.

"Well, you look like a typical American girl." The woman, who seemed like a respectable businessperson of indeterminate years, briskly handed me her business card. "Are you American? Scandinavian? Italian?"

I nodded. "All of the above. Half-Swedish, half-Italian, and all-American."

She looked slightly puzzled but galloped on unchecked.

"Over there across the street at the Excelsior Hotel"—she pointed—"they are doing Pepsi-Cola commercials. They want typical Americans. Now, I am an agent, yes?"

And I am an actress, no. But my interest was perking.

"You go over there and try out. If they want you, I will represent you. Not to worry. I am known, and you will not be cheated. You will not have to talk or sing. Just be natural and look happy. Go! Make some money!"

She had said the magic words. It was not that I was mercenary. I was nineteen and in love with Europe. The future could wait.

Within the next few hours I was launched on my career in show biz, smiling for Pepsi with a group of other smilers. There would be three commercials, my self-appointed agent informed me, each taking about five days to shoot and paying $25 a day.

Terrific! I thought. I'll just stay in Rome doing commercials at $25 a day as long as they last, and sell *International Herald Tribunes* on the corner after that.

I checked my battered suitcase into a *pensione*, $50 a month and bathroom down the hall, and congratulated myself on the economics of my new situation.

For months, I resolutely pushed all thought of serious work to the back of my mind. I did odd jobs. I traveled. I felt free. Europe was my home. Life was wonderfully unstructured. People seemed to be unrestricted and unafraid. It was all right to go anywhere, wearing whatever you happened to have. There seemed to be no pressure on young people to go to college, to get married, to choose a profession. Nobody asked, "What are you going to do with yourself?" It was a life for the restless and I was restless.

Nonetheless, I had made a decision. By Christmas 1968 I was home in Florida, starting to get my act together.

That period of my life comes back to me in a curiously fragmented way. I lived it in a kind of bewilderment. First, there were the months at college in northern Florida where I tried desperately to be a model student and hated it. Classroom learning struck me as artificial and impractical, alien to human nature. But no one else seemed to think so. I wondered if I had a serious character flaw or if I simply was not college material.

Then there was the flying with Ron Chapell, an instructor at the Gainesville airfield. At last, I had started taking flying lessons, and each hour strengthened my conviction that flying would be my life.

Another fragment is the college dress shop run by Mr. and Mrs. Frank, who paid me $21 a week, plus commissions, to work after school. Each flying hour cost me $19. I took one lesson a week for several weeks.

Within three months I decided that the only worthwhile thing I was doing was flying, and that it was not a moral failure to feel out of place in college. I dropped out and went home.

Next fragment: with the last of my savings I took another hour of flying instruction at Pompano airfield. At the end of it my flight instructor casually said, "If you'll give me your medical certificate, I'll solo you right now."

The medical certificate is the basis of the student pilot's license. One side testifies that you have passed a third-class physical; the other side, when stamped and signed, is an endorsement by the flight instructor that represents the student's license to fly alone within the vicinity of the airport and under the instructor's supervision. It is every civilian pilot's first license.

"Uh, no, uh, I don't have my certificate," I sputtered. "I sort of didn't bother. I didn't think I'd need it yet."

"Well, you do," he said cheerfully. "Just get your physical, bring the certificate tomorrow and we'll solo you."

"Great!" I said. "Terrific."

"See you tomorrow."

"Sure."

The next day I did not go to the flying field. I went to New York instead.

I was running.

All at once I had been faced with the reality of actually taking up an airplane by myself. I knew that it was no big deal to get a private license. Lots of women flew planes. But for me, the solo was symbolic. If I did it, I was committed to a profession whose doors were closed to women. It was more comfortable to dream of being an airline pilot than to try to become one.

A friend in Manhattan steered me to a job with a radio production company. At Cine-Vox I was an assistant to an assistant producer, helping to package commercials and country-western programs on cassettes.

The few months in New York were the most difficult and confusing in my life. I had to admit to myself that it was panic that had sent me scampering off to the big city to find out what was going on there. As if I really cared. What I had to do was to sort things out.

I wondered if I had been shooting off my mouth about wanting to be a pilot just because of my brother's success. I wondered why I was sure I could do the job and yet still harbored doubts. I wondered where my hopes and my sporadic efforts were taking me, and if I really had a goal. But eventually I became extremely impatient of my uncertainty and indecision.

In the summer of '69 I was back at the airfield at Pompano Beach flying a Cessna with yet another instructor. After exactly 1.3 hours Bill Carswell said, "Do you have a medical certificate?"

"Yeah," I said casually. "S'matter of fact, I do."

"Terrific. I'll solo you. You know what to do, okay? Three takeoffs and landings to a full stop. No touch and go's. Full stops."

"Got it."

I settled myself at the controls, alone in a plane for the first time. I would fly a big rectangle over the airfield: upwind, crosswind, downwind, base and final approach. Land, repeat; land, repeat. This time I was prepared—physically, mentally, emotionally.

Something inside me said, *"I am so ready!"* and I taxied to the active runway, almost singing as I reached for the mike.

"Pompano Unicom," I said proudly into the transmitter, "this is Cessna 10155 departing Runway Niner at Pompano Park for takeoffs and landings. First solo."

"Okay, Cessna 10155. Good luck!"

We soared into the air, the plane and I, and nothing else existed but the blue Florida sky and the thin line of voice contact with the Unicom.

I was in a mélange of all the planes in the sky, part of them but separate. It's me, I thought. I'm here! This is me!

I flew the broad rectangle, landed and took off again. There's nothing to this! It's the greatest thing in the world, and it's so easy!

I landed, took off, came in on the final.

"Pompano Unicom, this is Cessna 155 on final Runway Niner Pompano Park—full stop."

Bill Carswell's voice came in on the Unicom as the Cessna taxied in. "Good job, Bonnie. A-OK."

Body and mind tingled with pleasure. I had never been so happy. The only wonder was that it had taken me so long to take the most important step of my life.

3

A Flier's Apprenticeship

Getting a student pilot's certificate is like not flunking out of kindergarten. It's not a major achievement, but you can't get very far without it. It is a learner's permit. I still had to complete at least forty hours of flying time to qualify for a private license. Each hour could cost as much as $35, depending on how I spent the time—at ground school, or flying in a borrowed plane, or hiring an airplane with or without an instructor, or whatever.

At almost twenty-two, a young woman who has *au paired* in Paris and Pepsi'd in Rome prefers not to live with her parents, much as she might love them. But simple common sense dictated that I swallow my pride, and I resigned myself to staying at home. That resolved the problem of saving money on rent. The next question was getting the money to save. I applied for a job with the Tiburzi Travel Agency in Fort Lauderdale, promising hard work in exchange for a minimum wage and flexible hours at the account books and, luckily, Gus Tiburzi hired me. Then I went back to the FBO at Pompano Air Park and signed up for more lessons.

Tony Riccio, who owned Pompano Aviation as well as Buffalo Air Park in New York, was a slightly built, finger-snapping Italian who fiercely wanted his daughter Beverly to learn to fly. Two days older than I, Beverly had soloed and shown promise of being a more than adequate pilot, but she couldn't disguise the fact that she had no interest in racking up excessive amounts of time in airplanes. Her father, therefore, took a particular interest in me—an exuberant half-Italian who might well have been a second daughter to him—and as time went by he gave me a lot of privileges not generally accorded to students at Pompano. Initially that simply meant keeping a watchful eye on me and seeing that I got the best possible instruction, but later it meant extra flight time. For my part, I had the greatest respect for him as a father figure and mentor, and although he was Tony to almost everyone else at the airfield, he was always Mr. Riccio to me.

Pompano Aviation, like Tiburzi Airways of Danbury, operated not only a flight school but also a variety of passenger and cargo services—representing jobs for anyone with a commercial license. Getting the airplanes where they were needed was a major part of the operation. Tony Riccio would have his pilots ferry them back and forth between local airports or between Pompano and Buffalo, as needed for hire. He also managed a Cessna dealership, so planes would have to be picked up at the Cessna factory in Wichita, Kansas, and flown down to Florida.

Whenever I was ahead of my work at the travel agency I was at the Pompano airfield. It was like being back where I belonged. Small airports are much the same wherever they are. Same clusters of buildings, quiet outside and humming with activity within. Same strips of grass or blacktop with the same planes parked on them, same quietly competent mechanics, same mix of strong silent aviators, laconic charter pilots, wide-eyed kids and swashbuckling Sunday fliers showing their stuff. There is always a sense of relaxation about the places where the planes are, with an undercurrent of exhilaration and anticipation.

With every ounce of concentration channeled into what I was doing, I sat at the yoke of the tricolored Cessna 150 beside instructor Dan Rhea, learning how to get into and recover from stalls, side slips and figure eights. Practicing slow flight. Doing short-field takeoffs and landings. Touching down on soft-surface runways or against crosswinds. Repeating each move until it became second nature, until pilot and airplane were one.

Poring over charts, diagrams and weather maps. Studying schematics of the innards of machines. Talking to seasoned pilots, listening to mechanics, learning more and more about what makes machinery tick and getting grubby doing it. Watching the small airplanes touch down like butterflies and the corporate jets nose in like guided missiles. Catching fragments of airport gossip, overhearing pilots grumble about bad manners in the sky.

Doing my preflight checks. Gassing up the plane. Taking off, my slightest movement watched intently by Dan. Dodging other student pilots in the traffic pattern, eyes peeled and ears attuned to radio alerts. Interpreting and adding to the babble of sound coming from the cockpit speaker. "Wind is out of the east favoring Runway Niner, no reported traffic . . . Single Cessna 15015, five miles north landing . . . Wind is a hundred degrees at ten knots . . . Three reported airplanes doing touch and go's and one aircraft reported inbound from the northwest . . . Okay, Cessna 015, thank you . . . Cessna 015 entering left downwind Runway Niner at Pompano. . . ."

Being shown how; being tested and corrected.

"Let's go ahead and clear the area and then practice some slow flight," Dan Rhea would say. "I'll demonstrate, then you follow through with the controls."

Slow flight sounds easier than it is. What it is, is flight at minimum controllable airspeeds. The point of the exercise is to recognize imminent stalls and take the necessary action.

"Okay, power back to about fifteen hundred rpm. Maintain altitude as the airspeed falls off."

My thoughts parallel Dan's instructions.

Maintain directional control with the ailerons and rudders. . . . As the flaps come down, the increased camber of the wings causes momentary lift, but that's going to turn to drag. . . .

"See how quickly the airspeed bleeds off once you lower the flaps? We'll have to come in with power to maintain our altitude. Should be about twenty-five hundred rpm. Keep one hand on the throttle to adjust the power as you need it. . . . That's fine."

Gotta remember that the airspeed indicator in this plane is totally unreliable at this angle of attack. So, have to recognize minimum controllable airspeed when the controls start getting mushy—and the stall warning starts to sound.

"Now see how the nose wants to slide to the left? Just a bit more pressure on the right rudder—not too much, now. That's it. She's easing back nicely."

Keep her straight and level. You can feel it in your seat when the plane isn't coordinated . . . feel how sluggish the controls are. . . .

"All right, now, no changes—just keep her nose up, keep her straight. Okay, fine. Let's try some turns."

Sluggish. Like moving through mud.

"Come on, now—keep scanning for traffic. Now just ease in a bit more right rudder and release the pressure on the aileron. . . . There she goes—a nice, smooth, coordinated right turn. Just a *lit-tle* more power, now, just a touch. . . . That'll do it."

Release rudder pressure and add left aileron. Careful not to lose the nose. More back pressure in the turn. Gently, now. Keep working the controls. Keep them smooth. . . .

And more. And more. And more. Again and again.

"Hold it steady, keep it comfortable. . . . Okay, fine. That's nice. That's really nice."

It took me eight months of commuting between the Tiburzi Travel Agency and Pompano Aviation on my Honda 175 to accumulate my flying hours and basic skills. At the end of that time the FAA-designated flight examiner for the airport, a gnarled Italian with the un-Italian name of Ed Gargan, pronounced me fit to fly with a private license. That meant I could take family and friends up for flights, and even nonpaying strangers if they trusted me. I could not fly in instrument weather conditions or for hire; and I was limited to flying single-engine land airplanes VFR—visual flight rules.

For someone who had learned the basics of flying at the age of twelve, I had spent a rather long time in coming a not very long way. But at least I had a license to fly.

Now I could begin to see the goals stretching ahead of me, like truck stops on a highway. The test for the private had not exactly been a breeze, but I felt in my heart that I had done well. I believed that I was a better than average flier.

Where should I go from here?

Simple. I would work toward my commercial license.

This is where Tony Riccio helped by letting me fly his planes. Not far, at first, but every minute of flight time counted. To get a commercial license you need two hundred hours. I had forty, plus a few. If he needed an airplane taken to Fort Lauderdale, he'd let me take it. The flight was worth ten or fifteen minutes in my logbook, and it was free flight time for me.

Every once in a while Richard Grotke and I—he was Mr. Riccio's manager at Pompano Aviation at the time—would take a commercial flight to Wichita to pick up Cessnas from the factory for delivery to Florida. Trips like that made for a nice buildup of hours and also gave Gus Tiburzi something to think about.

My father the aviator declared himself altogether unconcerned about my ferrying flights. "What, me check up on you?" he'd say. "You're my baby—you're a good pilot. You don't need me checking up on you. Um . . . what time are you leaving?"

Richard and I, each flying a Cessna 150, used to file a joint VFR flight plan, which meant that only Flight Service knew approximately where we were at any time. I knew that my father had to know our exact departure time so that he could keep track of us. I'd call home and say, "Okay, Daddy, we're taking off tomorrow morning at eight o'clock." "Fine," he'd say casually. "Have a nice trip." And the next day he'd be keeping an eagle eye on his watch to track our progress via his own dead reckoning.

Every time we landed en route from Wichita to Pompano Beach we'd find that my father had called the airport. "Are they on time?" he'd ask. "How was her landing? How did she do? Is she okay?" One time we got weathered in at an unscheduled stop. We couldn't make it to our destination because of bad weather, so we turned around and landed at an interim airport. With the wind picking up and black clouds about to burst, I was tying down the airplane when the airport operator came out and said, "Is your name Bonnie?" I thought, Omigosh, I've made a violation. Wonder what it is? "Yes," I admitted. "Your father's on the phone," he said.

Sure enough, he was. "Nice job, Bonnie," he said. "I've been checking your flight plan and the weather all the way down the line, and you've been on course the whole way. Good work. Good girl!"

Good grief.

Another time he missed a cue but found me anyway. Richard had me make all the radio calls to Flight Service for weather advisories, pilot reports and the like. Tracking right along with me on his built-in radar, my father called the Flight Service stations en route and asked, "Do you have a flight of two Cessnas?" Typically, they answered, "Is one a girl? Doing all the talking?"

And Daddy said proudly, "Yup, that's my daughter!"

Through the summer of 1970 I picked up flying hours ferrying Tony Riccio's planes around Florida. Sometimes I was lucky enough to get a shuttle trip to Buffalo, collecting one of his airplanes at Buffalo Air Park and delivering it to Pompano Aviation. I went on working at the travel agency, taking my flying lessons whenever I could squeeze them in.

The hours accumulated slowly. By the end of summer I was

restless and dissatisfied in spite of the gift of extra flight time. I might as well, I thought, be flying around in circles. There must be different ways of learning by experience. What to do?

I did what I always did when in doubt. I left town.

Brussels in the fall. I loved it.

Friends from Rome had moved to Brussels and I had been getting glowing letters about how wonderful it was. NATO was there, they pointed out, and perhaps that meant job opportunities for me.

For some reason I thought that if NATO was in Brussels it would be virtually encircled by American companies. By another lost thought process I conceived the idea that I could therefore live in Europe for a while and build up my flying time there. Incredibly, I was right.

On arriving in Brussels I dropped my bags at my friends' apartment and went straight to the airport. Scouting around the general aviation area, I found a little charter company called Publi-Air and walked right in.

Eyebrows rose as I announced that I had a private pilot's license and would like a job. We all knew that jobs for private pilots were few and far between, if not absolutely unheard of, but I felt in my bones that I was going to get one.

"I'd like to fly for you," I said, with all the poise and confidence I could muster. "Is there any chance?"

I thought I saw the beginnings of headshakings and faint smiles. Some of the men listening were obviously pilots at least ten to fifteen years older than I: seasoned-looking, hard-muscled, no-nonsense guys.

"Fly copilot on your charters," I said boldly. And played one of my two good cards.

"Without pay, of course."

The looks now said, What's your angle, Yankee fly-girl?

"How would it be if I were to go to some of the American companies here and get charter work for you? As an American myself, I can go around and be your salesperson. I could go to BankAmerica, Levi, companies like that, and sell charters. And if I did that, would you let me fly copilot on those trips?"

In addition to wanting the hours, I wanted the experience of copiloting and I wanted to learn to fly instruments to get my instrument rating. For a beat of time there was a concerted look of astonishment. Then the manager said, "Take our brochures. See what you can do."

Levi was the first to become a client, followed by BankAmerica, followed by one or two others; and for every single charter flight I sold, I got to fly copilot.

Strictly speaking, those flights in airplanes like the Beechcraft Queen Air and Cessna 401 didn't really need a copilot. But the pilots, most of them airline pilots moonlighting for Publi-Air on their days off, seemed to like the idea. They had no objection at all to having me do the preflighting on those chilly autumn mornings. The colder it got the more preflights I did, hurrying around the airplane in the required skirt or dress while they, all snug in pants and flight jackets, grinned cheerfully at me over steaming mugs of coffee.

On boarding, I got into the copilot's seat, finished the checklists and did my number with the radio—"Brussels Tower, *c'est* Twin Cessna 3012, *nous sommes prêtes sur* Runway Two-Four . . . Okay, *merci et à bien tôt!*"—and off we would go with our load of businessmen bound for Liège or Cologne or Nuremburg. On reaching altitude I transformed myself into an air hostess, picking my way through the club-style arrangement of the plane's five or six seats to the minuscule, makeshift galley, where I assembled coffee cups, sandwiches and soft drinks. Then, for a while, I would sit on the little dual-purpose seat in the rear—unless someone else wanted to use it, at which time I would move off discreetly while the passenger raised the seat cover and drew the ankle-length curtain for a measure of privacy. When everyone was nicely settled I served the refreshments, went back to my potty seat until it was time to collect and stow the empties, then returned to the cockpit and the copilot's seat. Dignity suffered only slightly. I always got a kick out of going from potty command to second in command. There, in microcosm, was what one goes through in working one's way up. No job too small, no task too menial—so long as I could get some precious cockpit time.

Hanging around the Brussels Airport between flights paid off an unexpected dividend in the shape of a new training experience. Publi-Air kept a list of pilots as a resource pool, with a few heading the list who flew nearly all their flights. If the charter business got particularly brisk at any time, they could dig into their pool of other off-duty pilots and come up with as many as they needed. It was through this grapevine that I met a pilot who was, as far as I could gather, the one and only simulator instructor in Brussels. The simulator itself, an earthbound cockpit something like an outsized and very sophisticated Link trainer, was right there at the airport.

Here was a great opportunity for me if I could only figure out how to seize it. Simulator instruction is hard to come by for a private pilot. Not even all the airlines have their own facilities and instructors; some have to train their students in equipment leased from larger companies. None of the flight schools I knew of gave simulator instruction. It was the best way for me to become familiar with the cockpit of a large passenger plane. Furthermore, the Belgian instructor was perfectly willing to teach me. Trouble was, as usual, the lessons had a price tag, and I didn't have the price.

"There is a way out of everything," he said, with what might have been a suggestive smile.

"Ah, yes?" I said guardedly.

"My wife, she would love to learn English," he said. "I speak it okay, I think, but not well enough to teach her."

Light began to dawn, and he no longer looked suggestive.

"You mean—?" I began.

"Why not?" he said, with a Gallic why-not gesture. "You can teach, yes?"

"Yes, yes." Indeed, I was a veteran. "I'd be very happy to do it."

"Well, then, for every hour I give you in the simulator, you give her an hour's English."

It was a deal. He gave me fifteen hours of instruction in the equivalent of a multiengine cockpit, a preview of sophisticated equipment that added to my growing resolve to fly the big ones, and an experience that would be invaluable if I were ever to be considered for an airline job.

And his wife, getting equal time from me, was soon speaking extraordinary English. "Good" was not the word.

Meanwhile, short flights as copilot with Publi-Air were mounting up. Some lasted twenty minutes or less. Some were longer. Occasionally I drew a bonus in the shape of a pilot with his own small plane, who would invite me to lunch with him over the border in Lille and fly back to Grimbergen in the afternoon, giving me radio and instrument instruction along the way. I'd also get in at least a few minutes at the controls. All in all, during my fall season in Brussels, I added almost thirty hours of practical flight training to my slowly rising total.

But as winter approached, the trips got fewer and further between. Fog, rain and bitter temperatures set in toward the end of fall, and small-plane flying became increasingly difficult. The preflight walkaround checks, never a discomfort in balmy Pompano, were torture. By the end of November the weather pattern had become one snowstorm after another. Between the cold and the snow the charter flights became unpopular modes of travel. My flying minutes dwindled down to zero, right along with the visibility.

As before, I was reluctant to leave Europe. But there was no more flying in Belgium for me that year, nor was there any work to be found in France or Italy. It was time to go home.

Sunny Florida, in December 1970, was almost exactly like the Florida of a year before, except that I was now well on my way toward getting my commercial rating. The lessons grew more intensive and the flights grew longer. Buffalo in the winter is no more hospitable to flying than is Brussels, and before the weather became altogether impossible I was up there in a flight or two with Richard Grotke, picking up planes to fly down to Pompano for student use or charter hires. It was not paying work: I was getting paid in flying time, my services in exchange for the use of Tony's planes. And I paid for all my hotel accommodations along the way. But the arrangement was still cheaper than paying for thirteen or fourteen hours of flying time, and it gave me a sense of working directly for my keep.

The hours mounted, solo and dual. What I was learning at this stage—in addition to the seasoning that comes through repetition and experience—was much like what I had gone through for the private license, but with complex elaborations on the one hand and increasingly precise refinements on the other.

I brushed up on precision maneuvers and practiced stunts I hoped I would never have to use. I wish I could enjoy aerobatic flying: it looks so beautiful and so exhilarating. Unfortunately, it turns me inside out. Not even as a kid did I enjoy riding Ferris wheels or roller coasters. But some aerobatics must be learned, to prepare fliers to meet emergency situations and to get out of them safely. Unless pilots have practiced recovering from deliberately induced stalls, slips, spins and their more heart-thumping variations, they can't know what to expect or how to react. They must become familiar with unusual altitudes and abnormal conditions—so familiar that they can react to them instantly, instinctively and correctly.

I flew at night and in foul weather. I planned and flew long, cross-country solo trips. I pored over maps and charts, I studied and I practiced and got ready for what I knew would be an exhaustive battery of written, oral and practical tests. These would be important, because with the commercial license I would be qualified to take passengers up for hire—to fly people around on sightseeing or business trips and actually get paid for it. It was one thing to take a chance with yourself and your friends, and quite another to make yourself responsible for customers entrusting their lives to someone they had every right to assume was absolutely reliable and competent. The Federal Aviation Agency, trying to protect these people, was not going to pass a pilot who was inadequate in any way.

In February 1971 I took the tests and was checked out as a commercial pilot, this time by Tony Riccio himself. Now a new problem: Who was going to hire me after only two hundred hours? And a new thought—at least for me: there is no reason why I shouldn't be a flight instructor. I don't see any women flight instructors around, but so what?

By this time it was clear to me, from what I had observed at Pompano and gleaned from Ed Gargan, the designated FAA flight examiner, that the way to the full-time job market led from the commercial license to flight instructor to charter or corporate pilot to whatever presented itself next. The chances of there being any jobs for women in the category of "next" were negligible to nil, but even if I couldn't see the road ahead with absolute clarity I could see the ultimate goal.

It shone like the Grail, and it was a large jet airliner in the fleet of a major airline with Captain Bonnie Tiburzi at the controls.

Meanwhile, flight instruction beckoned.

Flight instructors occupy a curious position in the hierarchy of professional flying. As beginners, they are considered competent to teach others to fly, but not yet experienced enough for charter jobs. And when you're a two-hundred-hour commercial pilot, lacking that experience, there's not much you *can* do except ferry planes and work toward your flight instructor's ticket. So I did both.

Twenty-five flying hours after getting the commercial, I got through the FAA's two-part written exam on teaching techniques and received, in return, a flight instructor's certificate entitling me to take students through their private and commercial licenses. And since I had gotten all my licenses through Pompano Aviation, it seemed only natural to start instructing for Tony Riccio.

The transition from student-ferry pilot to instructor-ferry pilot was imperceptible. For the better part of two years I had been student-flying under the close supervision of Riccio, his manager, and one or other of his instructors. Now Mr. Riccio or Richard said casually, "Okay, Bonnie, take up a student and let's see how you do," after which I was an instructor, still flying under close supervision, until gradually I became more and more independent of scrutiny. The segue was as inevitable and effortless as having a birthday.

Yet there was a change nonetheless. To teach someone to do something you love very much is both engrossing and rewarding, and while I was instructing I thought of nothing but my student and the work of the moment. But during down times I kept track of the mounting hours and tried to calculate how quickly they were taking me along my personal road map. There I was, teaching young men to become commercial pilots and finding their progress enormously gratifying, but I was not yet making enough of my own career.

There was no need to push anything. Every flight made me more secure within myself and in my attitude toward my students, most of whom were older than I. We worked together toward achieving the smooth flight, the perfect landing, the ultimate in safe yet exhilarating flying. It was okay to pause for thought, and to expand awhile. There was time to think about obtaining other ratings, and figure out how to get them.

I was always at the airfield, surrounded by planes and by people who lived to fly. It seemed they talked and thought about little else, with me just as much as with other fliers. Access to a variety of aircraft was seldom difficult.

When I decided it was time to get an instrument rating so that I could fly commercially at night and in less than VFR weather, it was no trick at all to find someone I could make a deal with. A man who wanted his son to learn how to fly but preferred not to do it himself loaned me his Piper Tri-Pacer in exchange for the lessons. On top of the experience gained by instructing in an airplane that was instrument equipped, I got hours of extra flying time by simply paying for the gas and taking an instrument-rated fellow instructor for a ride. Depending on who the instructor was, we would either make a picnic out of it or I would repay him with babysitting time.

It was the same sort of thing, though slightly more complicated, with the Cessna 310. A serious pilot does not get very far without a multiengine rating. Once in a while I was able to borrow someone else's airplane, a Cessna 172 or a Piper Cherokee, but the insurance requirements and costs involved in using a borrowed multiengine aircraft—either privately or corporately owned—were really prohibitive. Only a very rich doctor, lawyer or company executive might consider lending out his plane, and such people seldom came my way. Thus the occasional multiengine lessons were so few and far between that my skills rusted from trip to trip.

No sooner had I begun to give this problem concentrated thought than several pieces of luck fell into my lap.

I was tying down an airplane late one breezy afternoon when someone I'd known casually around the airfield and flown with a time or two came over and started to chat. After a minute he began to lead into the part that counted.

"I hear you're looking for multiengine practice," he said.

"Uh-huh," I said absently. The wind was picking up and I was rather wishing he would help me tie down my airplane instead of just standing there shooting the breeze.

"I just bought a small business," he chatted on.

"That's nice. Oh—airplane business?" I said hopefully.

"No, but there's an old plane that goes with it. A Cessna 310-C. 1958. But it flies."

Yes, that was old. But age does not wither a good airplane if it's been looked after. And a Cessna 310 has two engines.

"Great." I made my final Tiburzi knot and dusted off my hands. "I'd love to fly her."

"Tell you what. If you can arrange for the lessons and pay for the gas, you can have time in the plane. I won't be using it much. But when I do, you can fly me for free. Then I'll pay for the gas, but you'll be the pilot."

In those days, nearly all general aviation pilots at the flight-instructor stage were trying to accumulate hours to earn higher ratings and better jobs. I was, and so were two other instructors at Pompano. Certified for multiengine instruction, they were happy to give me lessons in the C-310 while building up their own time. We made a deal where one or the other would go up with me whenever he could and give me instruction in exchange for flying hours, in much the same way that I had taught English in exchange for lessons in the Belgian simulator. I'd pay for the gas and buy sandwiches and we both profited. Especially me.

It was ten hours or so later that Ed Gargan signed me off as a multiengine pilot. Normally it would have cost me about $100 an hour to rent a multiengine airplane wet—with gas included—and pay for instruction. But, thanks to the barter system, my multiengine certificate had cost me about $90 in gas, plus a few lunches.

With the multiengine rating, I built up flying time at accelerating speed. Automatically, I became multiengine flight instructor and taught increasingly advanced students. My own experience increased as I flew the owner of the C-310 and groups of his friends on trips to the Bahamas. At about that time, another Cessna 310 owner leased his plane to the Powell Brothers Construction Company of Fort Lauderdale.

Powell Brothers had their own airplanes for ferrying workers and supplies to various sites, but sometimes the company planes were all in use. On those occasions, Powell used the leased C-310. And luckily I, as an experienced C-310 pilot, was hired to fly trips to Bimini, where they were doing a major construction job.

In effect, I was driving an airbus, and at first glance it seemed a costly proposition for the company to hire a plane and pilot to transport five or six construction workers from Fort Lauderdale to Bimini, wait for them until quitting time and fly back. But it was only a thirty- to forty-minute flight each way, the gas didn't amount to much and certainly my remuneration wasn't going to put anyone out of business. General aviation pilots, whether instructing or on charter, live uncomfortably close to the poverty level. Powell Brothers almost certainly found it cheaper to rent the airplane and pilot from day to day than to keep their guys in a hotel for weeks on end.

Although there were times when they *did* stay over in hotels for extended periods. On those occasions I airlifted special supplies. I remember that, more than once, some of the men had to stay through Thanksgiving or Christmas, and Powell Brothers would load the plane with frozen turkeys, pie and trimmings for me to deliver to Bimini. One of the guys from Powell would pick them up and take them home so that everyone could have a lavish dinner, and I'd fly on home to have mine.

Those men were gents. In the beginning they didn't quite know what to make of me. They had been told there was going to be a girl pilot, and when I showed up in my T-shirt and slacks they knew I was the pilot and were perfectly prepared to treat me as such—however you did that. They were big guys, all of them; huge, macho men with wide, wondering eyes that followed me around the airplane as I did my preflight check. They seemed to think they had to do something for me.

"What can I do to help?"

"Nothing, thanks. Why don't you just climb aboard and get comfortable?"

Okay, we're all boarding. One hangs back. Gallantry strikes again. "Need a hand?"

"Gee, no, but thanks a lot."

Okay. Everybody seated. Belt up, everybody. Y'all comfortable?

"Uh, fine, miss. Anything we can do?"

"No, thanks." The engine starts. Coughs. Stops. Ahem! Too bad. This never happens, truly.

Engine's obviously cold. Start again. "Everything's fine. Just relax."

They can't relax. Conversation buzzes. Muscular bodies strain against seat belts, desperate to do something useful. Nervous laughter, wisecracks, offers to get out and push. Engine goes into its overture. We taxi and pick up speed. Wheels leave the tarmac. Dead silence falls within the cabin. I glance around. They are gazing solemnly out the windows, looking their last upon home and family. Faces white, they are as quiet as mice. I sense their silent prayers.

After the first trip the boys got used to me very quickly, although once in a while they would reach out involuntarily to give me a hand and they were always rather quiet on the airplane.

4

The Glamorous Life

Thanks largely to Powell Brothers and the boys, I was doing a considerable amount of multiengine flying without actually having taken on a full-time job as a corporate flier. I caught myself thinking that those hours would look good on my résumé.

What résumé?

The one I intended to write when I had more experience.

My flexible schedule, crowded though it was, left me time to add a few numbers to my repertoire. The mythical résumé needed something more impressive than frozen-turkey flights on an old Cessna 310. The hours were beginning to spill into new logbooks, my ratings were mounting and I was teaching people how to become flight instructors. But all the same, I thought, I really ought to get some time on a more sophisticated, slightly bigger airplane.

Again I was lucky.

A construction company in Connecticut, Arute International, had bought a DC-3 back in 1953 and had never given it full-time work. Now, with the plane about nineteen years old, they decided to put it back to work flying air taxi in southern Florida during the company's slack season. One phone call led to another, and within a matter of days the DC-3 was down at Sunstream FBO, which was located just across the taxiway from Pompano Aviation at Pompano Air Park.

Arute's man at Sunstream was someone I knew fairly well, just from hanging around the airport. Pompano was still small enough so that we all knew each other at least by sight, and some of us had become good friends.

"How would you like," he said, "to get checked out in the DC-3? And then do some charter flying out of Sunstream?"

Before long, two of us and several other local pilots were attending informal but FAA-approved ground school classes. It was a great opportunity for me, because I was the youngest and least experienced of the group and had only a fleeting acquaintance with what looked like an awesome craft in comparison with the Cessnas and Beechcraft I was used to. The DC-3 was a hefty, chunky, nineteen-passenger airplane with an incongruously big wingspan that made it look short-changed in the rear end and earned it the nickname of the Gooney Bird. Its weight, its retractable gear and its relatively sophisticated systems put it in the category of complicated equipment.

As a corporate aircraft, it had been flown under general operating rules governing noncommercial craft. As a charter air taxi, its weight of more than 12,500 pounds and its complex systems put it in the category of an air carrier. As such it had to be modified to some extent and certified under much stricter regulations designed to protect the public. By the same token, those of us who were being trained to fly it had to be thoroughly schooled in the specific characteristics of its hydraulic and electrical systems and in the particular procedures and regulations applying to the type of operation for which the airplane was being adapted and certified.

Thus, while the old Gooney Bird was being overhauled, reequipped and provided with marked emergency exits, we were developing a manual covering its operation as a one-plane airline complete with a dispatcher to keep track of its exact location and condition at all times.

In the cockpit of the DC-3 I felt very much the professional pilot. Almost an airline pilot. The trips were much like the

Pompano charters. Most were day runs to the islands and back, although once we flew the governor of Florida and a group of people to Disney World. But the flying was vastly different. I liked being part of a flight crew, no matter that there were only two of us. I liked knowing that we had a second crew, our own scheduling operation, a ticket office and dispatcher. The *thrum* of the big low-wing engines had the sound and feel of a substantial flying machine. It throbbed and vibrated through me like blood circulating through my body. There was more flying to do in the big old workhorse than in the smaller airplanes. They were fun to fly—but this was *doing* something.

I yearned for a steady multiengine job. If only the governor of Florida would hire me as his full-time pilot. If only I could spend more time on the DC-3. As it was, I had to share it with the other crew, but at least I could look forward to many terrific trips on the Gooney Bird.

Wrong.

I happened to be away on the track of another multiengine job when the second crew ran the DC-3 right off the end of the runway in the Bahamas. Everybody was fine except the owners. They were hopping mad.

There were people who envied me my work. Oh, the glamour, the excitement, the romance of whipping around in those little airplanes! Yeah.

Much of it was hurry-up-and-wait. I did a lot of waiting for both Powell and Pompano. Most of my assignments involved taking people over to the islands, either for a day's work or several hours of fun and frolic. Charter parties would come to Pompano Aviation, for example, and hire a plane to take them to the Bahamas for an afternoon on the beach followed by dinner and an evening at the gambling tables, and then bring them back.

The airports in Bimini, Nassau, Chubb Cay, Freeport and

most of those areas are or used to be pretty deserted. I remember going over there prepared to sit and wait several hours for my human cargo to return, which they had every right to do at will and expect to find me there. Without a care in the world, I'd change into my bathing suit or shorts and lie down on the wing to get a suntan. After a while I'd rouse myself to read or study a little and have my picnic lunch, then turn over to tan the other half. Most of the time there was nobody else around: not another pilot or airport operator or mechanic or gas jockey. Just me, in the sun, waiting for a bunch of construction guys or scuba divers to come back at the end of the day. It never occurred to me that someone might come to that deserted airport and assault me or steal the plane or both. Nobody ever did.

Only one night did I really get concerned. I wasn't worried about being attacked, but it was way past my bedtime and I wanted to go home.

One afternoon Tony Riccio called on me to fly a charter to Freeport that evening in the Skymaster, a four- to six-seat Cessna 337 known as the Push-Pull because it has one engine in front and one in the back. At seven o'clock, as scheduled, two couples showed up and said they planned to have dinner at Freeport around eight, then do a little gambling, but intended to leave no later than ten or eleven o'clock.

We took off, landed in half an hour and off they went with a casual comment that they were going to a particular casino.

I sat. I waited. I got hungry. At about eleven I wandered over to the casino and saw my two couples having a grand time, eating, drinking, gambling and drinking some more, obviously quite oblivious to the clock. I had a little something to eat and walked around Freeport for a while. Shortly after midnight I went back to the casino. They were still drinking and enjoying themselves. Getting quite boisterous, in fact. As discreetly as I could, I pointed out the time.

"Want to go home pretty soon?" I suggested hopefully.

"Ahh, what's your hurry? Night is young."

"No, it isn't," I pointed out again. "You were going to leave at eleven."

"Oh, c'mon, Bonnie, sit down. Have a drink. Have something to eat."

"No, I can't, it's getting late. We're way past the time. Well, okay, a cup of coffee then."

Twelve-thirty.

"Hey, whaddya think, huh? Time to go, huh?"

"Jush a li'l bit longer, okay? In a li'l while."

Great. I could see they were going to be swell passengers.

One o'clock. I wasn't sleepy but I was getting tired and I'd rather not be tired when I fly.

Finally, at something past one-thirty, we all left the casino, full of jolly laughter. The five of us tumbled merrily back into the airplane, my peals of merriment sounding hollow in my ears.

The night was clear as a bell. Panel lights glowed warmly in the tiny cockpit. I took off gratefully, relieved to be on the way at last and happy with the beautiful clarity of the stars. I called Flight Service and filed an instrument flight plan.

We rose over the dark sea, stars above twinkling and panel lights . . . fading? Yes, fading . . . cockpit lights dimming, some lights going out. . . .

I'd lost an alternator.

Okay, I have a backup system. I have two alternators and two Nav/Coms—two sets of radios, each with a navigation and communications portion.

But I don't know why I've lost the alternator. Major electrical problem? If so, I could lose the second alternator and have nothing. Last thing I want to do is be over the open water with no electrical equipment at all.

So I should turn off nonessential equipment to conserve power for the other alternator. Turn off the two Nav systems and one radio and all but absolutely essential lights. Can't see much now as it is. Need a flashlight.

There was a flashlight in the beach basket I used as a flight bag, and if I could just dig that out I could beam it on the instruments. It was going to be awkward, holding the flashlight, working the radio and flying the airplane all at the same time, but I could clutch it between my knees or prop it somehow . . . or perhaps one of the revelers in back could steady it on the seatback for me. With that thought, and with my fingers on the flashlight, I half turned, involuntarily, to ask one of my passengers to give me a hand. With that, the flashlight slipped out of my fingers and rolled out of sight. Curses! I cursed.

I peered back into the little cabin, hoping to spot the rolling flashlight by the remaining dim glow. All I could see was a shambles of slumped people, a couple of them apparently asleep and the other two quite sick. And it wasn't even a bumpy flight. Well, so much for any chance of help from them. Thank heaven it was a smooth night.

When a pilot flies an IFR there are certain highways in the sky that controllers want her to use. They coordinate the various planes in the air, using the VOR—very high frequency omni range—to direct them. But, as I cut back on my electrical power, I couldn't see any of the VOR indicators. All I had was one VHF radio tuned to Palm Beach Center, and a clear sky.

If you're not able to fly on instruments, you fly by visual flight rules—if you can see. I called Air Traffic Control.

"Palm Beach Center, this is Zero One Hotel. I've lost one of my alternators, I've turned off all my nonessential electrical equipment, and I'd like to cancel IFR if I might and go VFR."

"Zero One Hotel, squawk ident. How do you plan to navigate?"

"How about pilotage?" I said.

A chuckle came from ATC. Navigating by pilotage means going by recognizable visual points below, but straight below was nothing but black ocean—deep, deep black from Freeport to the Florida coastline. But ATC knew what I meant.

"Okay, Zero One Hotel," said ATC "But monitor this frequency and we'll keep you posted on traffic."

"Fine, thank you, Zero One Hotel."

Now it was really dark.

Came an anguished voice from the rear: "Hey, Bonnie, what's going on? Something wrong? What happened to the lights?"

"Nothing's wrong," I yelled back at him. "The lights are out so you can sleep. Take it easy—we'll be home in half an hour."

He snorted and fell silent.

We were now about to accomplish something that would have been impossible in a different setting. Over mountainous country, we couldn't have done it. Over uninhabited prairies or sparsely populated farmland with a smattering of lights, we couldn't have done it. But over the black, featureless ocean and without a single onboard navigational device, we could do it. We could find our way home just by looking.

I could see every single light on the coastline and I knew exactly where I was going. I banked and peered ahead. Somebody moaned with the movement of the plane. Thirty miles across the sea I could see the green-and-white rotating beacon at Palm Beach. Neatly laid out along the brightly lit coastline were the unmistakable patterns of Boca Raton, Pompano Beach, Fort Lauderdale and the big blaze of Miami, great clusters of light drawing us to the mainland. We drew a bead on Palm Beach, then Pompano and homed in to the airfield, true as a well-aimed arrow.

My passengers seemed glad to be back on land. They all looked green and exhausted as they walked across the ramp to the parking lot, and even though they said nothing but a muttered goodnight, I don't think they felt at all well.

Some excitement. Some glamour. Some romance.

What interests me in retrospect is that no one, in those days, seemed particularly surprised to find a female pilot in command. Except one famous ballplayer.

His name sounded vaguely familiar to me but I didn't really know who he was until afterward. Perhaps recognizing him would have made a difference. Perhaps not.

Ted Williams called Pompano Aviation one day and said he wanted a charter flight for the following morning, to take him to his orange groves at Wauchula, Florida. Flight time was set for 7 A.M. in a Cessna 172.

As the available pilot, I was at the airfield at 6:00 in the morning. Ordinarily Tony Riccio or Beverly would open up Operations and start the business day at eight, but whoever had an early charter was given a key to unlock the office and get the day going. By the time the charter party arrived at 6:45 I had gassed up the plane—the gas man not having checked in yet—preflighted it and taxied it over to Operations. It was parked there, door open for passengers, as Mr. Williams and a business companion walked to the counter and announced themselves.

We exchanged good mornings and I wrote up the invoice, which I would complete with time and mileage at the end of the round-trip flight. Then I led them to the plane.

"Any bags?" I inquired, ready to pile them in in my role as Skycap.

"No bags, thank you."

"Okay, if everybody's ready to go," I said briskly, "why don't we hop in?"

Tall Ted Williams looked down at me with a puzzled frown.

"*We,* hop in?"

"Yeah, I'm your pilot," I said, just as breezily. "Shall we go?"

"Now just a minute," said Williams, his voice extremely firm. "You're the one just opened up the office? I'd like to see your license, if you don't mind. And your logbook."

As it happened, I did mind. *I'm a pilot, doggone it,* I muttered soundlessly. But indignation faded as I suddenly saw myself as he must see me. Half his size, half his age, white slacks, yellow top, asymmetrical pigtails. Perhaps I should have looked a little more professional.

I didn't have my logbook with me but I told him my hours and showed him my license. I figured he had a right to know if I was a legitimate pilot. He still wasn't too keen about flying with me, but when a desperate scan around the flying field failed to turn up a more substantial pilot, he decided to take his life into his hands. He was a Navy pilot, he explained, directing his colleague to a rear seat, and he was going to sit up front with me just in case.

We rolled down the runway and rose. The big Williams hands strained to clutch at the yoke . . . and gradually relaxed. About seventy minutes later we landed at Wauchula, and for all that he didn't care to admit it, Big Ted was hugely impressed that I found the airport at first try. It was a little grass field, almost indistinguishable from the air until we were nearly upon it, and we plonked right in.

He was relaxed and cheerful on the trip back, so deep in conversation with his colleague that he forgot to look out the window to see if we were about to hit something.

That was the only occasion on which my credentials as a pilot were ever questioned. One of my instructors had told me, "You gotta be ugly. A corporation's not gonna hire some chick who looks like anything, because some wife is gonna get on board and look atcha and say, 'You are not gonna fly with my husband on a three-day trip to the Bahamas. That is just *not* gonna happen.' "

I was skeptical. The work I was doing for Powell Brothers was corporate flying, even though I wasn't piloting vice-presidents around in a company Lear jet, and I hadn't seen a single outraged wife. Must be, I thought, because the boys go home and tell their wives I'm only part of the machinery—which, in effect, I was. But I did experience one curious case of wifely cold shoulder in the course of flight instructing.

A couple of men in the lobster business kept a twin-engine Skymaster at the airfield. One of them was planning to take the airplane on a two-day business trip to the islands, stopping overnight at Nassau. He asked Tony Riccio if he could take a flight instructor along with him, because he wanted to get his instrument rating and thought that as long as he was doing a flight of five hours each way he might as well utilize the time and get some instrument instruction.

Mr. Riccio had no objection, and scheduled me for the trip because I was the only instrument-rated flight instructor available just then. I was pleased, because I needed the instrument experience myself, and could use the ten hours to put in my log book. So my student and I plotted our trip.

The day before the trip, Mr. Riccio called me over.

"Trip tomorrow's canceled," he said, with what I thought was a rather sly grin.

"Howzat?"

"Guy called. Said his wife didn't want him going on an overnight with some woman flight instructor."

"But all I'm teaching him—"

"I know, sweetie, but she doesn't."

I cast around in my mind for a picture of her, and found it. She'd come to the airfield a time or two, and she knew I was an instructor. It hadn't seemed to bother her. She was in her early thirties, nice-looking, unremarkable. And there we were, in 1972, when a sense of sisterhood was sweeping the nation. True, I had been so wrapped up in my own concerns that I had little concept of women's lib, but I had never anticipated encountering old-fashioned jealousy.

Isn't that ironic? I thought. Here women are trying so hard to get someplace in life, and a man is giving me an opportunity to instruct him while learning something myself, a woman—his insecure wife!—doesn't want me with him for two five-hour flights. And an overnighter, of course, but that's just adding the ridiculous to the dumb. If there is a threat to her marriage, I am not it.

Billy Turner's wife was something else again. She also had a sense of competition, but of a much healthier variety. Billy, a car salesman in Fort Lauderdale, was a competent pilot without a plane of his own, and he wanted to hire one of Pompano's airplanes on occasion. Our insurance coverage required that we familiarize him with the traffic and communications patterns of our airport, and Tony Riccio naturally wanted him to be shown how we liked our airplanes to be flown. (Everybody has individual flying quirks, and we at Pompano had ours.) I was delegated to give him instruction and check him out.

He was a quick study and did a fine job. I told him so, and he went off wreathed in smiles.

The next day Mrs. Billy Turner came to the airport and asked to see me.

"Yes, ma'am?"

She looked me over and produced a hesitant smile. I was my usual impressive self: a pigtailed post-teenager tanned dark by the Florida sun, in Chinos and a smear of grease.

"You're Bonnie? My husband was checked out by a woman?"

"S'right," I said. "He was terrific."

"That's what he said." She was more confident now. "And he said you were good, too. Well. If you can do it, I can do it. *I* want to learn to fly. Will you teach me?"

"You bet I will!"

Mrs. Turner turned out to be an excellent student and a skillful pilot. She told me that she had a full-time job as a travel agent. It had never occurred to her that she could compete in any way with her husband, the strong male figure, the head of the household. Flying was something that he did and she couldn't. And then he had taken a lesson from a female.

Only then did she think that maybe she could do it, too.

Mrs. Turner flew a fine solo and I signed her student license. She smiled, thanked me and went away. She had done all she had meant to do: prove to herself that if I could do it, she could do it.

The Turners were rarities in my instructing experience, and it may be because they were a little unusual that I was struck by the thought of how many women instruct men who then go out and get enviable jobs while the women stay back in their instructing slots. I did not want that to happen to me.

But I knew it could, if I didn't fight it very hard.

I already had a number of jobs, of varying degrees of interest but none particularly enviable. I was flight instructing on all levels available at any airport school, and I was flying for Pompano, Powell Brothers and Arute International. The hours were irregular and long. Many of the charter flights started early in the morning. Some of my students could only come before or after work, so I was at the airport early and late for them. Quite late, in some cases, for people wanting night flying lessons or night checkouts. In Florida, in summer, it stayed light so long that it was well after nine o'clock before we could get going. And up again, early in the morning. And Saturdays and Sundays, when people wanted to play on the Bahama beaches or in casinos or go scuba diving, and wanted someone to fly them there.

I often worked such long hours that I could not take time out to examine my doubts and fears, but they were there. Was the hard work ever going to go anywhere? Already I could see some of my students running off with their brand-new certificates and popping into well-paying jobs. Goodbye, teacher. Hello, career. But how could I know that what I was doing was ever going to pay off? The boys *knew.*

What I needed was some form of moral support, somebody to talk to who had a degree of sympathy for what I wanted to do. And I had that support. If my father, for instance, had raised his expressive eyebrows at me and said incredulously, "Don't be ridiculous, Bonnie. Women don't do that, and you're not going to do it!," I probably would have said meekly, "Okay, Daddy." I might not have felt meek, but I would have had a hard time going ahead without his approval.

But he had always been encouraging. He was glad that I was a girl, proud that I was a flier, enthusiastic about what we hoped would be my career. I think perhaps he gave me even more encouragement than he had given my brother, because of the novelty of being able to introduce me as my daughter the pilot. He was gratified when I got compliments on my flying, and as self-congratulatory as any father when anyone —on occasions when I looked my best—flashed admiring glances my way or made flattering remarks.

He hadn't always been so pleased about those admiring glances when I was growing up. My very Italian father the pilot knew what men were like and didn't trust them at all. He thought that every male in sight was after his daughter.

But in becoming a full-time flier I had apparently matured in my father's eyes, and the trust that had always been between us matured as well. When I doubted, my father encouraged me; when I dated, he kept his own counsel. He knew that, since my life revolved around the airfield, virtually all of my friends were men, and it was only natural that I should see some of them outside working hours. I felt comfortable with guys like Richard Grotke, who understood my obsession with flying as few nonfliers could but didn't feel they had to talk about it all the time. And I liked romantic attention, as any woman would.

I also had a nonflying boyfriend who made heroic and almost successful efforts to comprehend what I was doing and why I was doing it. Bob was an attractive, unassuming, thoughtful guy who was trying hard to establish his own identity and career. Perhaps it was because he wanted so very much to be himself that he came so close to empathizing with me.

Dates were difficult to fit in. With the guys at the airfield I could make spur-of-the-moment arrangements, but it was harder to make impromptu dates with someone in an altogether different business or even to make plans for a Saturday night on the town.

"How about tomorrow night?"

"Not until ten o'clock," I'd say regretfully. "And then maybe just for a soda, because I have to be up at six to take a charter to the Keys."

"What about Sunday?"

"Sorry, no. I have a charter to Bimini."

So we'd meet for a hamburger and a Coke on Friday.

And sometimes I had a date with someone else.

But I got to see more and more of Bob. He was ingenious, he had the resources and he needed to go places. Also, he was intrigued with my flying, and supportive of my efforts to build time. Whenever he had business requiring travel, he would rent a plane from Pompano Aviation and ask for me to fly it. He also steered his colleagues to Pompano Aviation whenever they needed a charter flight and made sure I was the pilot. Once in a while we combined business with pleasure, as when he and his brothers—who could just as easily have piled into a car—hired me and a plane to take them scuba diving at Pennycamp, an underwater park in Key Largo.

So Bob was helpful. But he was concerned about my work schedule, which often meant fourteen- to fifteen-hour days and seven-day workweeks. In the nicest possible way, he'd ask, "Why are you working so hard? Why is it so important to drive yourself like this? Why does an airline job mean so much to you?"

It wasn't all that easy to explain. I was not consumed with ambition, although I had a goal. Nor was I a trailblazer, concerned about being first at anything. No matter to me whether I was the first or the ten-thousandth woman to fly for the airlines; it was the *job* I wanted, and the prestige and security I imagined went along with it.

"I need the security," I said.

He gave me a quizzical look.

"You don't exactly *need* it, do you? Anyway, if security is all you want, you've always got your flight instructing and your charter work. I'm sure you could get a great corporate job if you wanted it."

Uh-uh. Corporate flying? All those wives and no union? No, if you wanted to fly, airline flying was where it was at. You work for a company whose business is flying. You have a big, solid structure, you have a union behind you and one job—flying. You don't have to open up the airport, you don't have to write up the tickets, carry the bags, empty the honey buckets. There are other people to do those things, while you do what you are trained to do.

"If you really love to fly, and if you want to make something of yourself by doing what you're good at doing," I tried to explain, "then you want the best. And that's airline flying. I want the best that's available in my profession. I want the prestige. And the salary that goes along with it. Why shouldn't I aim for the best?"

He nodded slowly. "Sure, why not? But—*is* it really work for a woman? What sort of personal life can you have? What do you go home to?"

I knew what he meant. Married pilots go home to their wives, unmarried pilots go to their bachelor pads and live it up.

"It's a bit soon to worry about that," I evaded. "Let me get my job first."

"Security first, huh? You don't really need it, you know. Women don't need the security. It's the traditional role of the man to provide it."

"No! I need to have it for myself. I must have something I can do well, something that'll carry me through so that I won't have to depend on anybody else. I've got to be able to rely on myself. . . ."

And so on. It usually ended with me saying something, "Gee, Bob, you know what I mean."

Essentially, he did. He tried very hard to understand what

I wanted out of life, even though I found it difficult to articulate. He understood my love for flying. He understood having a goal. He understood self-reliance. He understood my enjoyment of what I was doing, and shared some of that enjoyment. Yet he could not completely accept that what I wanted was right for a woman.

I'm not sure that I even cared whether he understood or not. I was obsessed with airplanes, ratings and flying hours. I managed to grab some precious minutes on a Lear jet, and put the time in my logbook as proudly as if I'd been given a ring. ("Any jet time?" I would be asked when I applied for my next job. "Oh, yes," I would say airily.) For the time being, there was nothing else in my life I needed. Just air time, experience and, eventually, the big opportunity.

There was no one to whom I could admit that I vastly enjoyed being the only woman flier at Pompano. So far as I knew, I was the only woman flier in Florida—or for miles around, for that matter. When I talked on the radio I was instantly greeted by name, even by strangers. "Oh, that must be you, Bonnie." Yes, it must be me. Who else? Those were the times when women's voices were so unusual on aircraft radio that the men couldn't help but recognize me. I liked that.

I had not even known that other women were actually flying professionally until I started instructing. Then, at flight safety seminars, I saw a few women I took to be in their fifties and sixties, but somehow I did not relate them to anything besides teaching. They might have been famous aerobats or owners of regional airlines for all I knew. At the time I was oddly incurious about aviation careers other than my own. Cropdusters, helicopter pilots, aerobats—who cared about them?

Eventually, I would.

Meanwhile, I was enjoying the idyllic situation of being the only girl in the game; almost one of the guys myself, but treated like a women when it counted. The guys liked a woman who could fly, and to whom they could talk flying. Boy, had I been gutsy, battering through the fringes of that thunderstorm! Wow, had I greased that plane in on that soggy runway! Wonderful Bonnie had the pick of the guys asking her out, on those rare occasions when she was available, because there was not another girl on the scene.

Until, one day, Debbie arrived with her little Pitts and her entourage of slavish admirers.

I had started early that morning and was taking a short break before my late afternoon student arrived. Several of the guys—one or two other instructors and a couple of commercial pilots on their day off—were with me, all of us relaxing in lawn chairs on the ramp between the Operations building and the runways. As usual, there were a couple of specks in the sky, getting larger as they approached the airfield. We glanced up idly, then ignored them. Nobody we knew.

Suddenly, *Zoom! Blam! Boom!* Two exquisite little airplanes buzzed the airport one after the other and arced skyward, higher and higher, then arced again and fell together in perfect synchronization. Once more, the *zoom* around the airfield, and they were up, up and away, spiraling into a series of loops and gyrations that left me breathless with admiration.

As if to herald them in, several other small planes appeared in formation over the airport as the two Pitts Specials touched down and pulled up in front of Operations. It was quite a performance. "Must be the Jim Holland outfit," somebody said. "Touring aerobatic show. He's got some girl—wow!"

She stepped out of the airplane with a swagger and a flourish, like someone who's just swung down from a trapeze. For a moment she stood there in the imaginary spotlight, a vision with long blond hair, short-shorts, long legs, bestowing upon us a dazzling smile. Then, lithely, she walked toward us. Jim Holland got out of the second plane and some other people emerged from assorted cockpits, but all eyes were on the blonde. Guys jumped to their feet and rushed forward. Introductions were made. Hi! Debbie Gary. Nice to meet you all. Hello.

I was not one of those who rushed forward. I looked at her and devoutly wished she hadn't come. Why doesn't she jump back into her airplane and fly into the sunset?

Her eyes met mine. She gave me a chilly smile. An immediate circle of admirers gathered around to collect the gems that fell from her lips. Men materialized from all over the airport and fawned upon her. Instructors told her how wonderful she was. Airline pilots begged to take aerobatic lessons with her. It was awful.

Debbie made Pompano Air Park her headquarters for the winter. She kept her plane there, and she was at the airfield almost every day with her gaggle of friends and fellow fliers and my old friends falling all over her. I wondered what I had done to deserve having that woman land at my airport, flashing her looks and her talent. The place had been mine, *mine.*

Tony Riccio made matters worse by hiring her as an instructor. In addition, she taught aerobatics for Jim Holland. She seemed to be around all of the time, nearly always in the center of a fascinated group.

Amazing, I thought, how much more interested people seem to be in blond aerobats than in a person with a slightly queasy stomach who wants to be an airline pilot.

5

"She'll Never Get Off the Ground"

The antagonism was mutual. I couldn't imagine why. Debbie and I did not like each other at all, and it showed. We could have been two cats. As the weeks and months passed we had no social contact except for exchanges of very polite hellos and how are you's, even though we now knew nearly all the same people. At best, we tolerated each other's presence.

Only once was there a flicker of anything like acceptance. I had done some aerobatics with Jim Holland, which made me all the more aware that stunting wasn't really my thing. And one day, after Debbie had come down from an even more spectacular demonstration of grace and skill than usual, I said spontaneously, "Gosh, I'm so jealous of you! I really wish I could do something like that." She flashed me a look of near-approval and was starting to say something when one of her fans butted in with a question. So that was that.

For me, Debbie's very existence as an acclaimed aerobatic pilot was a revelation. The only woman aerobat I'd ever heard of was Mary Gaffaney, an older woman whose long career was so star-studded that she had become a legend to me, even though she, too, was a flight instructor in Florida. Debbie, my age and ever-present, was no legend. She was indisputably real, as I was to her. How very interesting, to run into another professional woman flier. How comforting. How annoying.

We were not in professional competition. Our career goals were completely different. But in our own little world, each of us was the Other Woman.

In addition to sharing our friends, we shared the experience of being minicelebrities. Many people in Florida at that time found women pilots unique. Debbie and I were repeatedly asked to appear in TV segments, or to be interviewed for articles or to pose for either advertising or ornamental pictures. The job supposedly made the person interesting: Bonnie Tiburzi, pilot and flight instructor, models Alfonso's latest jumpsuit! Once I even made the cover of *Gold Coast Pictorial,* right along with tennis star Rod Laver. Debbie and I were minor social items, both of us, without ever really becoming part of the local social scene.

Even before Debbie arrived I had started getting a little paranoid about why some individuals asked me out or why I was invited to participate in certain events. I felt that people, other than Bob and my flying friends, didn't especially like me. They liked what they thought I represented—whatever that was. When Debbie came along and was similarly deluged with calls from instant friends, I wondered if she had the same misgivings I had—or if she really was the most popular person in the Pompano–Palm Beach area.

Bob, for one, thought she was just marvelous.

Funny, that. And I didn't want her at the same airport or in the same profession.

By the spring of 1972 I was getting edgy. I had almost a thousand hours of flight instruction time and several hundred hours of straight flying time in dozens of different plane types, from the Cessna 150 to the DC-3, and I was getting no closer to my career goal. My advanced students kept going off and getting good jobs, many of them on regional airlines and some of them on the majors, but I simply couldn't seem to find out how to do it. The fellows managed to find out, and tell each other, but they wouldn't tell me.

Not that there was a conspiracy of silence against me. They just didn't take my ambition seriously. I asked airline pilots, FBO managers, flight instructors and FAA inspectors what the requirements were, and how to go about applying, but nobody had the answer. I couldn't believe I needed more flight time, but I didn't know if I had all the right ratings or what I might be missing.

Several years later a woman pilot hired by American Airlines, Leslie Rasberry, told me that she had had similar doubts. She had gone on accumulating time until she had logged around 4,500 hours in general aviation prop airplanes—but not a minute in jets. Her experience, barring the small gaps, was three times what she needed. She hadn't known when to stop.

The difficulty for me was that I was operating in a vacuum. How can a man tell a woman how to qualify or apply for a job that has never been available to women? It was like applying for the post of Santa Claus.

None of the men seemed to have any history of aviation to draw from. They had heard of Amelia Earhart and Anne Lindbergh, just barely. They hadn't heard of Helen Richey, who flew for Central Airlines for a year in the 1930s and was squeezed out of her job by the all-male Pilots Union. Nor did I know much about women pilots of the past, other than Jacqueline Cochran—yet another Floridian—and Jacqueline Auriol of France, but I knew that the tradition of women fliers was almost as old as aviation itself. By my day, a woman pilot should not have been regarded as a novelty.

Yet I could think of no one to point to as an example. The only contemporary woman pilot who came to mind was Turi Wideroe of Norway. Turi, I had read somewhere, had flown for eight years with her father's feeder carrier, Wideroe Airways of Oslo, until the company was absorbed into SAS in 1969, when she began flying a Convair 440 turboprop out of Oslo for the major Scandinavian airline.

"Welcome aboard. This is your captain, Margaret Williamson speaking."

Drawing by Richter © 1973 The New Yorker Magazine, Inc.

Yesterday's cartoon, happily, is today's reality. At American, we have a woman pilot: Bonnie Linda Tiburzi.

We were the first major U.S. airline with a woman pilot. We have men serving as flight attendants. We have a woman facilities architect. We have both men and women working as Flight Service Directors. If you want to help us fly one of our planes. Or if you want one of our planes to fly you, call American.

If you want to take off right now and pay after you get back, why not charge your flight with an American Airlines Vacation Card. Write to American Airlines—P.O. Box 920, Bellmore, New York 11710.

American Airlines

To The Good Life.©

American Airlines ran this ad in *Ms.* and other magazines in 1973.

At least she made my job prospects seem remotely possible. A woman had been found capable of handling an airliner. But her name was not a household word around Pompano Beach, and on the home front I could find neither inspiration nor precedent for what I dreamed of doing.

Most of the Pompano-based fliers who sought better jobs were older than I, and certainly more impressive physically. Some of the instructors had more hours and broader experience. And a lot of the other fellows who used to hang around the airfield were already airline pilots. There were a number who flew or had flown for United, and several with Delta and Northeast. Some had their own planes, a Pitts or a Cub, some came to take aerobatic lessons—mostly from Debbie Gary—and some belonged to a flying club. But mainly what they did, after flying for an hour or so, was hang around Operations, drink coffee and talk. Man talk.

Bob Serling's book, *She'll Never Get Off the Ground,* came out at about that time, and although the fictional heroine—the first woman airline pilot in the United States—did indeed become a member of a flight crew, she was grounded because of her love for a man. Her captain. Whose life she saved. By jeopardizing her passengers. Something like that.

She, Dudney Devlin, was held up to me as an example of what might happen to me if I persisted in my fantasy. The title was their favorite part.

They teased. They even jeered. They called me "Dud."

I must admit that the book discouraged me a bit. Poor, presumptuous Dudney had been put very firmly in her woman's place. And yet there was a contrary gleam of encouragement in the fact that someone had considered putting a woman in an airline pilot's seat.

"But she did get off the ground," I reminded them. "She flew as well as any of the guys, and she was just as cool."

"C'mon, that's just fiction, some guy making it up. That's not gonna happen."

The more the fellows brushed me off, the more serious I got. It got to be a major challenge.

"Okay," I'd say. "Never mind I'm a woman. How would *you* go about getting an airline job?"

"I don't know—I don't *want* an airline job."

Or: "How did you get your job with Delta?"

"Years of experience in the military, honey."

Oh.

We would be taking it easy between flights or jobs. One of the guys would say, "United's hiring." And another, who may have earned his commercial or flight instructor's license through me, would ask, "What are the requirements? Who do you write?" Then heads would go into a huddle while information was exchanged, and somehow I never overheard the answers.

"Hey, fellows! What about me?"

"Oh, Bonnie!"

I got plenty of useless advice from people who meant well. "Look, you're just going to get hurt if you have this ambition. Try to be satisfied with being a flight instructor or a charter pilot, or try for a corporate job. Women don't become airline pilots."

"Well, I'm going to."

Firmly: "You aren't going to be an airline pilot, because there aren't any women airline pilots."

It was all beginning to sound like a broken record.

There was one little tiny ray of light, one man who offered a small spark of encouragement. He was an Eastern flight engineer, a glider enthusiast who flew out of Boca Raton and came over Pompano to show his stuff. He was in love with soaring. He used to call me on the phone before being towed at Boca Raton, and say he'd soon be there. "Look out for me—I'm going to do some wingovers and chandelles and stuff. Just see how pretty it is."

He was a nice and gentle man. I remember looking up at

his small white airplane against that clear blue sky and thinking, "Yes, it is beautiful." And even from the ground I could sense how much he loved what he was doing. Every once in a while when he came down to earth, he would say to me, "You know, Bonnie, it would really be a howl if you applied to the airlines and got hired. Wouldn't that be something?"

Oh, yes, indeed it would!

Finally, I asked, with a sort of despairing wail, "But what do I *do?* How do I know who's hiring? *If* anybody's hiring?"

He looked at me as if I were an idiot.

"You write the companies. You spell out your qualifications. If they're interested, they'll send you an application. Is that hard?"

"No," I whimpered.

First, find your companies, then their addresses. "Easy," said my father. "They're all in the *Official Airline Guide.* Use the copy in the office."

Of course. Every travel agency has an *Official Airline Guide.*

"Neatness counts," my mother said. "Your letters must look nice. If you don't know how to spell something, look it up."

Aided by a pair of assiduous proofreaders, I wrote to every single airline in the *OAG,* the minors and regionals as well as the majors. To my astonishment, I got acknowledgments or application forms back from every one. Some replies were form letters requesting that I fill in and return the accompanying application blanks. Many of the acknowledgments said, Thank you very much for your interest, we regret we are not hiring at this time. TWA and American Airlines replied with personal letters. TWA cordially requested me to keep them updated on my progress. American said that a number of their pilots were actually on furlough but that they expected to be hiring later in the year or early in '73, and would I please complete the enclosed application. They would notify me if a suitable opening developed.

I set up an alphabetical filing system and typed up applications to American, Aspen Airways, Continental, Eastern, Pan Am, TWA, United and all the other airlines I knew anything about, and then to all the ones I didn't. All these applications would remain on file for a specific length of time, usually for six months, during which time I would be under consideration should anything arise.

My files began to bulge with copies of letters, applications and more acknowledgments. I started feeling that I was getting somewhere. There seemed to be a hiring slump, but I was confident that my deluge of applications would turn up a few job interviews.

I confided my hopes to Allan, then flying copilot on the DC-8 for Seaboard.

Very seriously, he said, "Oh, they're not going to hire a woman. That's a man's job, and men need those jobs. They have to support their families."

I stared at him, my beloved brother, who had always thought it was so great that his little sister loved to fly. We had flown together, and that had been terrific. He had been pleased with my hours and ratings, seemed almost proud that I was instructing and charter-flying. But for me to be an airline pilot —I guess that was going too far. To work was okay, but to aspire to a job that a man might consider desirable was not okay.

"But what about me?" I demanded. "What about me, taking care of myself? Don't I need a decent job, too?"

He shrugged and didn't say he expected me to get married and get taken care of although I could read it in his mind. Instead, he said, "Well, I think you're being unrealistic. Airlines don't want women pilots."

I was sure he was wrong. I reread my letters. TWA had gone so far as to send me height and weight requirements for females. They had said they were very interested. Unfortunately, they had people on furlough and might not be able to hire for as long as a year or two, but they were encouraging. American had been very positive. There was a definite indication that women were being considered.

But how long would I have to wait . . . ? I couldn't wait a year or two.

As the weeks and months went by, I began to think that Allan was right. The deluge of correspondence stopped. It was too soon for me to update, useless to prod, and I had already written my follow-up letters to what had seemed the most likely prospects. (Answer: "We're still not hiring!") But I had been given no reason to believe that women applicants need not apply.

I waited as patiently as I could. I went to the airport and did my various jobs. I went home and checked the mail. Nothing. I worried it around with Bob, who was sympathetic but ambivalent. I bored my long-suffering parents. The *OAG* did not disclose any new addresses. My files revealed nothing I had overlooked. The result of all my efforts was nothing, nothing, nothing. One big fat ZERO.

"After all these years," I complained. "Working and slaving. Studying, teaching, doing all these grungy jobs. When's it all going to pay off? Is this a way to spend a life?"

Bob looked at me critically. "Just be glad you're not studying to be a brain surgeon," he said coolly. "Furthermore, you're only twenty-three. And I thought you liked your jobs."

I did, but now I wanted more. Certainly twenty-three was old enough to leave home, and if I could find a job that paid any more than three dollars an hour I would do just that. It seemed to me that my career was stalled. During the two and a half years at Pompano I had developed skills and experience, but I seemed to be running in place. I was work-weary. I was going to blow my savings on a vacation in Europe. Interesting things always seemed to happen to me in Europe.

Bob half offered to go with me. I declined. I still thought trips were better solo, especially voyages of discovery.

"Well, have fun," said Bob.

And I did. First in Spain, and then in the South of France. But nothing really significant happened to mold my future. On the way back home I stopped in New York to visit Anita, my sister, who, as a gorgeous blonde taking after the Swedish side of the family, is utterly unlike me. She was already well established in a glamorous public relations career, handling top accounts and meeting fascinating people.

It is ironic that Anita, who had no interest in aviation and whose friends were mainly in the arts and the media, should have been indirectly responsible for the opportunity I was looking for.

That opportunity came heavily disguised in the person of James Brady, the publishing personality who was then the editor of *Harper's Bazaar.* Anita had plans to spend an evening with him and some friends, and invited me to come along.

Coincidentally, *Harper's* was planning a Florida issue for publication in January of 1973. A reporter and camera crew would be down in my area within the next few weeks, working on a profile of people in southern Florida. Brady looked me over appraisingly as he told me this, and then asked if I would like to be interviewed for the issue.

"Why, sure," I said. "That'd be terrific."

I went on home, and the *Harper's* crew came down in November with their cameras and tape recorders. For a few wonderful hours I was the glamorous center of attention, all careful makeup and graceful poses, after which the crew turned its attention to bigger game and I went back to work.

My brief vacation had recharged my flagging batteries and sent me back to my application files to get a fresh slant on them. The more I reviewed them, the more it became clear that my avoidance of higher education had left a blank in an important space. I knew that most, if not all, of my flight students who had found airline jobs were college graduates. By now I also knew, from bits and pieces I had put together, that a flight engineer's ticket was considered highly desirable. That was not something I could get at Pompano.

I applied for admission to the Miami extension of the Embry-Riddle Aeronautical Institute to plug up some of the gaps in my knowledge. My jobs would cover my tuition fees as long as I continued to live at home, and I could commute to Miami fairly easily. Being accepted was a shot in the arm. Equally pleasing was the course credit Embry-Riddle was giving me for my ratings. At least I wouldn't be starting from scratch. Graduation with a two-year associate's degree would be only months away.

While waiting for the term to begin I went about my usual business. I flew my bricklayers and my turkeys, took my socialites to Bimini, started studying for my flight engineer's written exam. Debbie Gary made her lazy circles and heart-stopping side slips through the sky, giving me her veiled looks whenever our paths crossed. Word went the rounds that the governor of Florida wanted a pilot for his Queen Air, and I was told that I was in the running for the job. Aspen Airways gave me a tremendous boost by accepting me as a candidate for their training program. I was thrilled, but I had committed myself to going after the majors. With all respect and gratitude to Aspen, I did not want to tie up with a small airline flying DC-3s. I *knew* something would happen with the Big Ones.

Bob was his usual steadfast self, encouraging me to do what I felt I should and yet not wildly enthusiastic about my goals. He continued to help me, and he continued to doubt. We talked about his work and about mine. He thought mine was fun—which it was—and yet he took it seriously. It was when we discussed my long-term future that he was very much a gentleman of the old school. With all his heart, he wanted me to have what I wanted, including a flying career, but I don't think he could bring himself to believe that a woman's career could or should be of primary importance to her. For a while, perhaps. But eventually she must become domesticated.

Once he asked, "When are you going to make a commitment?" I could have said, "What do you have in mind?" Instead, I went into my airline pilot routine; I had this to do and that to do, people to see and places to go, and I already had commitments if anyone had. He looked at me as if I were seriously lacking somewhere. Maybe I was.

The January issue of *Harper's Bazaar* came out as scheduled. I appeared in a couple of very soulful photographs, all long hair blowing in the machine-made breeze and cheekbones accentuated into nobility by skillful makeup and photography. The story was headed, "Bonnie Tiburzi: In Control," and described me as "—A dynamic woman . . . with a commercial pilot's rating. Only one major obstacle in her way . . . the commercial airlines will only accept a woman as an attractive order-taker for 'coffee, tea or milk.' Bonnie aims to change all that and be the first woman in the cockpit."

It went on: "Her goal: to be a commercial jet pilot. Today, 10 percent of all the world's pilots are women, but so far, the airlines in the U.S. have been negative to the idea of women captaining their flying ships. She has applied to all of them with no success. Answers have been polite but have always been 'No.' " And it ended: "*Bazaar* is betting that she will pilot that commercial jetliner yet!"

I looked at myself and didn't know me, but I thought the pictures were great. I loved the one of me in the cockpit, a fashion model with rings like knuckle-dusters on my fingers and a squinty look in my luminous eyes. Now if that were the cockpit of a commercial jet . . . I'd probably be told to get the hardware off my hands, cut my hair and attend to my instrument panel.

The *Harper's* story rapidly inspired a spate of articles in the local newspapers and wire services about the jet-setter who flew her own jet and dreamed of flying for the airlines. Debbie sniffed disdainfully, the fellows at Pompano outdid each other in hilarious comments and even I was a bit embarrassed about the jet-setter part. On the whole, though, I felt good about the *Harper's* piece. It helped to bring me into focus. Never mind that it read like a society page; that was the fun of it. There, in black and white, was my ambition, and it didn't look unlikely or silly. It made perfect sense. It also gave me the feeling that I had arrived somewhere—not in the jet set, which had made me laugh, too, but at a place where I could be seen as an individual trying to accomplish something.

With this cheering thought in mind, though rapidly fading, I continued doing exactly what I had been doing. Any day of the week the jet-setter could be seen copiloting a DC-3 carrying groups of fun lovers to the Bahamas or ferrying fishermen, gamblers, surfers, politicians, landowners, businessmen and ballplayers to their desired destinations in and around sunny Florida, the envy of her earthbound peers. It was business as usual for me while the airlines of the nation gave the distinct impression of being monumentally uninterested in hiring me.

6

"Eastern's Hiring"

His name was Gene Steele and he was a lawyer with the FAA in Washington. He was calling, he said, because he had seen my picture and the accompanying story in *Harper's Bazaar*. I had an instant pang of uneasiness. Could it be that I had done something to offend the FAA?

He was a furloughed United pilot, the voice was saying, and he'd been most interested in my efforts to get a job with the airlines. Even though United was still not hiring, there might be jobs available.

My brain came alive.

"Jobs? Where?"

"American's hiring," he said.

"But I applied to American," I told him. "They said they'd let me know if an opening developed. That was at least eight months ago."

"Yes, but you've got to keep updating. They want to know what you've done lately. Haven't you been doing that?"

Actually, no. Not systematically. True, the letter from American had said something like, feel free to send an update to your application from time to time should any information change, but I thought it was just the personnel department being nice.

"They don't say things like that to be nice," said Gene. "If you add hours and experience, they want to know about it. If

I were you what I would do is write to the Chief Pilot in New York, Captain Dan Wetherbee. Send your update to him. I know they'd want you to, and I know they're hiring now. So do it, and good luck."

I had goose bumps when I hung up. The idea that a stranger would take the trouble to call me with a gem of advice was as heartwarming as his information was welcome.

On January 29, 1973, I wrote my letter to Captain D. A. Wetherbee at La Guardia Airport in New York, noting that since sending my initial application I had increased my flying time to more than 1,400 hours, taken on a copilot job on a Douglas DC-3 for a charter company, gotten checked out on seaplanes and obtained my instrument instructor's rating.

Captain Dan Wetherbee wrote back on February 6 informing me that since I resided in Florida, my application had to be processed not in New York but at Dallas Love Field and that he had redirected my updated information there.

A week later—now things were starting to move fast!—I got the phone call.

I was at Pompano Aviation waiting for my scheduled student to arrive when Reception called out, "Bonnie, line two, you have a phone call."

The next voice said, "Hi, Bonnie. This is Ben Tillman, American Airlines Pilot Recruiting Office, Personnel Representative. We'd like you to come down to Dallas next week for your interview, a little test, and a miniphysical. It'll only take one day. How about the twentieth?"

As I hung up, my screech of delight sent shock waves across the room and out over the runways. I started gabbling to everyone in sight. "Oh, wow, guess what! Hey, listen!" I told so many people within the next few days that I had laryngitis by the time I left and still had it when I arrived. My voice was two octaves lower than usual.

Before leaving, I did some homework. I had flown on American only once in my life and I knew very little about the airline. I looked up where American flew, found that the company was based in New York City and had no Florida connections, that it was a conservative airline with a fine safety record and that it employed nearly 3,800 pilots flying Boeing 727s, 707s, 747s and DC-10s—all the things I thought a prospective employer might like me to know.

Early on the morning of February 20 I was on my way, conservatively dressed in my one good outfit. Ben Tillman had told me that I could arrange all my own transportation to Dallas Love Field or make my way to the closest airport serviced by American Airlines and pick up a pass on American for the rest of the way. Of course I elected the latter, not so much to save money as for the sake of getting acquainted.

By the time I got to the ticket counter in Nashville and asked for my pass, everybody seemed to know who I was. They said, "Oh, are you the little girl who's going down for pilot training?" I was introduced to all the ticket agents and taken into the offices to meet the secretaries, and greeted by American's Chief Pilot in Nashville, Dave Chambers, who wished me the best of luck. I thought, Oh boy, what a friendly family this American Airlines is. I just know we're going to have a wonderful life together.

But I wasn't all that sure. It was fun to be fussed over, but at the same time it was odd to be singled out as "the little girl who. . . ." Like any job applicant, I was nervous about the upcoming interview, especially since none of my previous jobs had required any formal application, yet there was something dreamlike and unreal about the journey and my reason for making it.

Nervousness rose above the sense of unreality as we landed at Dallas Love Field and I was ushered behind the American Airlines ticket counter to the offices. Jets blasted overhead as Ben Tillman welcomed me to the personnel department, asked me a few opening questions and handed me some forms. While I filled them out he looked at my logbooks with, I thought, a noticeable lack of interest.

I finished the forms. Tillman gave me some more. "This is

just a little preliminary test," he said. I looked at the questions. Vocabulary, mathematics, general knowledge, space perception, starting easy and getting progressively harder. Maybe a hundred questions.

"It's a time test," said Tillman. "Twenty minutes. Eighty percent is the minimum passing grade." He looked at me quizzically. "There's a lot of math in this test."

My instant reaction was the thought, Oh, I'm terrible at math! I looked at Tillman. He was expecting me to say something. It struck me that almost every girl I'd ever met would say, "Oh, I'm terrible at math!" Most women seem to think they are, while men are usually very confident about numbers—if not downright obsessed with them.

"I hope you do well," Tillman said gently.

"Oh, I'm terrible at math," I moaned involuntarily.

"Well, good luck."

I was expecting algebra and trigonometry, both of which were mysteries to me. Instead, there were practical questions in addition, subtraction, multiplication, spatial and depth perception; nothing requiring much more than a working knowledge of numbers, shapes and basic mechanics.

I was so relieved that I sailed through the whole thing in the required twenty minutes and got what Tillman said was a good grade. First hurdle over.

The next was Captain A. B. "Chubby" Crimmins, Chief Pilot for the Dallas–Fort Worth area. Ben Tillman took me to his office. This would be a very important interview.

Crimmins. Captain Crimmins. The name was tough and intimidating. Captain Crimmins rose behind his enormous desk. He was a good-looking silver-haired man, unusually tall and broad, with the straight no-nonsense look of the typical senior airline pilot. He looked down at me and smiled. "Bonnie—how are you? Please sit down." Well, pleasant enough.

I sat down and started to gabble in my hoarse voice: about the airplanes I was flying, and American Airlines is so wonderful, and I've always wanted to fly with American Airlines and so on and so on and so on.

He wrote and wrote and wrote. Why doesn't he ask me anything? I thought desperately. I had researched and rehearsed it all so carefully. He was going to say, "Well, tell me what you know about American Airlines." I was going to tell him how terrific it was and how long I'd looked forward to working for them. But he didn't ask me anything. He just sat there and wrote.

What was he writing? Why didn't he ask me any questions?

I started to fade. It was obvious that I was nervous, but all applicants must be nervous. Surely, even if he couldn't get a word in edgewise, he must have a general idea of my profile through my application, my test, my general appearance and attitude, my interview with Tillman, my flying hours, my . . . I ran out of steam while I worried. There was a silence while Captain Crimmins finished writing.

He got up with a big smile and, still without asking me a single question, thanked me for coming and wished me luck for the rest of the examination. "Hope everything works out," he said, shaking my hand.

I squeezed back firmly, to show I was a solid individual and not one of those limp and fishy handshakers. I still had no idea what he thought of me, except for the handshake and the smile, which I'm sure he bestowed on everyone. The big unknown was whether he was genuinely considering a female applicant—and why he hadn't said anything.

Little did I know that he had two or three daughters and a wife at home. When he told them that he was going to interview a woman that day, they had said, "You'd better pass her, or don't come home!" He told me that months later. And, of course, the reason he hadn't asked me anything is that, unasked, I told him all he wanted to know and a whole lot more.

Tillman walked into the chief pilot's office as I walked out, and I waited awhile for him in the corridor. He came out shuffling a sheaf of papers, his face wreathed in smiles.

"Terrific interview," he said. "Captain Crimmins gave you a very good report and wants to know if you can stay for the regular eight-hour physical instead of taking the miniphysical this evening."

Standard procedure was for the applicant to be given a brief preliminary checkup after which he would go home and wait while a pilots' board reviewed all the application and interview material, analyzing and assessing each candidate against the others. I had not seen any others, but I had heard that there had already been several thousand applicants for something like two hundred slots. Any candidates considered by consensus to be particularly promising would be notified to return for a marathon physical. Being asked to stay seemed like a good sign. Or was it?

"Well, can you do that?"

"Oh, sure, fine!"

Of course, expecting to go home that night, I'd brought no extra clothes or overnight gear, nothing but a toothbrush and a few incidentals, but my wardrobe could not have mattered less to me at that point.

Tillman sent me to a nearby hotel, and I fell asleep wondering how a physical examination could possibly last an entire day.

Next morning the Fort Worth limo service picked me up and took me to the American Airlines Flight Academy. My sense of unreality came back as we drove through the gates toward the vast expanse of the academy, at first sight a series of huge interlocked boxes gleaming white in the early sun. As instructed, I reported to Health Maintenance at eight o'clock sharp.

"Health Maintenance" had struck me as an odd piece of airlinese, perhaps something adapted from the military services. Pilots identify with the word "maintenance," Tillman had explained. "Medical Center" just didn't sound like pilot talk. The term sounded mechanical to me. But that was okay. A body is a machine which should be fine-tuned periodically and carefully maintained.

I reported in yesterday's discreet little black-and-white outfit and sat down on a bench outside Health Maintenance waiting to be called in. The facility was an enormous, streamlined place that looked like something out of *2001,* full of people in uniform or white coats or neat suits gliding up and down quiet corridors past rooms full of futuristic equipment. A constant stream of purposeful-looking individuals flowed in and out, men and women who I later discovered were pilots, flight attendants, administrative and other personnel getting checkups or some form of medical attention. All American Airlines personnel in the area, including the applicants to the academy's Stewardess College or Learning Center—affectionately known to irreverent locals as the Charm Farm, there being no male flight attendants at that time—came to this one enormous place to have their health maintained. But the pilot physical was especially rigorous, for a pilot's health is as vital as a pilot's skills.

We sat together on the bench, five or six of us, with me on the end. I looked down the row, and the row looked back at me. Everyone else had gray suits, gray vests, freshly close-cropped hair with white patches of skin where sideburns and mustaches had been shaved off, black socks and shiny polished wingtip shoes. They looked so exactly alike they could have been clones.

After a few minutes we were all called in, the clones and I, and shown to the changing rooms.

Once again I was bemused and gratified by unaccustomed attention. The nurses and doctors had known that I was coming, and they all seemed excited about it. In one of the little changing cubicles I put on my paper robe and slippers. Coming out, I saw the guys milling around in the same attractive costume and casting looks and tee-hees over at me. This was the peach-fuzz set; surely they were too young and silly to be here.

I, mature and sensible, was firmly led off in one direction while the boys were taken off in another, presumably so there would be no naughty peeking. When I was lying down for my cardiogram I caught glimpses, through a gap in the curtain, of the male applicants going by, ushered past by the nurses so that none of us would meet at any point.

The game of hide and seek went on all day long, interspersed with blood taps, knee taps, the standard eyes-ears-nose-throat examination, a urinalysis, a glucose test, a lung capacity test and a lot more. From time to time a technician or a nurse would comment on how odd it was to be giving the pilot's physical exam to a woman. There were no other female applicants, and apparently never had been. Flight attendants, yes, in groups completely separate from the men; pilots, no.

Just before lunch I was given an electroencephalogram, in part to detect epilepsy and in part to determine my normal brain pattern so that, in case of an accident or other incident, they could come back to this scan, repeat it and detect any brain damage or clotting. To set me up for the electrodes they slathered my hair, which was down to my waist at that time, with a thick gluey substance that sank right down to the scalp pores. Clumps of gummy hair stuck out in all directions as if tied to stakes. I made the Bride of Frankenstein look good.

I showered afterward. There was no shampoo. I sudsed and sudsed with soap. The male assistant kept stopping by, offering arm's-length assistance of some sort. "More soap!" I kept begging. "Could I please have some more soap?"

I got most of the mess out of my hair as best I could, but it was still greasy when I towel-dried and pulled my lank locks back and tied them in a waist-length pony tail. It was time for my lunch break, according to what I'd been told earlier, so I shuffled back to my changing cubicle and tried my hardest to put myself back together. By the time I had dressed and applied a little makeup, my hair had started to dry. And as it dried, the gummy substance turned to a stiff and chalky crust, like well-whipped egg white. Swell. Glamorous jet-setter will now enter the cafeteria, and all heads will turn with admiration.

All heads turned.

By this time, everybody seemed to know there was a female applicant at the academy. I click-clacked up the long hall from Health Maintenance, around the corner and through the large glass doors into the cafeteria. Silence fell as I walked the endless gauntlet, heavily conscious of my curiously piebald hair with its drying pony-tail tip looking as if it had been dipped in a pail of whitewash. Out of the corners of my eyes I glanced at the fellows. None of them had white spotty heads. But none of them had pony tails, either.

Click-clack from me. Silence at the tables.

I reached the food line and a buzz-buzz of conversation started up behind me. At last, everybody was making normal sounds again. Yet I still felt painfully self-conscious, as if I were a visitor with some physical defect while all the others belonged there and were perfect. All I wanted to do was sit down as soon as possible and fade into the crowd. Even choosing something to eat was a problem. The simplest thing, as I scanned the bill of fare and the confusion of dishes in the counters, seemed to be egg salad. "I'll have an egg salad sandwich, please." I said boldly.

The woman behind the fast-food counter slapped an enormous ice-cream scoop of egg salad on a piece of bread and handed it to me in one swift fluid motion. I finished loading up my tray and walked back into the dining area, a lull falling ahead of me like grass bending in a wind. Sound started up again as I found a vacant table and sat down, except for the little bubble of quietness immediately around me. As soon as I dug into my sandwich the egg salad spurted through my fingers and dribbled down my arm.

Wonderful. It's probably one of the most important days of my life and I'm sitting here with white gummy hair and egg salad all over me.

Several youngish men with trays suddenly appeared beside

me, said Hi, and sat down at my table. They said they were new hires, going to classes at the academy. Was I the woman applicant they'd heard tell of? Yes, I was. The ice broke instantly. One, a Southerner who introduced himself as David Rottgering, was especially pleasant. He was a thirty-three-year-old former Navy pilot who had flown with the Blue Angels, the Navy's spectacular exhibition team, and had since been flying for World Airways.

Dave was thrilled about being hired by American. He'd always wanted to get on with American, he said, and was surprised and happy that he'd made it. Airlines don't, as a rule, like to hire pilots as old as thirty-three, and he felt that American was giving him the opportunity of his life.

I liked Dave on sight and I was pleased for him, but he gave me pause to think. If American was hiring Blue Angels, crack pilots with years of Navy flight experience and even more years with another airline, they surely couldn't think too much of my background. Suddenly, all my ratings, my 1,400 hours and all my little flying jobs shrank down to nothing.

By this time my table was not only fully occupied but surrounded by guys with interested faces, standing around chatting away with friendly curiosity. I went on biting into my huge sandwich not knowing what to say, still dripping egg salad down the back of my hand and making a thorough mess of myself. I was sure they must be thinking, "Oh, God! Why *this* woman?," but they gallantly overlooked my table manners. "Yes, I'm going for my interviews," I managed. "Isn't this exciting?"

"Heavy odds," said somebody. "You don't want to be too disappointed if you don't make it the first time. Lots of guys do several interviews, maybe with different airlines, before they get on. This isn't a great hiring binge—only two hundred and fourteen slots. And fifteen thousand applicants."

Fifteen thousand! Conversation seemed to stop as I stared across the roomful of confident young men. I can't take this seriously, I thought. I'm the only woman among fifteen thousand applicants. I'm a token woman. They must be interviewing me as part of a quota. It's because of the women's movement. It's a gesture toward minority hiring. They have to show they're willing. They don't really mean it. They don't want me. Nobody wants a woman airline pilot. Nobody—

"—Emily Howell," Dave was saying. "Frontier's just hired her, is what I hear. So it isn't as if nobody's hiring women."

"Frontier?" I said. "Denver? They hired a woman? What'll she be flying?"

Dave shook his head. "Dunno. Think they have mostly Convair 580s."

Hmm. Nice work, Emily, whoever you are.

Cheered by the thought that my interview might be something more than a sop to women's lib, I relaxed into the conversation. The fellows were wonderful, as encouraging and enthusiastic as they could be. By the time we finished lunch, I was soaring with happiness.

I floated out of the cafeteria with a group of young men, all of us chatting away like old friends. They were on their way to the simulators and I was heading back to Health Maintenance for another battery of tests, feeling higher than a kite and ready to tackle any psychological quizzes or exercise-cardiograms they could throw at me.

We paused where our paths diverged and made parting chitchat about hoping to see each other again. A second group came out of the cafeteria and walked toward us, wearing an air of authority—even a touch of arrogance.

"Instructors," said one of my new friends. "Those guys are line pilots called in to teach the simulators. That guy in back there, Chuck Somebody, he was a Blue Angel, too, hired here a few years ago. Macho type. He's teaching 727 engineers."

I glanced at him. Very macho male type.

My friends and I exchanged warm goodbyes. Life was great, everybody was wonderful, I felt completely accepted and really up.

I took a few steps down the corridor and turned around to

wave at my lunch companions. Chuck Somebody, walking along behind them, slowed down and gave me an appraising look.

"Oh, by the way," he said coolly, "Eastern's hiring." And walked on.

I looked at him with my mouth open and my heart plummeting. My balloon of happiness burst. I walked back to Health Maintenance with my tail between my legs. Some chance I'll have of being hired with guys like that around.

7

The Inn of the Six Flags

Back home at Pompano I settled into my old routine of taking any flying jobs available, dating Bob and one or two casual boyfriends and keeping a grudgingly respectful eye on Debbie Gary. No doubt about it, she was a superb stunt flier. Pity she couldn't have found some other place to park her Pitts.

Nobody showed much interest in my interview, and I was reluctant to volunteer anything. For the time being there was nothing I could do but wait for word from American. If it ever came. There were times when the trip to Dallas seemed like something I invented. Surely it was impossible to have so many hazy, conflicting feelings about something that had really happened.

First, there was my memory of the Flight Academy. It was simply too enormous and too streamlined to be real, like a TV space station. Then there was the contrast between the macho Blue Angel and everybody else at the space—um—Flight Academy. That was fairly easily reconciled: one sour note was not representative of the majority. If Chuck Whatsit felt like putting me down, that was his problem. On the other hand, his negative attitude might have been the expression of a hidden animosity that could surface on a larger scale if I was actually hired.

Then there was Rod, another applicant. He and I had shared a ride back to the airport and ordered a couple of sodas while waiting for our respective flights home. As we sat and sipped our drinks I asked him about his background. He was twenty-eight years old, an Ozark copilot wanting to get on with a major. With about five thousand hours behind him, he flew first officer on the DC-9 and was rated on an F-27—a twin-engine Fairchild—as well as on this, that and the other classy airplane.

I stared at him as he unreeled his wonderful career and thought, My God, somebody like that's a shoo-in. Here I am, twenty-four, and with nothing but general aviation time. Sure, I'm a flight instructor, but who cares? And I've got only fourteen hundred hours to his five thousand.

"That's sensational," I said enviously. "I wonder how many other applicants have qualifications like that."

"Oh, lots of guys," he said with some surprise.

Yes, of course, like Dave, the nice Blue Angel. Lord, if I'm rated against Blue Angels . . .

I picked up an airline magazine on the homebound plane. It was a brand-new issue. In it was a little squib of a story about Emily Howell having been hired by Frontier Airlines as a flight crew member only a couple of weeks before, on January 29. Emily, the story said, had been an aspiring stewardess when she took her first airplane ride and decided that she'd rather do the flying. She had begun lessons in 1958, became an instructor at a flight school near Denver in 1961 and the manager of the school in 1969. Ultimately, she would be flying Boeing 737 twin jets, Convair 580 propjets and de Havilland Twin Otters in Frontier's fleet of fifty-two aircraft. There was also mention of a Barbara Barrett flying for Zantop, a small Michigan regional that apparently spent a lot of its time going in and out of business.

Well, good luck to you both, I thought. Maybe I do have a chance in the majors.

But it was a very slim chance.

One in fifteen thousand.

Or maybe half a chance in fifteen thousand.

The doorbell rang. It was ten o'clock at night and I was sitting home alone. For a change, my parents were out for the evening and I was the stay-at-home. Bob was out of town. I had an early student the next day, if the weather cleared, and meanwhile I was content to be in out of the drizzle.

My heart leapt, and so did I. People in Pompano Beach don't call after nine o'clock, much less come knocking on your door.

I dropped my magazine and tore out of the room.

"Who is it?" I called at the door.

"Western Union for Bonnie Tiburzi!"

I knew what that was. A yes or no from American.

I opened the door, seized the telegram from a startled-looking young man, raced about the house to find some change, gave it to him, shut the door and ripped open the telegram.

> CONGRATULATIONS. [Oh, yes, *yes*, wow!] YOU HAVE BEEN SELECTED AS A FLIGHT CREW MEMBER TRAINEE PENDING RECEIPT OF SATISFACTORY REFERENCES OF FORMER EMPLOYERS. PLEASE ADVISE IMMEDIATELY BY RETURN WIRE WHETHER YOU ACCEPT THE OFFER AND CAN REPORT FOR CLASS MARCH 30, 1973.
>
> [Signed] JOHN D. HODGES AMERICAN AIRLINES
> 633 THIRD AVENUE NEW YORK NY 10017.

I was ecstatic. Adrenaline jolted through me. I walked around the house picking things up and putting them down, thinking about who I could call. Mom and Dad, come home so I can tell you! I picked up the phone and called my sister in New York. She was out. As usual. Who could I call in Florida at that hour? Nobody. I called Allan at his home in New Jersey. No one answered. Too restless to sit, too excited to read, watch television, eat or drink, I kept bobbing up and down from one chair to another until at last I heard a key rattle at the door.

Now I was going to be very cool. I was just going to be calm until they were inside the house, and then I was going to tell them the news casually.

The front door opened and my parents walked in. I flung myself at them, thrust the telegram in their faces and said, "Guess what! Guess what! I've been accepted!"

It took a few seconds for them to read the telegram and grasp what I was going on about. But even before they sat down my father, tears of happiness in his eyes, was saying, "Well, you've got my pilot's sunglasses and my flight computer, and now you can certainly use them, and if you have any questions you can call me and I'll help you through school." Mother said, "What are you going to pack? What do you have to wear to class?"

I didn't know. All I knew was, I was going to send my return telegram first thing in the morning, and then spend the next two weeks gearing up to change my life.

Rain had puddled the Pompano runways the night before and was beginning to fall again as I took over from my student and taxied the airplane onto the wet blacktop. There was a possibility of dry skies later in the day, but there'd be no more flying for a while yet. Most of Pompano's regular airplanes were on the ground, except for those whose owners had taken them for the weekend.

"Nice flight, Don," I said.

My student gave me a modest smile. "Thanks, Bon. See you Wednesday?"

I nodded. "Fine."

He headed for the parking lot and I walked toward Operations. Not many more Wednesdays here for me, I thought, and my heart gave a little leap. While I was working I had pushed the excitement of last night to the back of my mind, but now it all came rushing forward.

Bubbling with excitement and the joy of having friends to

share it with, I opened the door to Ops and bounced in. A lot of people were there—students, flight instructors, airline pilots on their days off and, over in the corner, the insufferable Debbie Gary and her inevitable circle of groupies—sitting around having coffee and playing cards. There's not much else to do in a small airport in bad weather, so I had a ready-made audience.

"Hi, guys," I trilled across the room. "Guess what? I finally got a telegram from American Airlines. I'm going to flight training in a couple of weeks! Isn't this exciting! I'm going to be an airline pilot! I'm hired!"

I stopped. I was the only person in the room making a sound. There was not so much as clink of coffee cups. Heads turned, eyes looked, eyebrows were raised, but no one stood up and cheered. No one even cracked a smile. "I'll be leaving on the twenty-ninth," I said feebly.

At last one of the airline pilots said tonelessly, "Hey, that's great." There was a faint, echoing murmur of, "Oh, yeah, yeah, terrific," and then the heads turned away and shut me out. Conversation started up again.

Oh, by the way, Eastern's hiring, I told myself sourly, and slunk away.

I was staring at what looked like a break in the weather when light footsteps came up behind me and someone grabbed me by the arm.

"Come on outside." Long blond hair swirled beside me. "Let's get away from these jerks. They really give me a pain."

Debbie dragged me through the doorway and turned an incredible smile on me. Still clutching me, she said, "I'm so happy for you. I'm *so* happy you've got this job. Those jerks in there have no idea where you're going or where your head is at—or where *my* head is at. You shocked them, you know that? They never really believed you." She pumped my hand and hugged me. *"I am thrilled for you!"*

I was so surprised and delighted that all I could do was laugh and babble incoherent thanks.

"Also, they're jealous," she added, with a big grin.

I had a sudden sense of relief that our ambitions went in different directions. Debbie was formidable competition.

"You know what I thought about you?" Debbie said later. " 'Who needs her?' That's what I thought. I'd always been at an airport where there was only one woman—me—and I land here, and here you are. Another woman flier! I couldn't stand it. So glamorous, and all the guys falling all over you. You put my nose right out of joint."

Who, *me?* I *did?*

Now we were friends. Having a woman friend was a novelty for each of us. Even more novel was how the two of us, female rivals, suddenly stood together. Of the men, only Tony Riccio, Ed Gargan and Richard Grotke—who had not been present at the time of my triumphant announcement—were almost as happy for me as were Debbie and my parents. To my gratification, they had mixed emotions: they were pleased for me, but sad that I was going. They, too, were friends, true friends.

After a while a few others, mostly the younger fellows with very little flying time, said, "That's great, Bonnie. Congratulations." But there was no general acclamation for the hometown girl on the verge of making good. I was uncomfortably aware that some of the guys resented me. Even among my own students—the advanced ones who had gone on to get much better jobs than I had—there was a strong undercurrent of envy, even indignation. *How dare she get that job? Why didn't I get it?* I found it depressing. Even though I had taught them how to fly, and even though they had far less time and experience than I, they felt slighted because I had gotten an airline job and they hadn't.

If I had felt like making them feel better I could have pointed out that many new hires scrub during the training period, and I might very well be one of them. And even if I made it through the course, I would be on probation for a year. Instead I meditated on the sorry lot of instructors everywhere.

Flight instructing is an important and vital part of flying, and yet people minimize it just as they so often minimize other forms of teaching. *Oh, you're a flight instructor. That's okay—I can take lessons from you, but you're still not as good as I am.* Flight instructing, to me, was an enormous pleasure and also a means of financing experience. Flying is costly, in the learning and the doing, and to many fliers flight instructing is a necessary step, which sometimes becomes a permanent and valuable career.

The two weeks between the telegram and my departure date were difficult and anxiety-ridden. Miffed as I was about being cold-shouldered by my buddies, whom I had always thought of as the rest of the guys, I realized that their reaction was partly because, as Debbie had said, they had never taken me completely seriously when I talked about my ambitions. Now I wondered if I had ever really believed it myself. Those everlasting doubts seemed impossible to bury. This opportunity was something I had worked hard to get, and I felt that I had earned it. Yet it was one thing to work hard for something, then fall comfortably back on the excuse that I didn't get it because I was a woman, and quite another to face the fact that —good God! I've got it!

What was it going to be like? It was going to be tough: eight to ten weeks of intensive training in every aspect of the Boeing 727 aircraft and every detail of a flight crew's duties; learning an entirely new job, that of flight engineer; becoming accustomed to airline procedures after freewheeling around Florida and the islands like a gypsy. There was going to be some really hard material that I'd never covered before: a complex electrical system, with generators, circuit breakers and other mysteries . . . pressurization and air conditioning . . . a new hydraulic system . . . fuel management of three engines . . . a mass of performance data . . . and everything from fixing the coffeemakers to ditching the airplane in an emergency.

I was petrified that I might not pass. Imagine, after all these years of wanting to accomplish something and actually getting accepted, how would it be if I couldn't pass the courses? Or if I didn't fit in? Or if I didn't like it? *If I didn't like it.*

That was a hard one to cope with. I fought it back while putting in extra hours to finish up all the students I could and grooming the rest for other instructors. This was my big chance. This was Equal Opportunity time. The airline wasn't handing me a freebie as a token woman; I knew I had done well in all my tests. But what happens if I don't like it? You can't guarantee to yourself or anyone that you're going to like a job once you get it. What if, after all these years, it's really not what I thought it was going to be?

The possibility lodged uncomfortably in my mind. I couldn't let anybody down by not liking it. Or by failing. Or by being barely acceptable, and then not being able to cut it when I got on the job.

Several people outside the aviation community had commented on what my hiring meant in terms of the women's movement. "What a plus for women's lib!" they enthused. "One more proof that women belong everywhere, that they can do anything they set their minds to. You're doing something for every woman, everywhere."

I am? In that case, I'd better do it right. God, I've got to succeed. If I don't, women all around the country will be saying, Shoot, she flunked out, why couldn't she have been better. What a blow for women's lib! And men all around the country are going to say, See, women couldn't make it to begin with. It's a man's job. Told you so.

If I really didn't like it, I wouldn't be able to quit until I'd shown I was good at it.

The pressure was enormous. It was compounded by the realization that I would be leaving Pompano Beach and my parents forever. Sure, I'd be coming back on vacations, but I wouldn't be living in Florida anymore. At twenty-four years old I was finally grown up and leaving home. All by myself. I had signed away my options. American had no bases in Florida. There was no way I could be close to home. I had guaranteed to American that, upon completion of training, I would be prepared to accept assignment to Boston, New York, Washington, Buffalo, Chicago, Nashville, Dallas, Los Angeles, San Diego or San Francisco, and that I was willing to move anywhere.

That was indeed the case, but now that I was face to face with the future I realized that it wasn't going to be as easy to come home as I would have liked it to be. I would miss Bob, and the neat little structure of life I had built up in Pompano. I wouldn't be piloting the governor's Queen Air. I wouldn't be going to Embry-Riddle. Suddenly everything was different.

I hoped I was prepared to leave my nest, to leave what was so secure for me, to go off into an environment that was totally foreign to anything I'd ever known: a vast, nationwide corporation that was a complete and complex world in itself. I'd be a very small fish in a very large pond and, unless I failed to make the grade, it would be a lifetime commitment. Airlines don't hire temporaries. When they hire a flight crew trainee, they are hiring a potential captain upon whom they are prepared to spend thousands of dollars before putting her to work. Many pilots never leave the line they first hire on with until they reach retirement age, and a good many others only leave if they are furloughed. It's a little like marriage: you don't know exactly how you're going to like it, you hope it's going to be permanent, and only if the relationship proves unbearable do you end it.

Pangs of premature loneliness hit me once in a while, not only for my family and friends but for female companionship I had scarcely known. It was odd to think that I would be the first and only woman trainee at the academy. It was hard to decide whether I liked the idea, but I did have a sense of being the only woman on the space station. Nobody was going to come dropping in to share my space with me. You're *it,* kiddo. The girl.

For all the jumbled thoughts I had about stepping out of my familiar world, I knew I would go. Nor did it cross my mind to ask Bob how he felt about my leaving. We were close, but I didn't feel we were all that close. Anyway, my career was waiting. He already had his.

Finally, Mother and I had to worry about what to pack. I rummaged through my closet wondering what the well-dressed student would wear to class at American Airlines. Not this, I told myself as I sorted, and certainly not that. Shirt and tie for the male students, I mused, American being such a conservative airline, and I suppose I'll have to look basically dignified through the whole thing.

Hardly anything I had was basically dignified. Finally I ran out and bought a few pairs of slacks and several shirts and blouses. That should do it. I packed them, some heels, my bathing suit, a couple of my Lily Pulitzers, my tennis racket and my jogging shoes, and I was all set.

I said my goodbyes and off I went, Delta to Atlanta and change for Nashville, and Nashville to Dallas via American. I went up to the cockpit and introduced myself to the pilots and engineer. You can only do that if you're a fellow professional. It was wonderful. I quite forgot what I'd been worrying about.

"You mean the Flight Attendant College?"

"No, sir, I want to go to the Inn of the Six Flags."

The tall man behind the counter on the little podium looked at me quizzically, still doubting. But my written instructions were very detailed and explicit. Limousine service was available between Dallas Love Field, the American Airlines Flight Academy and the Inn of the Six Flags, where American's trainees were housed. Upon arrival at the airport I was to contact the Brown Limousine representative at his station next to the American Airlines baggage pickup counter.

"I'm an American Airlines student," I added. "I'd like the airline rate to the Inn."

"You're a—?"

'I'm an American Airlines new hire," I said firmly, "and I'm going to the Inn."

"Oh. Okay."

He directed me to a long, off-white limousine with Brown's name painted on it. The car was already almost full. I found a seat in the last row in the back and squeezed in between two neatly dressed young men.

Doors closed. The driver called out, "Where does everybody want to go?"

There was a chorus of "Flight Academy" and "Six Flags."

"Six Flags!" I piped.

The driver turned and looked at me. "You mean the Flight Attendant College, young lady?"

Here we go again. Was it always going to be like this?

"No, sir," I said, getting louder with every word, "I want the Inn of the Six Flags."

With that, all the other heads turned and looked at me. For a moment I wondered if I'd said the wrong thing after all. Surely it couldn't be so unusual for a woman at least to visit the Inn. No . . . I'll bet they've heard there's a woman hire. They figure I must be it.

Okay, so I am.

There was hardly any talking as the limousine left the airport behind, swept past the gleaming expanse of the Flight Academy and its enormous grounds and eventually pulled up in the semicircular driveway of the Inn of the Six Flags.

We carried our baggage into the lobby and looked around uncertainly. Restaurant to the left, magazine and candy store straight ahead, reception area and offices to the right and a number of unsettled-looking young men milling about. I walked up to the reception counter and waited my turn. The young woman glanced at me inquiringly.

"Tiburzi," I said. "I believe American Airlines made a reservation?"

"Um, let's see," she said, running her finger down a column of names. "Yes, Tiburzi's with Rogers. He's in room one-thirty-one, B Wing."

I gave her a blank stare. "You mean I have a roommate?"

The clerk looked up from her list. The by-now familiar phenomenon occurred: everybody, from the reception desk to the candy store, stopped moving and talking. It was like the who's-your-broker ad—everybody listens when E. F. Hutton talks.

The receptionist and I stared at each other. She said, "You're Tiburzi?"

"Yeah, I'm Tiburzi."

A faint, bemused smile raised the corners of her mouth. "Well, in that case . . ." She started rummaging through her files again.

By that time the reception area was like a busy if unusually quiet bar, the counter three or four deep with people waiting to see the outcome of this episode. The woman looked up with a grin and handed me a key.

"Okay, we've got you in another room. Wing D. I'm sorry, it's completely separate from the new hires, but it's the best we can do right now. It's a suite. Enjoy it, because we're going to have to move you in a day or two. When we've figured out exactly what to do with you."

The lobby relaxed. "Wing D," I said."Where's that?"

"Just going that way," someone said.

Two of the guys grabbed my bags and started off with them. "Come on, we'll walk you down to your room. You starting class tomorrow?"

We chatted for the three or four minutes it took to reach my room in a more elegant wing than those reserved for students, laughing about the sudden kink I had put into the Inn's room assignment routine. My escorts were bombarding me with questions when we arrived at my suite. I was exhausted, not because the day had been strenuous—it hadn't—but because it had been jam-packed with novelty.

"Look, fellas, can I meet you on the limo tomorrow morning and we'll talk about everything? And maybe have breakfast together at the academy?" We were due to report to the training service center at the Flight Academy at 0800 the next morning, but we had already discussed breakfast and decided that, since we were paying for our own meals, we had best do most of our eating at the company cafeteria.

The first thing I did, after admiring my luxurious quarters and taking a few things out of a bag, was to run to the phone and call my parents. I thought I'd say something terribly profound when they answered, possibly along the lines of One Giant Step for Womankind, but when my mother picked up the only thing I could do was squeak, "I'm here, I'm here!"

I could visualize my mother as I heard her voice, a little faster and higher-pitched than usual in her excitement; she was holding her hand snug against her cheek and she was beaming with pleasure as she said, "Oh, Bonnie, I'm so proud of you." Then I heard my father on the extension, and I could see that little giveaway shine in his eyes as his voice cracked slightly and he said, "You're my baby." I was always moved when he said that. We talked and giggled for a while, and I told them about Brown's limousine, the friendly guys I'd met in the lobby and my elegant suite, and then we all realized that it was probably time for me to get organized and get some rest for the next day.

That set a pattern for the weeks to come. I had flown the nest, but almost every day I called home and told my parents what had been happening lately and how I was doing with my courses. My father never lacked a response to what I was learning. He always had something a little extra to tell me about technique or finesse, or a little nugget of explanation that helped me tremendously.

Early in the morning of March 30, Brown's Limousine Service picked up a batch of us in the carport of the Six Flags and took us to the Flight Academy. Again I was driven through the gates to the vast, multileveled structure with that clean, gleaming look that had impressed me so much before, setting off the color-coordinated red, white and blue of the company insignia. But now, for some reason, it looked more friendly and accepting than at interview time.

The car pulled up at the administration building and we all piled out. I looked up at the building as we went in, and it seemed to me that it was all windows full of eyes peering out at me.

You're paranoid, I told myself. You always think people are staring at you. Conversation stops when you come in, and people stare out windows.

But it was true. People did stare. And this time they weren't staring at a woman who might have come in to apply for a job in any one of a number of capacities. They were looking at American's first female pilot hire.

8

A Woman in Their Midst

There were twenty of us in Class 73–9, an apparently random selection of ex-military pilots and general aviation fliers. At twenty-four, I was the youngest. The rest ranged in age from twenty-six to thirty-three. All but two or three were married, and already had children or were on the verge of becoming fathers. This much I learned the first day as we sorted ourselves into a group amid the 214 hires and took the first tentative steps toward getting to know one another.

I was relieved to see that the form of dress was neat but casual, although I was the only one in pastels.

Our priorities were getting to the cafeteria in time for breakfast and learning our way through the long, sleek halls to the classrooms, the simulators and the airplane mockups. American's priorities were to photograph us for our I.D. cards and have us fitted for our uniforms. The uniform was a problem.

Standard procedure was for the manufacturer's tailor to measure each student for a standard uniform. For the men it was run-of-the-mill. For me it was a little different, and the manufacturer's man let me know it with his expression as he measured me. Something told me that I didn't measure up to his idea of a pilot. I wondered what in the world he was going to come up with for me.

Fortunately, the men in the ivory tower shared my doubts. The Vice-President of Flight, Captain Ted Melden, called me into his office and sat me down. He was a man with a rich and colorful vocabulary and a bark that was far worse than anybody's bite, and—inevitably—he had a heart of gold beneath that gruff exterior.

"I want you to look at this," he said, handing me a newspaper photograph. "She's a woman pilot."

I could see a tall, apparently shapeless woman in a male pilot's uniform that had evidently been very slightly modified to conform to her contours. *Very* slightly. It was topped off with an unbecoming man's hat. The woman looked bulky, ungainly and absolutely sexless, very much my idea of an Iron Curtain military policewoman.

"Transylvanian Airways?" I inquired.

"Huh? Oh. No. Looks like [bleep], doesn't she? Oh, excuse me. Point is, we don't want you to look like that. Not like a female *male* pilot. We want you to look like a professional pilot who happens to be a female. You try to come up with something. So will we. We'll get samples made. I'm assigning Bill Copeman, Manager, Flying Procedures, to see you through. He'll call you. In the meantime, any ideas?"

I returned the picture. "How would it be if I went over to the Charm—to the Stewardess College? Maybe their outfitters can help."

Melden slammed a heavy hand on the desk top. "Absolutely not. No [bleep] pilot of mine is going to look like a [bleep] stewardess. I want a nice sophisticated professional-looking woman's uniform. No frills. But feminine. Copeman will be in touch. You go back to class."

"Yes, sir."

I took the elevator down from the ivory tower to the real world and click-clacked along the long corridors in my high heels to join my classmates in an orientation lecture.

So ended my first day.

Next day we started settling in and looking around at the other classes. To my surprise, Ozark Rod of the five thousand hours and multiple ratings was nowhere to be seen. He had not been hired. Neither had a number of other applicants whose credentials had seemed awesome to me. I asked around, finally broaching the subject directly to an approachable instructor. Why hadn't some guys with enormous experience been hired instead of me? The fear of tokenism had suddenly struck me again. I was rebuked for even thinking about it.

"Look. In this business, lack of the right kind of experience is not something to play around with. Okay, the women's movement definitely had something to do with your being hired at this particular time. But not as a quota of one, okay? If you didn't qualify, you wouldn't be here. We've got lives in our hands—safety is our primary concern. So. No token hires."

"But what about the guys with thousands—?"

"Okay. You've got your credentials. We know you're a good pilot. The number of hours isn't as important as the *quality* of the time. Another thing. We don't particularly want to retrain veteran pilots. Every airline has its own techniques and style. It doesn't matter if you know how to fly an Ozark 727 or a Delta 727. We want you to fly *our* 727s, and we want to teach you the way American Airlines flies. We have our own way of doing things, and we want all three crew members working in exactly the same way. Our main concerns are cockpit coordination and how you're going to get along with the rest of the crew on a day-to-day basis. Okay? Because you might fly with a different crew every time you fly, and you've got to have that innate ability to get along with all those guys."

He went on.

I had four hundred hours more than the minimum requirement of a thousand hours. Furthermore, I was in robust health. 16American wanted to be sure, when they hired me at twenty-four, that with all the money, time and effort they were about to invest in me, I would retire a healthy captain at the age of sixty. Furthermore, their medical retirement plan was so generous that they could scarcely be faulted for wanting healthy specimens.

Both for their passengers' sakes and for their own, American didn't hire people with a family history of diabetes, heart disease, cancer or any other ailment that might possibly be hereditary or suggestive of family predisposition. Emotional stability was essential. Eyesight had to be 20/20 uncorrected. The company was looking for flexible but not floppy individuals with excellent physical and mental health and good attitude, more than for military pilots. Other airlines might have slightly different requirements. Even American might change some of the requirements and hiring procedures in the future. Meanwhile, let one thing be perfectly clear: I had been judged qualified for training, and that was it.

Now all I had to worry about was keeping up with my fellow students, just about all of whom seemed to be college graduates or to have done their training in the military. I knew that one or two of them had been combat pilots in Vietnam, and a few of the others had majored in aeronautics at such schools as Purdue or Embry-Riddle. The competition was going to be tough.

In fact I did have something else to worry about. I had never realized how much of a fishbowl existence I would be living. Reporters called and asked how I thought I was going to get along with all those men and if they were accepting me. *Newsweek* called and wanted to do an article. American's P.R. department said, "We don't want to do anything until after school. Then we'll have a press conference." *Newsweek* did a piece anyway, a little squib in its "Newsmaker" section. A newspaper columnist observed that a "leading fashion magazine, *Vogue,* has already asked if they can have a reporter and photographer follow Bonnie through her indoctrination," and added, "American Airlines is apparently not too keen on the idea. They want no publicity about her until she graduates in June. There is always a chance she might flunk out." The column, originating in Washington, D.C., happened to be syndicated and was read not only by my old friends in Pompano Beach but also by my very new ones in Texas.

To their uproarious amusement, it was headed, "Jet-Setter Pilot Studies for Wings with Major Airline." "Jet-setter" broke them up. They wanted to know who else was in the set, besides the frozen turkeys I'd told them about. They quoted paragraphs out loud. "Bonnie Tiburzi, featured blah-blah in *Harper's Bazaar* as a jet-setter who flies her own jets, has been hired by American Airlines as their first female pilot trainee. She begins a blah-blah . . . If the twenty-four-year-old aviatrix completes it successfully, she will become the first woman to help staff the cockpit of a jet liner for a major U.S. passenger carrier. With the aura of glamour that already surrounds her, she seems likely to become an overnight celebrity and the best-known woman in flying since Amelia Earhart." This made them fall down and roll in the aisles. There was something just a little hollow in their laughter.

To me, the prospect of celebrity and fame seemed most unlikely. True, there were spurts of publicity throughout the training period, plus countless calls and letters from strangers, bare acquaintances and reporters in search of a story—"Lots of rumors going around that you aren't going to make it through school. Care to comment?"—but, although they kept me busy explaining or denying or declining comment, they did not thrust me into coast-to-coast stardom. They merely added a little discomfort to my daily rounds.

My classmates, when they got over their initial rather forced hilarity, were not unanimously delighted about the attention I was getting. They had to put up with me standing out like a sore thumb in class and with having other classes ogling us as we tramped off to the mockups or the cafeteria. American had made it clear that there would be press coverage of my graduation, if I made it, and everyone knew that arrangements would be made in connection with my presentation to the press.

Then there was the business of my uniform, and American's big question: How are we going to have you look? Bill Copeman, a genial line pilot who'd been upped to the ivory tower, got onto me soon after my first dressmaking discussion with Melden, and it was perfectly obvious to everyone at the academy that I was being singled out for special attention.

It was surprisingly difficult to come up with a uniform design that maintained the American Airlines image of sturdy proficiency and yet permitted me to look feminine. We turned down the efforts of the regular manufacturer and spent hours thumbing through catalogs to find uniforms, hats and blouses that looked adaptable to women pilots' wear. We prowled together through the Mall of the Six Flags looking at hunting caps, red-white-and-blue scarves, ascots, ties and button-down shirts. We came back from our shopping expeditions and spread slacks and blouses all over Bill's desk, discussing them as earnestly as if we were trying to solve a knotty aeronautical problem. We wrote letters to various manufacturers, inviting them to come and look me over. We had weighty discussions about footwear. Since the male pilots wore black socks and black patent-leather shoes, should I wear black stockings and black shoes? Should they be flat and sensible, or stylish and with a little narrow heel?

The uniform question was to go on through my weeks at school and even afterward. It was no wonder that some of the other trainees resented my special treatment just a little bit. They were indulgent, they made jokes and they were never ugly, but I could tell they had reservations about the extra attention I was getting. To my classmates, we were in school together, a unit of twenty people supposedly undergoing exactly the same training for exactly the same purpose, with nobody singled out for privileges. They may have wondered, though nobody ever suggested it to me, if I was going to get special treatment throughout the training course and be judged by a separate standard.

In fact, the meticulous attention devoted to my uniform was

the only preferential treatment ever given me by American. I was the same pilot material as the other students, except for my different physique, and the ivory tower knew it. But the executives at American also knew that they were establishing some sort of precedent in outfitting a woman, and they wanted to do it right. Whether I passed the course or not was up to me. Yet the spotlight obviously set me aside a little. I liked it, and I didn't.

My classmates were unaware that they themselves were treating me in a special way. Sure, I was just another trainee, but a gentleman holds a door open for a lady. A male student carries the coed's books. A man with any manners ushers a girl into her seat and slides it gracefully beneath her. They were always holding doors open, but they didn't quite know what to do about the other chivalrous gestures. They made them tentatively, as if I might be insulted, or they went to extremes to avoid having to do anything. Having only one coed in class put us all in a faintly ridiculous position. I enjoyed all the little courtesies but was torn, myself, between gracefully accepting them and indicating that they really weren't necessary. At least, not on the job.

The men started getting letters from their wives and cute little finger-painted notes from their kids. I started getting letters from my family, from the boys back at Pompano, from American Airlines personnel who were pleased that I had been hired and from old-timers who remembered the old golden days of women fliers. The letters from retired American Airlines pilots were a boost to my morale. "I wish I'd had a copilot that looked like you." And, "I'll never get a chance to fly with you, but good luck." They were getting a kick out of what I was doing, and they had a frame of reference that included female fliers.

The guys in my class were a whole different breed: cool, skilled professionals, whose knowledge of women aviators was limited to Amelia Earhart and the closing incident of her career. "Oh, she got lost somewhere, didn't she?" Older fliers, whose experience dated back to World War II, knew that women had flown for the British Air Transport Service and the WASPs, the American Women's Airforce Service Pilots. The young men, not knowing, made it clear by their attitude that they thought I was barging into a male preserve and had no business being there, no matter what Gloria Steinem or Betty Friedan might say.

I was not trying to make a point. I kept telling them that. I was just being me. But they were politely skeptical.

They were also intrigued. If I wasn't trying to prove something, why was I doing this? Was I doing it for the publicity? Did I really think I was as good as a military pilot? Did I think I would have been hired if I had not been a woman? Did I have any boyfriends? What did they think about it? Most of my classmates were enormously inquisitive about my private life. I answered everything they asked, but they always seemed to think there must be something more.

Maybe they were right. But was it really so hard to find a motivation for wanting a prestigious, exciting job with built-in challenges and opportunities, doing exactly what I loved to do and getting well paid for it? To me, flying was not a closed profession. Obviously, American Airlines felt the same.

But the guys had always thought of themselves as special, and my presence somehow made them a little less special. I remember one of them saying—and others agreeing—"If you're going to be an airline pilot, look like one. Wear a suit and tie, wear a hat like ours." I said, "Hey, wait a minute! Why does an airline pilot have to look like you? Anyway, you don't have your uniform yet, any more than I do."

And then some others said, "I suppose you're going to want a maternity leave clause in your contract."

None of us would be eligible for a union contract until the end of the probation period, which would last for a year after the completion of flight school. I had not yet begun to think of maternity leave. Now I did.

"Sure, I think maternity leave should certainly be in the contract."

Big grins from the fellows. "If you get maternity leave, *we* should get maternity leave, too."

Small smile from me. "Okay, then *you* have a baby, too."

All this chitchat was outside of class. In class, we worked intensely. There was never any attempt to upstage or downgrade me. Only two distinctions were made between me and the rest of the class. One was in the matter of the ritual off-color joke, and the other was the strength test.

The tradition was that, after each break between our fifty-five-minute classes, the instructor would open the session with a lively story to get things going. Naturally it was on the raunchy side. Conscious of my delicate sensibilities, my fellow students made me stand out in the hall—with my fingers stuck in my ears—while the warmup anecdote ran its course. There was a small glass pane in the door through which I peered at them and they cast roguish glances at me while muffled gales of masculine laughter filtered out into the corridor. When the joke was over, they signaled me to come in. Oddly enough, I did not feel excluded. It was rather like having a lot of older brothers, whose enjoyment of their dumb jokes was enhanced by stopping up the ears of their innocent little sister. If they wanted neither to offend me nor to give up their male ceremony, that was okay with me.

They had already eliminated one other tradition on my behalf. Every once in a while the lectures were accompanied by slides demonstrating the hydraulic system of the 727 or the cockpit configuration or something of the sort. In pre-Tiburzi days the instructors had been accustomed to slip a shot of a nude and nubile female into the series of ten or twenty unexciting aircraft scenes just to make sure that everybody was awake and paying attention—especially after lunch, when there was a tendency to nod—but they dropped that practice for Class 73–9.

Apparently Eastern Airlines had the same tradition, and also suspended it when they hired Barbara Barrett as their first female pilot. Barbara, a little cleverer and more innovative than I, snuck into the slide room one day during a break, found a view of a nudie in a *Playboy*-like pose and slipped it into the slide sequence. Came the hour of the slide presentation. Barbara sat there among the men. An unsuspecting instructor breezed through his lecture and clicked the slides through their paces. Then all at once there was a roar of laughter, and he looked up to see a naked lady on the screen. According to Barbara, who was laughing harder than anyone, he was suddenly all thumbs, trying to turn on the lights and turn off the film switch at the same time and succeeding only in calling more attention to the naughty picture. It's funny, now, to realize how old-fashioned some of those men were. Old-fashioned, decent and rather charming. The instructor was mortified when he thought it was his fault, and doubly mortified when he discovered that it wasn't. But the rest of the class got a kick out of it, and the incident nicely broke the ice for Barbara.

My first challenge came with the strength test.

I, and only I, was called out of the class one morning for a special trip to one of the simulators, a scale model of the 707 cockpit which duplicated all the machinery, instrumentation and movements of the real thing. It had suddenly occurred to somebody that, in case of the loss of a couple of engines or of a complete hydraulic failure, I might not have the bulk or the strength to manipulate the flight controls manually. "Oh, it's not just you," I was told when I got there. "Anybody under five-ten or a hundred and forty pounds."

Huh. I saw no one else that size around.

I sat in the captain's seat feeling a trifle surly. I had been flying for years, and strength had never been a measure of getting an airplane off the ground or back down onto it.

With an instructor at my side, another in the first jump seat, and Captain Al Brown, the check airman, to supervise, I took the simulator to flight altitude and airspeed.

The instructor killed the two engines on one side, leaving me with two on the starboard wing.

Suddenly I was flying an airplane that yawed toward the two dead engines, and fighting the rudder pedal to keep directional control. It takes leg strength to compensate for the thrust of an aircraft with one-sided power, and I felt my leg muscles straining and beginning to quiver. But after the first instantaneous swing to the left we recovered direction, and now all I had to do was maintain it. I straightened my leg and locked my knee to keep the rudder where I wanted it. Years of tennis and swimming and surfing, plus just having been trained on the DC-3, had conditioned my legs so that I had no difficulty in holding the rudder and keeping us straight.

"All right, now . . ." said the instructor. "Just hold it right there." And he trimmed the aircraft in such a way that the stabilizer was locked into an extreme nose-down position. We bombed toward earth at a dangerously steep angle. He took his hand off the trim. "You've got it!" he said cheerfully. "And there's no electric trim."

No hydraulic power. We'd reverted to manual. With two engines out and my right leg clamped to the right rudders.

I yanked the yoke back and reached for the hand crank between the pilots' seats to manually retrim and stabilize the airplane. Whoops! This is harder than I thought! The manual trim crank is like a big fishing reel, and it was as tough to turn as if I had hooked a giant tarpon. I really needed an extra hand, although I could just manage to turn the thing . . . whoops again! I couldn't hold the yoke with one hand—the airplane shot back into an acute nose-down angle. I grabbed the wheel with both hands until we were flying level again.

Now for the hand crank. This is ridiculous. I need another limb. Arm, leg, anything will do. So happens my left leg isn't doing anything at the moment. Still clutching the yoke with both hands, I positioned it precisely and wrapped my left leg around the yoke column. Left hand grabbing my ankle to lock myself into place, I let go with my right hand and applied the full leverage of my right arm to the hand crank. It turned obediently.

All this had taken seconds. I had control of the airplane, and I would know exactly what to do next time.

My instructor gave a throat-clearing or maybe a choking sound.

"That's the silliest thing I've ever seen in the cockpit of a 707," he remarked. I followed the direction of his eyes: one leg encased in a bright pink Lily Pulitzer trouser locked around a yoke column, an open sandal revealing brightly painted toenails and a clutching hand with long fingernails to match.

"Well, I wasn't exactly planning—" I began.

"That's all right. Whatever works for you," he said ambiguously. "Let's go to lunch."

And so we did.

I heard no more about my strength test. A little while later, another of the 214 hires who was shorter than 5 feet 10 inches went through the same procedure and also passed. I suspect his method was more orthodox than mine, but no matter—if it works, it works. American subsequently incorporated the strength test and other simulator procedures into their interview program, thus presumably weeding out the weaklings before hiring them. Other women on other airlines have similarly been asked to prove themselves—including women as short as 5 feet 3 inches and quite delicately built—and, to the best of my knowledge, all have found efficient ways of coping. Muscle sometimes helps to make things easier, but it doesn't solve problems.

As for myself, it had never occurred to me that I might lack the strength to do anything I might be required to do, but passing this first test gave me a little cushion of confidence.

After that simple trial of strength in the simulator, I was never officially called upon to demonstrate that I, as a woman, could do what every pilot should be able to do. Small adaptations were useful sometimes but not vital. Class work turned out to be no problem: I already had more than the basics of navigation, hydraulics, electrical systems and the use of radio aids. We all knew how to fly a variety of airplanes; but I found, to my surprise, that I had more ratings and hours than many of my classmates. Those who had come up through the superior training offered by the military did not, in large part, have multiengine experience, and none had the variety of flight time earned through charter flying and instruction.

The civilian—general aviation—pilots lacked the tremendous discipline of the military, the extensive jet time and the action flying, but our general knowledge was broader. We had not leapt up in the icy—or steaming—dawn to the sound of reveille, bootcamped our beds into smooth perfection, gone to mess hall for breakfast and taken off into combat. There could be nothing to compare with that. But we had gotten up at ungodly hours to be at the airport at six, to fly odd loads to unprepossessing places or instruct students who were due in their offices at nine, then stayed late to teach instrument flying in the darkness. We'd begged and scratched for jobs, taken everything that had come to hand, just to fly the airplanes. So we had been through a similar trial by fire.

It was interesting to observe that, initially, the civilian pilots, of whom there were three or four in my class, excelled in the simulators. They were so accustomed to flying anything they stepped into that they adapted easily and flexibly to the unfamiliar controls of the 727. As I saw it, much of our training was based not only on our background as pilots but on simple mechanical facility, hand-eye coordination, the ability to apply logic to changing sets of circumstances and the kind of practicality characteristic of so many housewives and mothers. My own small ability to find round pegs to fit into round holes helped far more than my lack of higher mathematics hindered me. We *made* things go right.

I had one little problem in the simulator, which no one else seemed to have and which required some form of compensation. There was one circuit breaker way up high in the left-hand corner of the cockpit, near the ceiling, set flush with its surrounds at too awkward an angle for me to reach without rising from my engineer's desk and twisting my body in such a way that my leverage was wrong for grasping the switch or leaving me enough hand strength to pull it. The first time, I was slow and clumsy. Every time after that, when I had to pull that circuit breaker during practice, I grabbed my pliers, reached up and popped the circuit breaker and put my pliers back in place with absolutely no waste of time or motion at all. It amused my training partners, but they could appreciate the practicality of my method. In time, I found that there is nothing a woman—a trained pilot and engineer—cannot overcome with a little ingenuity, plus a particular flexion of the body to gain leverage, and maybe a pair of pliers. Or a screwdriver, a magic tool which seems to fix everything in the cabin from stuck galley drawers to stubborn seat backs.

Training in the simulator got us accustomed to teamwork, each of us learning all the tasks to be done by the flight crew as a team. With the engines roaring and whining, the instruments indicating a range of conditions from altitude through airspeed to fuel flow and cabin pressure, we learned to cope with every problem that might arise. Hail lashed on our fuselage, cloud cover enveloped us, instruments failed, compasses went crazy, radio communication was lost, engines caught fire, simulated scenery swerved past our windows as simulated ground rushed up to meet us and wheels came off as we made emergency crash landings. Throughout it all we worked with growing smoothness and proficiency. But after a while I became very conscious of the fact that, whenever I was in the engineer's seat, one particular instructor would stare at me in a puzzled, dissatisfied way.

It was hard to figure out what I could be doing wrong. In fact, he usually stared at me when I wasn't doing much of anything, so I thought perhaps I was supposed to be doing something. But when the pilots are doing work that does not involve the engineer, the engineer simply remains immobile but attuned to whatever is going on. I would sit at my desk with my ankles crossed and my hands cupped in my lap, watching the pilots and awaiting my cue to action.

Boyd Dollar was the instructor's name; Boyd $, as he liked to sign himself. He sat behind me in the jump seat, squinting over my shoulder and giving me worried looks. One day he could contain himself no longer. He got up abruptly. "Something's wrong," he said, frustration in his voice. "I don't know what it is, but something. You just don't look like an engineer." He grabbed my hands out of my lap and redistributed my arms, one on the desk and one on my seat arm, took one leg and propped it up against the back of the copilot's seat. I was half hunched over my panel and half out of my seat, just as if I were about to leap up and yell "Action stations! All hands on deck!" Boyd made a couple of minor adjustments and then stepped back with a satisfied, slightly smug look. "That's the way an engineer's supposed to sit," he said triumphantly. "That's the way you're supposed to look!"

He was so pleased with himself, so relieved that he'd put his finger on the problem, that I could scarcely demur. Next class, I made sure to hunch myself over in the required manner, even though I felt as if I were bellying up to a bar, and Boyd repeated proudly, "Now, *that's* what an engineer's supposed to look like."

Things went more easily after that. He seemed more comfortable with me, as if he had transformed me into a professional with that one inspired moment of instruction.

Classwork was intensive. There was no time for much personal interchange, either at our desks or in the mockups, but my fellow students never gave any indication that they thought of me as an intruder. We worked together without friction. But it took them awhile to realize that I was participating in class just as actively as they were and passing the graded tests with scores that compared favorably with theirs. It was only then that a couple of them admitted to me that they'd been sure I was hired because I was a woman and not because I knew my stuff. That made no sense, in terms of comparative test scores and quality of experience, yet the admission was more valuable than the error and did not send me into a frenzy of resentment.

For the first week or two I was left pretty much to myself outside of class, except for the rides in Brown's limousine and the meals in the cafeteria. Then, apparently having proved myself, I began to be absorbed into the mainstream of the class. Groups of us went out to dinner and went back to the inn and studied together. We did sports together, too, and I had no compunction whatsoever about beating the socks off them at tennis whenever I could. We jogged, swam in the pool under the Six Flags, played golf and touch football. I have never been modest about my athletic proficiency; it came with the genes, and I have never, for the sake of any male ego, pretended to lose at anything. By the same token, I admitted a preference for being a cheerleader rather than a fullback for the football games.

I helped them sew; they helped me study. We all did our laundry together to cut down on expenses. Some of the men had brought their cars with them, and we pooled rides when we tired of the limousine service. We congregated in one another's rooms, mended clothes, quizzed each other, cut each other's hair and professed poverty.

That is where we began to differ. I professed poverty along with the rest, but the $650 a month I was earning—never mind that it had to cover my uniform costs and other expenses—was about $300 a month more than I had ever earned with all my previous flight jobs combined. For the men, the money was negligible, a pittance to get them through their training and probationary period. Most had families to support on their $650, their savings and whatever their wives could earn, and most had been used to well-paid corporate or military positions that covered all their living expenses. Now here we were, making six hundred and something a month, and giving each other haircuts. But I felt like a millionaire.

In addition to financial security, I now had the support of a cherished group of peers. The guys were protective of me. There was not really anything to protect me from, but we developed a sense of being united as a class group that was slightly different from the other classes. Individuals outside Class 73–9 still appeared to regard me as something of a freak, and it was against that attitude that we presented a solid front. If I needed defenders, they were there.

Yet the sense of togetherness and sameness of purpose was not full-time. Most weekends, when the male students went home to be with their families and arrange their business affairs, I stayed at the Inn of the Six Flags and studied, either in the small room to which I had been reassigned or on the deck of the swimming pool. Usually the latter. It was when the fellows went off to North Dakota or Ohio and came back talking about mortgage arrangements and putting their homes on the market that I realized how we differed. I had no such arrangements to make, or any obligations of regular payments to bank or school or insurance company. In spite of my first feverish feeling that I was burning my bridges I really didn't have any to burn—and, if I had, I wouldn't be burning them. There was no guarantee that I would pass the flight school course, and no reason to make any changes in the life that was waiting until or if I got back to it.

The men were different. With unshakable confidence, they were selling their houses back home, getting their wives to give notice from their jobs, reviewing their banking arrangements, making inquiries about grade schools in various areas and trading in their cars for better ones. *They knew they would be transferring.* I remember saying to them, "How can you be so confident you're going to get through flight school?" They looked at me in disbelief. Why shouldn't they be sure? It was a step they had deliberately chosen, toward a planned career advancement about which they had no doubts; it was a standard move up for a professional man and head of a household.

To them the transition was normal, natural and inevitable. They were sure it was going to come about. I was not sure. For me, failure was not inconceivable but would be devastating; success would be a great yawning leap into the unknown.

I studied my brains out, alone at the inn; hopeful, but unsure.

9

Leroy Remembers

Jacob Reed's Sons
Manufacturers of Fine Uniforms
Since 1824

April 17, 1973

Miss Bonnie Tiburzi
American Airlines, Inc.

Dear Bonnie:

It was a real pleasure. . . .

As you concurred, the garments looked most attractive and we were very delighted to find the slacks were the best fit ever.

Needless to say, the safari to the shopping mall was most enjoyable and rewarding, in that the striped scarf you selected went over so well with Captain and Mrs. Melden.

You will be happy to hear the coat on which we decided to slant the lower flaps is completed and is being returned to Bill Copeman. We feel confident it will be to your liking.

We trust . . .

The pants were a terrific fit, largely because they had no pockets. Bill didn't like the scarf. We went back to looking at ties and ascots.

Flight school in those days consisted of several weeks of ground school training, using mockups, systems schematics, slide presentations and the cockpit procedural trainer. After that came an oral examination, then a solid twenty-five hours of simulator training. When finally permitted on a real aircraft, we were each given an airplane checkride or rides in the position of pilot number three, or flight engineer, and if we performed satisfactorily we were adjudged worthy of our wings. The training ride was the formal, actual end of our work at the academy, but it was not the ultimate test. The true test would come on our first on-the-line flight, with a full load of passengers—and a crew consisting of two seasoned pilots and an ever-alert flight engineer instructor.

So much happened during every one of those instruction-crammed days that I can't, looking back, sort it all out. Fortunately, Leroy remembers things I don't, and some, perhaps, that I never even knew.

Leroy Leddon, a slow-talking Texan with a twinkle in his eye, was the supervisor of the flight engineer instructors. At the time I went through, that was a group of about fifty men, including all the instructor examiners designated by the FAA, the simulator instructors and all of the check airmen. The first time I saw him was when he walked into the classroom carrying a stack of pink slips, and briefed us as to what we could expect after ground school.

"Now these pink slips . . ." I didn't notice the twinkle then. I just knew that it was important to match up to Leroy Leddon's high standards, and that if you fell short in any way you got one of the dreaded pink slips. That was not necessarily fatal. You could repeat an unsatisfactory performance by working a little harder and shaping up your act. But those unpleasant little pieces of paper were rejections to be avoided at all reasonable cost.

There was a lot of nervous speculation about the oral,

which was to be the first major test of our mettle. It was given, on an individual basis, by an FAA inspector or one of the six FAA designees at American, of whom Leroy was the most senior.

But when the time came it seemed to be less of an ordeal—for most of us—than anticipated. Those of my classmates who were tested ahead of me came out with big, beaming smiles. "Oh, it was a cinch," they said, "It's only thirty, forty minutes. They ask you just a couple of systems—electrical, fuel, pressure, you know. They just pick out a system at random, and if you do a good job with it, they figure you probably know the others. Then they may take one more system, and if you do a good job with that, too, well, that's the end of the oral. Hey, nothing to it!"

I got asked *everything.*

Most of the orals were given by a designated examiner who worked for the company. I got mine from Leroy, with the FAA sitting in.

I was apprehensive, more so because the FAA man was late. Or I was early. I remember hardly anything of what followed because I got asked so many questions and the thing went on so long. I couldn't understand why they wouldn't just let me out of my misery.

Leroy remembers.

"D'you remembah what ah said to you befo' ah gave you the oral?"

"Uh . . ."

"Well, you walk in, and of co'se the FAA was not there yet. You bring your kitbag in, you set it down, you walk across the floor two or three times, just very nervous. And ah said, 'Well, Bonnie, you don't really have to be nervous about this, because it's just another part of training. The FAA will be here, but they'll be watching me, so don't worry about it. Ah'll be asking you the questions. Ah'm sure you feel the pressure, and it's obvious to me that you're different from the students ah've had in the past.' " Big grin when he says this. " 'But all ah ask of you is performance.' Ah said, 'You perform, you pass. You don't, you don't pass. Is that fair enough?' And you said, in a very small voice, 'Yessir.' "

Oh, yeah, I remembah.

Then the FAA man walked in. His name was Al Polton, although I didn't hear it at the time or notice what he looked like. I would be seeing rather more of him than I actually cared to.

My oral took a little over two hours. I'm sure that part of the reason was Leroy's very slow and deliberate speech. And then of course being asked every question known to man was not conducive to speed.

"Well," Leroy admits, "I did give you a thorough oral. But part of that time was you going on about more than we needed to know. There was a couple of things we had to take a li'l longer at because you explained in more detail than was necessary." Another big grin.

"Remember one question that I asked you about a warning light . . . ? You talked so much, you lost me. Finally you said, 'If the pressure is not what it's supposed to be, the light will come on.' and I turned around to the FAA inspector and said, 'I don't know what else she said, but that part's right.' " Leroy chuckles.

"And the next question that you had a little problem with was on the electrical panel. Do you remember that?" he says indulgently.

I do remember. It was just a word I was groping for and couldn't find, so I had to go through a lot of others to get near it.

Leroy, in asking his questions, was using a mockup of the cockpit with all the panels enormously enlarged, all switches operable and each system distinct: the electrical system, air conditioning, pressurization, fuel system and so on. He would start at one panel, ask questions about everything on that panel, and then go on to the next. And the next. And the next. Not just the flight engineer's panel. All the panels.

"There was a switch," says Leroy, "that I was trying to get you to tell me that if you operated it when the engine was running, it would disconnect the drive to the generator. That's the CSD switch—constant speed drive—you remember that question?"

I nod.

"Well, you just couldn't think of the word *disconnect.* So you thought about it for a while and finally—I'll never fergit! —you said, 'Do you really want me to tell you how that thing works?" Leroy laughs immoderately at the recollection. "And I said, 'Yes, Bonnie, I really want you to tell me how it works.' And then you said, 'Well, it has this little jackscrew arrangement, and it unscrews itself.' That was your final answer!"

"What was wrong with that?"

"Well, we decided that was close enough to 'disconnect.' "

At about that time, roughly midway through the interrogation, we took a break. Leroy and the FAA left the room, and Glenn Miller, an instructor who had been waiting anxiously outside, came in.

"Bonnie, what's the matter? What's taking so long?" he said. Glenn was manager of the ground school at the time, and felt that how his students did was a reflection on him. He was looking very worried.

"Oh, Glenn, I don't know. He asked me about the CSD, and I said it unscrews itself, but I don't know what he's looking for."

Glenn gave me a stricken look and backed out of the room without saying a word. He couldn't help me, couldn't even give me a hint; just had to go away and suffer until my ordeal was over.

"So, anyway, we went on and completed the oral, and you went on through your classes and the simulator training. And one thing I remember about you, Bonnie," says Leroy, looking serious for a moment, "is that you came to me and requested a briefing room to study in. You wanted to come out early, and one of the simulator briefing rooms was not being used, and you used it to study in. This was something I noticed right away that none of the guys ever did. They never came out early to study on their own. So you were beginning to make me feel a lot better about you at this point, because you were working so hard at it!"

"Well, after a two-hour oral, who wouldn't? And you still haven't told me why it took so long."

Leroy chuckles and changes the subject.

"The company, as you probably know, requested that I give you all your checkouts and checkrides"—I hadn't known that —"except the line checks. So, my answer was, 'If I'm going to give Bonnie her simulator and aircraft checks, then I'm going to give her the line qualifying checks, because the line flyin' is something special, and I felt I should do all of it.' And that was all right, because it was reasonable for me, as the supervisor, to follow you all the way through. And naturally, because you were the first female American Airlines had hired, a lot of the fellows had strong reservations. Most of them didn't come right out and say it, but several guys came to me and asked me if I was really going to let you pass. At least you shouldn't be able to pass an exam or a checkride the first time around! You can understand this was new to a lot of them. They just felt like this was not a woman's job. But I told them, like I told you, 'If she performs, she passes.' "

"Well," I say understandingly, "it was something different for them. The men had to be educated just as much as—"

But Leroy is not interested in my observations about male education.

"So the next thing we did together was your simulator checkride. You remember? When Boyd Dollar recommended you for your simulator check?"

Yes. Boyd had not only taught me to sit like an engineer in the cockpit; he had taught me to work like one. In some areas he had drilled me relentlessly, with an intense and worried look on his face. He had been very nervous about signing me off for the ride, because he'd never had a female student before and he'd never had a failure. And I don't believe he had anticipated that the FAA would be sitting in on the simulator check, because he hadn't had that happen before, either. All in all, he was almost as apprehensive as I. Certainly my heart sank when FAA inspector Al Polton joined Leroy and me in the simulator. Even I knew, by that time, that the FAA did not send an observer to watch every student take every test. Ordinarily, they would watch perhaps one out of ten checkrides. But here he was again, just for me.

Leroy put me through the check remorselessly, from system to system, leading up to a heavy concentration on electrical problems and emergencies. I thought I knew what was coming: a two-engines-out, single-generator operation.

"Now the company had an agreement on that," says Leroy, "because it's a lengthy and complicated procedure which takes a whole team effort and quite a bit of checklist reading. We do it in the checkride for a captain, but it's not required for engineers. So we had agreed that the engineers would be fully trained in this procedure but wouldn't have to go through it on the simulator check. At the same time, the FAA wanted to be sure you could do it. So Boyd had been instructed to make sure that you were able to do it, and I'm sure that he drilled you quite extensively."

Indeed he had. He had drilled me like crazy. I was surprised, therefore, when Leroy said, "Okay, that's fine—the check is over," without even asking me about the procedure I had studied so exhaustively with Boyd. I could have done it in my sleep. I was dying to do it. I was rather pleased when Al, the FAA examiner, said to Leroy, "I'd like to see her do a single-generator operation, two generators out."

"No," said Leroy. "The rest of the guys didn't have to do it, so Bonnie's not going to have to do it."

"Oh!" I said eagerly, "I can do that!"

Leroy gave me a look that could have pinned a butterfly to a board.

"I know you can, but you're not going to," he said flatly.

End of simulator checkride.

"But I was so ready!" I tell Leroy.

He smiles. "Oh, I knew you were ready. But, you see, we had already planned that. We were not going to have you do anything that the guys didn't have to do. Watch you a little more closely than anybody, mebbe, but that's all. Because it was a new experience for all of us.

"Then of course the next thing was the aircraft check," he goes on. "The training checkride. We did that out at Greater Southwest, you'll recall."

This, of course, was the airfield adjacent to the academy.

It was my first flight in the cockpit of a 727 as a working crew member. We all spent minimal training time in the airplane, the simulator being the far more practical training tool, so now for the first time I would be putting together the complete sequence of a real flight from the preflight to the landing check. The first necessity was, of course, an available airplane.

"I believe we did this on a Saturday," Leroy says reflectively, "because the Vice-President of Flight, Captain Ted Melden, had a press conference set up for you on the Monday. So you were scheduled for your checkride Saturday. The problem was, we only had one other engineer scheduled for that day, and no first officers. Normally we do not fly airplanes just to check out one or two people, and we don't fly airplanes just to check the flight engineers. We always check engineers when we're doing pilot training for upgrading. That's the economical factor. So when Scheduling told me that we did not have any pilots that Saturday, I canceled the checkride. I said, 'We'll do it when we have someone to fly the airplane, so it's not so costly.' You probably didn't know about that."

Leroy's right. I never knew the flight had been canceled. I distinctly remember taking it.

"But then, after I canceled, I got a call from the vice-president's office, asking me if there wasn't some way that we could check you out. I said, 'Well, if Captain Melden wants her checked out, then he will need to authorize us flying the airplane at least two hours.' So I got the report back, and he said, 'I don't give a damn how long you fly that airplane, just check her out!'

"So we went out to the plane. Scheduling did manage to round up a first officer, to give him some landings, so I felt a little better about getting a plane and captain up to check out a very junior flight engineer.

"Well, there was our FAA man waiting for us. First thing we do, of course, is your preflight walkaround. One of my concerns about you being the first female to operate as a flight engineer—we're all entitled to certain reservations, I guess—was if you could close the E and E compartment door. I was standing there beside the airplane watching you and naturally I couldn't help or say anything."

There is a door on the bottom of the airplane, in the belly, like the hatch of a boat but on the underside. Its handle is flush with the skin of the airplane, so you have to depress a release button to make the handle drop down. When it does, you grip it with both hands—it's a T-bar, about the size and shape of a flattened lawnmower handle—and rotate it 180 degrees.

"I was watching and thinking," says Leroy, "how's she gonna do this? Because it takes a little bit of strength, and a bit of height doesn't hurt either. Most of the guys'll just reach up and turn the handle in place. But you—you swung your weight on the door and you kicked your legs around so your whole body made a hundred-and-eighty-degree turn!"

I still do it that way. It's the well-known leverage trick. The guys usually swivel the handle with one mighty twist of the arms. But if you're not that strong—and not all of them manage it easily either—you just use your whole body to turn it around. There's always a way to compensate for being under 5 feet 10 inches and less than 140 pounds.

"So then, in the cockpit, you were going through the checklist. There's five of us in there. The check pilot's in his seat, next to him a copilot being checked out, you in the engineer's seat, I'm in one jump seat and the FAA guy's in the second jump seat watching me give you your check. You remember in the before-landing checklist, when you came to the item 'altimeters'?''

It comes back to me.

''When you call out your checklist items, the captain and the copilot are supposed to respond, right? They say, 'Altimeters checked and cross-checked.' But this captain either didn't hear you or he ignored you. You called a second time. Again he didn't answer. I'll never forget the look on your face. You called 'em out, and he didn't respond. You gave me this questioning look, like, What do I do now? And of course I wasn't allowed to instruct you, but there's nothing to say I couldn't ask you a question just to lead you a little bit. So I asked, 'Well, did he answer you?'

''And you reached over and tapped him firmly on the shoulder. That got his attention! Then you said 'altimeters!' real loudly, and he finally answered. Now this is not normal procedure, but it was effective. He told me afterward that he'd never forget that.''

In being reminded of this, I wondered what his problem was. Did the captain really not hear me? Was he ignoring me? Was he testing the new girl in his own way? Whatever the answer, I later found him to be a really nice fellow, an okay guy.

We completed the checkride. Thanks to the presence of the ubiquitous Al, I received my FAA rating on the 727 right on the spot. I went back to the inn and waited for Monday.

Monday was more than a press conference. It was my graduation day. And only mine.

Flight academies do not have a commencement ceremony. As each pilot completes his training, he is signed off and leaves at once for his assigned base. There, with a minimum of flourish, he receives his wings from the base's chief pilot and goes to work. For his first trip or two—or up to a total of twenty to twenty-five hours—he flies under the surveillance of a check airman from his own base. But things were going to be a little different for me.

As the youngest class member, I occupied the last slot in the training hierarchy. I'd had to wait my turn for training in the simulators, which were used not only by American's students but by trainees for many other airlines that didn't have their own equipment, and for the past two weeks my classmates had been packing up and peeling off, one by one, to their base assignments. By Sunday, I was the only one left.

And of course I was the only woman. That made another difference.

No wonder Ted Melden had been anxious. The press had already been notified that I was due to get my wings on the morning of June 4, and it would have been tough all around if I failed.

I hasten to point out that I really did earn them. Leroy would have had no compunction in having the whole hoopla called off if he had felt I was not ripe for signing off.

It has been suggested, or so I've heard, that I must have squeaked through by a narrow margin or been carried through by kindly males. Not so. No squeaking through. You do it right, or not at all. And there was a measure of male courtesy, but no carrying—except for my flight bag, once in a while. At the rise of appearing immodest, I quote part of American's press release:

" 'We hired Miss Tiburzi because she is proficient and because she possesses all of the qualifications we expect from our flight officers,' said Donald J. Lloyd-Jones, Executive Vice-President, Operations. 'Her record at the academy was outstanding, and she will be a fine addition to the pilot corps.' "

It was silly time for the press again. My departed classmates had taken the buildup very tolerantly, and I could hardly wait for the moment when I would finally be accepted into the ranks of qualified pilots of American's fleet of 727 Astrojets.

The ceremonies were mercifully brief and there was a select group of newsmen around. It had been determined by American that a little bit of fuss but not too much was to be made over my acceptance as a different kind of jet-setter. All department heads and recipients of press releases had been firmly told that my public appearances—supposing any were requested—must be kept to a discreet minimum. As one memo noted rather primly: "Although we desire to publicize the fact that she is the first woman pilot hired by a major U.S. carrier, her prime purpose as an employee of American Airlines is that of a pilot."

The moment came. For the first time in recorded history, a Vice-President, Flight, conferred the honors upon a graduating student. Captain Ted Melden, wearing a warm, relieved smile, pinned my flight wings to the front of my new blue jacket, leaned down from his great height—and kissed me.

(Hot news, folks! Pilot kisses pilot!)

Naturally, I giggled, and there was some more giggling at the short press conference that followed. I tried to say intelligent things about the possibility of adverse reaction to a woman pilot by crews and passengers, and insisted that the world was ready for me. "I think women are accepted in aviation now," I declared boldly. How quickly we change! Only six months before, I'd been thinking exactly the opposite.

But did I think I was different in any way? "Well, I don't think you can ignore the fact that I'm a woman," I said seriously, at which there was some laughter. "But women fly no differently than men."

Had American made any special allowances for me? "Only in the uniform. They took it in a bit here, let it out there." Chuckles. Actually, none of us was too crazy about the uniform even yet, even though Captains Melden and Copeman and I had been mulling it over for almost two months. They weren't satisfied with the hat, which was a cute mock-derby but looked a bit too much like the hats worn by the stewardesses of another airline. The tunic looked terrific. The fit was elegant, if unrevealing, which was what American wanted. But it had no pockets at all, in either the jacket or the pants. My hands kept groping for them, but there was nothing there. The blouse, which was custom-made by d'Armigene and lovely, also presented a potential problem. Replacements of a short-run design item made especially for me were going to be very expensive. That was the core of the whole uniform business: all the guys wore clothes that were exactly alike except for size, mass-produced, and therefore relatively inexpensive. That mass-production was not available to me. Well, these were things we'd have to see about eventually.

The little bit of fanfare was soon over, and then the papers came out. "American Beauty Is Rose in the Cockpit," said one. "She Flies by the Seat of Her Panties," observed another. Headlined a third: "Kissing, Press Conference—Somehow Ceremonies for Pilot Un-Standard."

"Everyone kept trying to say that B. L. Tiburzi's Flight Academy graduation was just like everyone else's," began the "Kissing" story.

"Of course, no one could quite remember the last time an American Airlines vice-president leaned over and gave a new pilot a kiss.

"And no, it was not standard for new graduates to have press conferences.

"For twenty-four-year-old Bonnie Tiburzi, it might have been the hardest part of becoming the first woman pilot for a major U.S. airline.

"The reporters kept wanting to know if she felt she was striking a blow for women's lib.

" 'I'm not really trying to strike a blow for anything,' she said. 'I've been flying and loving it since I was twelve years old. I just want to fly.' "

But, I thought, if there were any spin-off benefits for women, so much the better. I'd do us all a really bad turn if I goofed up.

"Normally, I would carry a lady's bag," said Leroy, as we walked out to the airplane. "Bein' a Southern boy and helpful, y'know, you would lift a lady's bag. Well, I thought of it, and I said to myself, 'No, this is different. I can't show any special treatment. So you're going to have to carry your own bags.' "

"Well, that's perfectly fair," I said approvingly, bending slightly under the uneven weight of my kitbag and my suitcase. I had deadheaded back to Dallas to do my on-the-line checkride with Leroy, my first trip with passengers and revenue, and I certainly didn't want to establish any precedent of being waited on. It was bad enough that we had already bent standard procedure by having Leroy assign himself to give me the line checks instead of having them done by a check airman in New York, where I was to be based. And that there had been quite a bit of advance publicity about the flight in some of the papers, noting that it was my first flight, explaining that it was a checkride for me, and giving date, time, flight number and destination. That was more than enough special treatment for me, and I devoutly hoped that I could soon go to work without attracting newspaper attention.

Admittedly, I had enjoyed much of the coverage. Among the subheads coined by artful writers was one that had become my favorite slogan: "I'm Bonnie, I'll Fly You!"

Any day now, I would do just that.

A cheerful young man in American Airlines flight uniform caught up with us.

"Hi, Bonnie," he said. "I'm Waco Hungerford, your copilot. Carry your bags?"

"No," barked Leroy—if there is such a thing as a drawling bark. "She carries her own. She's just like the rest of us."

Waco looked at me and grinned as I thanked him and staggered on.

Shortly afterward the cockpit preflight procedures got under way. The flight attendants had greeted me with perhaps more interest than they usually accorded a new engineer, and the captain with a formal acknowledgment of my presence and very little interest at all.

Leroy told me afterward that he had said he would not fly with a female in the cockpit and was outraged when he learned that he would have to.

Passengers boarded. We proceeded with our checklists. Flight attendants hung up garment bags. A man in a neatly tailored suit came into the cockpit.

Oh, no! Was the FAA going to be in on this, too?

This was definitely not standard procedure.

Leroy, in the first jump seat, looked at him with surprise.

"Well, Al, I didn't know you were going to ride with us . . .?"

"You here?" said Al. "I didn't know you were on this trip."

"Al, I'm sure you didn't know," Leroy said, even more deliberately than usual. "It's only been in every newspaper in Texas!"

Al shrugged, and sat down behind the pilots.

We were beginning to start engines. There is a lot to do at the beginning of a flight. Everything moves fast and has to be done with uninterrupted, methodical speed. I did not need the FAA there to watch me under a microscope. I thought I saw Waco and the captain exchange eyebrow-raising glances, and I felt guilty about subjecting them to an additional presence. With all due respect to the FAA, pilots are not wildly enthusiastic about sharing the cockpit with an unexpected FAA inspector, who is as likely to inspect captains as anyone else.

Leroy, silent for a moment, said, "You really have no particular reason to be here, do you, Al?"

"Just getting a ride to Tucson," said the FAA man, including us both in his glance. "I'm not here to observe." He settled as comfortably as possible in his jump seat.

"Not watching Bonnie or anyone?"

"Nah," he said, unconvincingly.

We worked on. Leroy prepared to launch into speech.

"Well, Al, you're really not here to give anyone a check? You really didn't come to watch Bonnie?"

"Oh, no, no, no, no!"

"And you're going to Tucson for other reasons?"

"Yes."

"Well, then," said Leroy, "in that case, you won't mind riding in the back."

Al sat in silence for several long seconds. Then he gave a small grunt. Slowly, very slowly, he got up, ambled out and made his way into the passengers' cabin. Leroy closed the cockpit door behind him and beamed at me.

"That's better," said the captain. He turned to Leroy with a look of relief.

Then we were up and away. For the first time it was all coming together for me in my full role as a flight engineer working with a line crew and a load of passengers. All the separate pieces, including me, were forming the whole, fluid procedure of getting an aircraft safely from point A to point B and to points beyond.

My heart soared along with the airplane.

"Ten thousand feet, lights and altimeters," I called out.

Captain and copilot both responded.

"Altimeters reset, three-zero-one-five."

We climbed through thirteen thousand, coming up to eighteen, reaching for cruise altitude.

"Flight level one-eight-zero, radio altimeter switches off, and twenty-nine ninety-two on all the altimeters."

"Checked and cross-checked."

We reached cruise level. With a tap of his hand on the throttles, the captain gestured for me to set cruise power. "Any time you get point eight-oh," he said.

Watching the speed, I reached my left hand to the console between captain and copilot to set the throttles accordingly.

"Cruise power set," I said in my most professional voice.

Fine. Everything going smoothly. But why were the captain's shoulders shaking as if he were . . . laughing?

He was laughing. He was laughing very hard.

I was glad to see he was happy, but I did think he could share the joke with the rest of us.

The flight was otherwise uneventful and we glided comfortably down at Tucson, the first leg of a three-day trip.

The FAA man vanished into the departing crowd, never to be seen by me again. Captain and copilot gave me comradely looks as we left the airplane.

I suppose they thought I couldn't hear them, but shortly afterward Leroy and the captain had a chat.

Leroy: "Ed, what was so funny, you were laughin' so hard?"

Captain: "Well, I've never had that experience before. It was the darnedest thing. I look over at the console and there was that feminine hand with the painted fingernails setting cruise power! For a moment I almost forgot where I was. I looked around in *my* cockpit, and I saw *that*." He chuckled again. "I couldn't help laughing, it was just so funny. What's the world coming to!"

You would never have known that he hated the idea of flying with a woman flight officer and had been prepared to resent me bitterly.

The rest of the trip was pleasant and uneventful, except for one little cloud.

Toward the end of the second day I used the company radio frequency to talk to Operations in St. Louis, customary procedure being to call each destination twenty minutes or a hundred miles before landing. I gave them our ETA and requested the current altimeter setting, gate assignments and so on. Operations gave me that information and then asked Flight Engineer Leddon to come inside when we landed, because he had to call the academy. To me, that was ominous. The call, I was certain, had to be about me. I started a slow burn.

When we were on the ground in St. Louis, Leroy went inside and returned his call.

This is his story: "It was the Director of Training, Captain

Walt Moran, calling. He said, 'How is your student doing?' I said, 'Jes' fine. Needs a little more experience, a little more practice, and she'll be all right.' And he says, 'But you're not ready to sign her off?' So we discussed it and didn't really make any decision. I did comment that if she keeps on improving, by the time we get back to Dallas tomorrow, I think I can probably release her.

"Well, I went back to the airplane and you were sitting there in your seat. And you had been very cooperative, very ladylike, until that point. But now you lost your Italian temper. You turned to me, and you said, 'That call was about me, wasn't it?' You said that. You said, 'Y'know, what makes me mad about them is, I don't know how many you've checked out before me.' You says, 'I bet you, they've never questioned your judgment before. And they had to call you to ask how I was doing!'

"And I said, 'Oh, it wasn't anything like that, Bonnie!' "

Huh. It was, and I knew it. I felt demeaned.

"So we get to Cleveland," says Leroy, "where we were scheduled to lay over that night. Sure enough, when I got to my hotel room, I had another phone call. And this was the Manager of Training, Captain Mel Burton. 'Leroy,' he said, 'I talked to Captain Walt Moran and he says you're thinking about releasing Bonnie when you get back.' I said, 'Yuh, I prob'ly can, don't know yet, but if she continues doing as well tomorrow as she did today, she'll have enough hours and I can probably release her.' 'Well,' says he, 'Captain Moran says you shouldn't be in any hurry about doing that. Maybe you ought to ride with her another trip.' I says, 'Well, we'll see how things go tomorrow.' "

They must not have gone all that well, although everything felt pretty good to me, because when we got back to Dallas next day Leroy told me that we would probably take another trip together and he would let me know when it was going to be.

I left Dallas and sizzled all the way to New York. I knew

that I was going to do another checkride, and I was furious. A three-day checkout should have been plenty. I couldn't imagine where I had gone wrong—and I didn't believe I had. Big Bird was watching me.

But I was on the last lap.

Leroy called a couple of days later.

"We're going to take another trip together," he said. "Where would you like to go?"

"San Francisco!" I chirruped, happy over having a choice and never having been there before.

"Okay, come on down."

I deadheaded to Dallas.

The last checkride was distinguished by a particularly unusual crew. I was doing the cockpit preflight preparations under Leroy's watchful eye when a couple came on board and looked in.

"Hi, Bonnie," said a male voice.

I looked up, saw a young fellow in the uniform of a flight attendant and gave him a surprised greeting. Behind him was the standard female flight attendant.

"Congratulations," he said. "You were first, and so are we."

"Uh . . .?" Okay, male flight attendants were new to the airlines, but what was this "we"?

"This is my wife," he said, and introduced the young woman. "We met in training and got married before school was over. So we're the first married couple flight attendants!"

The novelty of it made me feel like an old hand in the cockpit and took some of the heat off my own newness. Some of the questions that might have been asked of me were diverted to them. "Say, what does it feel like to be . . .?"

In the limo going into San Francisco, one of the crew members said, "How is it being married and flying together, and being on layovers together?"

The young couple murmured something. She made a quiet little sound, and he said something like, "It's kinda nice."

Leroy looked them over and, for once, completely lost his manners.

"Sounds to me like, it's kinda like taking a sandwich to a banquet," he announced, and almost everybody roared. The young man did not. The young woman did.

With those two trips, I made my debut. Wherever we went, a ground-to-air or an air-to-air voice would be saying, "Are you the flight with the female crew member? Is Bonnie on board? Welcome, and congratulations. Hi, Bonnie!" Passing through Cincinnati I was presented with an enormous bag of popcorn. On a layover in Chicago, there were two gallons of ice cream—one chocolate, one vanilla—waiting for me, because somewhere along the way I had been thoughtless enough to mention that I'm addicted to the stuff. At another layover, there were flowers for me in the bridal suite and many nice young men scrambling for my bags. "No, no!" I would protest. "Well, okay." (When I got my wheelie the tables were turned. I wound up carrying everybody's.)

"You did get a lot of attention," Leroy complains. "A lot more than I ever got, and I'd been around for fifteen years. Nobody ever gave me popcorn or flowers. They say ev'body's supposed to be equal. There just isn't any way. Remember the mechanics?"

"Ummm . . . which mechanics?"

"Well, mainly all of them, but there was one place it was particularly noticeable. We were doing the preflight in Cleveland. You were almost finished with your walkaround. I wasn't going around with you, you remember. I said, 'You go ahead, and I'll watch from a distance.'

"So you went around and you saw some cowling that was loose on the engine. Some of the fasteners weren't holding tight. So you came back to me saying, 'They're loose.' I say, 'Well, Bonnie, don't tell me, tell the mechanic. You've gotta learn how to get these things done.' Well, you went and found a mechanic, and told him you had that problem. Now, if it hadda been me, I would've eventually gotten one mechanic out there to fasten the cowling, just before departure. Well, no. Not you. See, you tell the mechanic you need the cowling fastened, and there's *three* mechanics climbing all over themselves trying to get up to fix that cowling!"

That's right, there were. They were really very sweet.

"Well, I think some o' this ought to be brought out," says Leroy, "how *I* was discriminated against. I think it should. Reverse discrimination, that's what it is!"

It was nostalgia time, when we were talking about all this. I had not given a thought to the constant presence of the FAA man throughout my checkouts, not since his departure in Tucson. Now I gave it thought. He had spent an awful lot of time with me, when in fact he had not been obliged to observe any of my checkrides. Thinking back on his trip to Tucson, I wondered again why he stuck with me like a shadow.

"Leroy," I begin, "do you think he wanted to see me fail? Or was he just curious? Or was he actually assigned to follow the first female around and make sure she knew what she was doing?"

"I think he felt it was his duty." Leroy says seriously, "and that he should be present in case anything went wrong. Because you can imagine what would have happened if you had not passed, and if I would've had to have said, 'No, she's going to have to have more training,' and then *you* would have gone to the press or somewhere and said, 'Well, this company has been mistreating me and been unfair and etcetera.' I'm sure that was his reason for being there—as a backup, in a sense, in case something went wrong. It was in your interests, too, that he was there. He could testify that you really knew your job.

"Oh," I say inadequately. I had always thought he wanted to see me fail. Instead of that, he'd been a self-appointed watchdog and safeguard.

"It may be, too," Leroy goes on deliberately, "that he wanted to be in on something new. Because in a way you were part of airline history. I always felt that I was. There's been several licensed women pilots, but prior to that, there's never been a need for a woman to have a flight engineer's license. I'm sure you were the first female to receive a flight engineer's license in the United States. So I always kinda felt I was part of history in this, because I wrote the first ticket. And on top of that, we had to be sure. We had to be really sure of you. Maybe in some ways we had to bear down a little harder and take a little more time, just to be sure."

A small lightbulb lights up in my brain. "Is that something to do with why I had a two-hour oral?"

Leroy smiles. "That's something to do with it."

10

"I'm Bonnie, I'll Fly You!"

This is it. Here I go. Bonnie Linda Tiburzi, girl pilot, enters an airline Operations Room on her very first working day, alone, no Leroy Leddon to hold her hand, about to embark on the great adventure. Any minute now, people will turn around and stare, and I will blush and drop something.

No one turns. There is not a glance in my direction.

I have butterflies inside. I look around at a familiar yet unfamiliar scene.

It is one of orderly confusion, probably more orderly than confused but utterly baffling to me because I don't know where to go or what to do. Pilots in blue with silver stripes are picking up various sheets of paper at a long counter and having quiet discussions with each other. People behind the counter move about and hand out material with the casualness of comfortable routine, apparently doing some kind of briefing that, judging by the acknowledging nods, is instantly understood. Attractive young women, some in red dresses, some in navy blue, go around introducing themselves. They seem friendly, competent and thoroughly at home even though they do not know one another.

I suppose I should be introducing myself to somebody. But to whom? Where do I go? Whom do I go up to, and what do I ask? Why have I suddenly become so shy?

I stand near the entrance to Flight Operations, feeling bewildered and lost in this maze of red, white and blue. I can imagine myself standing here forever, never coordinating with anybody, just looking eternally foolish.

But nobody sees me looking foolish. I wait here, as if in a dream, watching people in this busy but quiet room go easily about their business.

I was at Boston's Logan Airport, having deadheaded up the day before and spent the night at the airport Hilton. Although I had been assigned to New York and expected to fly out of La Guardia, where I had gone through my indoctrination with the base chief pilot, the fates had decreed that pilots were, for the time being, in greater demand at the Boston base. I was among those selected for temporary duty—TDY, in airline and military shorthand.

So it was that the first time I reported to an Operations at the airlines, it happened to be in—for me—completely uncharted territory. And reporting to Operations is something they don't tell you about in ground school, presumably because anyone can easily figure out how to do it.

Not me. I knew my flight sequence was a two-day trip going to Chicago and Cincinnati. I knew the flight number, but I didn't know who the captain was or exactly how to get myself started. Nor did there seem to be any focal point in the room to give me a clue. There were charts and weather maps on the walls, and racks stacked with pilot information, but there was no sign that said anything remotely like PILOTS CHECK IN HERE.

I would simply have to find my place in the scheme of things. What was going on here was something like an orchestra tuning up. Everybody was intently pursuing his own theme, not necessarily in unison with the others but toward the same purpose. The dispatcher checking the flight plans, copilot marking in the revisions, flight attendants reviewing their briefing books, captain going over the weather charts—all were playing their particular theme in their own time and in their own way, getting ready for their cue to snap into action as a professional and harmonious unit. That cue, that maestro's tap of the baton, would be unseen, unheard, prosaic but electric: departure time.

And if I didn't do something soon, there'd be a gap in the orchestra.

I was moving hesitantly toward one of the faces behind the counter, framing a question that began with "Er . . ." when a distinguished-looking man with captain's stripes came purposefully toward me with an air of something close to recognition.

"You're Flight Engineer Bonnie Tiburzi," the stranger announced. "How d'you do? I'm Captain Almeida—Ed Almeida. We'll be flying together. Welcome aboard."

I stammered a relieved greeting, wondering how in the world this clever man had known who I was and that I was his flight engineer. No one else did.

"You'll be wanting to learn the ropes," he said. "Come along, I'll show you."

He smiled, took me by the arm and guided me to the first stop at the counter.

"This is the sign-in sheet for our flight, Number 115, and this is where you sign. See: Captain, Copilot and Flight Engineer, Tiburzi, B. L."

I signed.

And there were the dispatchers, the weather briefers and the crew schedulers; here was additional briefing information, hot off the Telex; and here was where we checked our flight plan.

He guided me through it all, as gently and meticulously as if there was nothing he would rather do than break in raw young flight officers. I began to feel at home.

"This is Chuck Hill, our copilot." I shook hands with a sturdy young man who gave me the once-over in a rather pleasant way. "And our flight attendants. Number One, Jane Howard . . ."

These were the young women in the navy blue and red dresses. I thought they looked terrific.

". . . Joan Rothenmeyer . . . Karen Nordlie . . . Judy Wickham."

Again, the friendliness tinged with curiosity.

"And now you'll want to get on with your preflight. You go through that door over there and just keep walking straight till you get to the gate where the airplane is, ship number 802. All right?"

All right!

I found the airplane, and as I did my walkaround I thought about Captain Almeida. What a nice man! And wasn't that exciting, the way he came right up and introduced himself!

Dazed with admiration for his perspicacity, I proceeded with my preflight. Very, very gradually it dawned upon me that, even if Captain Almeida had not known almost everyone in the room, at least by sight, he did know that he had been assigned a female engineer—the company's one and only—who would not be wearing a pretty red or blue dress, but a pilot's uniform complete with silver stripes.

I suddenly realized that I had an enormous lot left to do, and not much time left to do it in. I hurried.

Throughout that trip, I hurried, and I worried as I hurried. It puzzled me that everything I did seemed to be going so slowly. I never kept anybody waiting, but I had to break my back to get my checks and various other scheduled duties done before others suddenly turned up. I was always finding something that needed to be done right away or that I had temporarily forgotten, such as filling in our scheduled and actual flight times in the ship's logbook or writing up the maintenance squawks or monitoring the temperature controls so that the flight attendants wouldn't have to keep calling and saying, It's too hot in the back, or It's too cold in the front, or Could you please cool it off, or Everybody seems to be smoking today, we need more circulation or something along those lines.

And now that I was actually on the job, I was concerned about my image as a female pilot. Not very, but enough to give me a little something extra to think about as I scrambled to do justice to my multiple duties. As a member of a cockpit crew, I had breached the tradition of the masculine domain and been made to feel, at the very least, quite warmly accepted. But I dreaded arriving in Chicago—*infamous* Chicago. The crew lounges at O'Hare Airport were, I knew, segregated by sex, and I wondered repeatedly what I was going to do when the captain and copilot headed for the lounge bearing the implacable sign MALE CREW MEMBERS ONLY and the flight attendants went off to their own lounge. As a matter of protocol I belonged with the flight deck crew, but in a narrow sense . . . did I?

I really was not looking forward to O'Hare.

I was not sure how the flight attendants were accepting me, or how they expected me to act toward them. So far as I could tell, they had no objection to having me up there in the cockpit. Everybody was being wonderful to me. But maybe I was just seeing things through rose-colored glasses. New as I was, I did supposedly outrank the cabin crew, and I wondered how they liked the idea.

One of the news stories I'd read after getting my wings kept nibbling away at the back of my mind. I remembered a few lines of it vividly. "Some airline employees feel that resentment of Miss Tiburzi will come not from the men, but from some of the stewardesses." And then somebody—a male employee, I think—had said, "Sure, some of the girls are going to resent her. You get used to a certain image of a pilot, and for some, it just isn't a girl." After that came something about, She's going to have the authority, but she's also going to get a lot of attention and that's not going to go down too well.

To counter that sort of stuff, I'd had a number of encouraging letters from American's stewardesses, offering me congratulations and welcoming me to the company. "All of us have been pulling for you," one wrote. "Good luck in your new career." Another had very specifically said, "I don't think you'll find any resentment among our girls." The general attitude was warm and positive. One way or another, all the letters said the same thing: "Glad you made it. Hang in there."

I was hanging in there, all right. Of course, it was early hours yet, but I'd cross my bridges as I came to them.

The time sped by. I was busy, busy—busy in a way I could not recall having been in the simulator or on the line checks, although I was doing exactly the same things at what I thought was exactly the same pace. It's the difference between a drill and the real thing, Bonnie, I told myself sententiously, and applied myself to my panels and my paperwork.

Chicago had weather, which worsened as we approached. It was one of my duties, as engineer, to contact the company on the company radio frequency about twenty minutes before landing. "Chicago Operations," I'd say, "American 115, changing over, estimating Chicago at 23:55 Zulu"—that is, Greenwich Mean Time. Chicago Operations would come back and say: "American 115, understand changing over, estimating at 23:55. Altimeter settings are three-zero-zero-three, five-seven-seven above, converted to two-niner-three-zero . . ." and so on. I'd read back the information, and that would be that.

But I kept having to delay the call. Thunderstorms and rain came up to meet us, and Captain Almeida decided to add about a hundred miles to our course in order to circumnavigate the worst of the weather. Calculations about arrival time went by the board. Preoccupied with my flight engineer's tasks, I wasn't keeping track of the navigation, and for much of the time it was unclear to me exactly where we were and when we were likely to arrive.

"Do you want me to change over now?" I asked every few minutes. "Now do you want me to change over? Should I change over now? Is it time for me to change over?"

"No, no, no, don't change over yet," he kept saying. "It's not twenty minutes. But go ahead and give me the fuel remaining, and how much time before we have to go to our alternate."

Time ticked by as I figured out our fuel position and kept recalculating it while keeping up with my standard duties. This situation was really not standard at all—not for me, anyway—because when we practiced all possible contingencies and emergencies in the simulator, we dealt with them as distinct episodes. Now we had, if not an emergency, a special contingency that I found distinctly nonstandard. I felt as if I were running in place to keep up with the sequence of events. A seasoned flight engineer takes these things in stride. In time, all the bits and pieces fall into place, and various circumstances and procedures can be anticipated and handled automatically. But I was really working at it.

"Want me to change over now?"

At last it was time. I was able to radio Operations.

As we arrived at our gate in Chicago I put the finishing touches on my day's notes in the E-6 logbook, one side of which is the maintenance log and the other the paysheets for the crew.

There we are, exact arrival time to add to all the other times. Very important, because we get paid according to flight and overall duty time. All very neat and nice. I was pleased with my handiwork.

Everybody else, crew included, left the airplane. Several minutes later, after meeting the outbound engineer, I followed the crew into the terminal. My feet lagged as I wondered again where I was expected to go. I did not look forward to walking into either of the crew lounges.

Deep in my heart I knew where I wanted to go and felt I belonged, in terms of having earned the job of flight officer. But damn! In terms of being a woman, it was awkward.

I headed for the male crew lounge, knowing—because my checkrides had prepared me—that virtually all company personnel at O'Hare would know that I had arrived and were expecting me to show up at . . . well, wherever.

There it was. And there was the sign, in big, bold black letters. MALE CREW MEMBERS ONLY. It looked very crisp and forbidding.

Except that beneath it, penciled in equally bold lettering, were the added words: AND BONNIE TOO!

I felt my face split into a smile.

I stood on a cloud, looking in through the open door, feeling elated but suddenly struck with shyness. Faces turned to me with broad grins. Greetings filled the air.

"Hello, Tiburzi . . . Hi, Bonnie . . . Hey, we been waiting for you—where've you been?"

Incredibly, I was too shy to go in.

"Hi, guys," I said, with a little wave and a bashful smile. "I'll be back in a bit. See you all later."

And I hastened away, as if I had an errand to do and had just happened to be passing by.

That was the last time I had to worry about segregated crew rooms. Right after that, company crew lounges at all airports were opened to cockpit and cabin crews together.

Some hours later, it was on to Cincinnati, and the next day, back to Boston. Once again, the trip was hectic, although fortunately without the complication of weather, and I kept wishing for another pair of hands or an extra set of brains. There was always a checklist to be read out, always something to be reviewed in a manual, always a request to respond to and a switch or a knob to turn and never any time to choke down a snack.

I seized a brief quiet spell to go back into the cabin and stop at the galley for a moment of relaxation. The flight attendant gave me a slightly amused smile.

"Busy?" she asked.

"Phew! Am I ever! Father didn't tell me it would be like this."

Her smile broadened. "I always know when we have a brand-new engineer, even when he's not a woman—"

"Oh, something wrong back here?" I said anxiously.

"No, no, everything's fine. Better than usual. See, the new engineer is always incredibly conscientious. The uniform is as clean and as pressed as can be, and the creases in your shirts are right out of the manufacturer's package—I like your ascot, by the way—and they're always so earnest. Not only that, but they are *always busy*. They're always reading the manual, redoing a checklist, calling back to find out if the temperature's okay—they just don't have that relaxed, cool manner that the rest of the pilots have."

I felt a little better about my scrambling pace.

"Always busy, hmmm?"

"Always. Until they get over it. And always hungry, always ready to eat everything in sight."

I was startled. "Not me. I don't have time to eat. I don't even *feel* like eating."

She laughed at me. "Just wait. You'll see."

I glanced at my watch. Heavens, I'd wasted forty-five seconds. I hurried back to work, wondering if perhaps I was hungry. Ordinarily, there's nothing wrong with my appetite. Was I sick? Anyway, I was really happy that the F.A. had been so friendly.

At the end of the trip I paused at my desk to do my last little job: completing the E-6 logbook. Captain Almeida stopped to say goodbye on his way out, for it was the termination of our sequence together, and as he did so he glanced down at my paperwork. His expression was solemn.

"Now that," he said, running his finger down a column on the paysheet, "is probably the most serious error you could ever make."

Before I had a chance to panic, I saw what he meant.

I had transposed our names on the crew listing, so that I was the captain and he was the flight engineer.

"Always remember," he said gravely, "that it's very important for the captain to get his proper pay."

He kissed me lightly on the forehead, and walked away smiling.

I sat there beaming to myself, feeling wonderful. It had been a hectic first flight, but a very pleasant and encouraging one. No one could have asked for better treatment.

On my way through the terminal to the crew lounge near Operations it occurred to me that perhaps Captain Almeida had been especially briefed to keep an eye on me. I rather doubted it, because captains are expected to handle their crews according to their own judgment, but I thought it was a possibility.

In the corridor I ran into the crew scheduler I'd met briefly a couple of days before, when the captain had shown me where to sign in.

"Have a good trip?" he asked.

"Terrific," I said happily. "I had a great time."

"How did you get along with Captain Almeida?"

"Wonderfully. He was really nice to me."

The scheduler grinned. "Thought he would be. He's a great guy. But you should have seen his face when he looked at the sign-in sheet and saw where it said Flight Engineer, Tiburzi, B. L."

"Oh, really?" I was interested. "How'd he look?"

"Petrified! No, just kidding. Dismayed. Concerned. He didn't say anything, but it was written all over his face. Then he kind of braced himself and went looking for you. So I wondered how it went . . . And what about the passengers? How did they react?"

I stared at him, mouth open. Passengers! "Y'know, I never saw a passenger. I went back to do my cabin check before takeoff, I went back to the galley, but I didn't notice any passengers. They were all a blur!"

"Well, that's a first trip for you. They'll start getting faces one of these days."

We parted with a chuckle. Other than having failed to notice the passengers, I felt that I had established some sort of new-arrival rapport with my job and my work associates. The whole crew, headed by Ed Almeida, had been easy to work with and, in parting, had scrawled warm messages on my flight plan—it looked like an autographed plaster cast—saying It's been a real pleasure, Hope we get to fly together again, Best of luck, and other encouraging things.

So Captain Almeida had been worried.

It was very much like the days at the academy, I thought, checking my mailbox for messages. I don't always know what to expect, but neither does anyone else. Nobody knows what it's going to be like, until it happens.

June 28, 1973

Mr. Peter Bay
Jacob Reed's Sons

Dear Pete:

Once again I would like to thank you and Jacob Reed's on behalf of myself, Bonnie Tiburzi, and American Airlines. . . .

There is one problem area, however, and I'm sure it can be rectified easily, depending on . . . First of all, Bonnie's jacket does not have any inside pockets or a protective patch to cover the wings. I am sure this was just an oversight, as we were running close to our target date when the uniform was needed. As Bonnie's blouse and pants do not have pockets, it is imperative that she at least have some in the jacket.

Now that I have mentioned the pants with no pockets, I imagine in our zest to produce a fashionable and fitted trouser, we overlooked the pocket requirement. I'll leave this up to you and Bonnie to work out. . . .

Best regards,
Bill Copeman

TDY Boston had lasted only as long as that one trip. Back in New York I had to start getting my act together—deal with a pile of mail, look for an apartment of my own, shop for basic furniture and generally get into a settled routine. But the uniform, in which I would be spending a great deal of time, was still one of my priorities.

I appreciated the company's wish that I appear in a fashionable and well-fitting "trouser." I shared it. But the lack of pockets in both jacket and pants were proving to be quite a problem. The guys were festooned with pockets, both visible and concealed, in which they crammed wallets, coins, keys, cards, pens, pencils, snapshots, handkerchiefs, toothpicks, gum and other small staples of daily life without unduly distorting their well-cut uniforms. And ordinarily I would have carried a purse for such items. But purses are not standard issue for airline pilots and I didn't think a trend was likely to develop.

Keys were my main problem. I would also have liked to carry my own pen, but that was less important. Every time I went out to the airplane to do my preflight walkaround and open up, I carried my jet bridge keys and cockpit keys in my hand or pinned on my pants until I could put them on my desk, where they'd slide around during flight.

This was impractical, so I protested a little.

Another thing was, it was getting warm. Pilots, along with the rest of New York, were taking off their jackets. They still looked well dressed in their tailored shirts with the epaulets and the neat breast pockets, even when the pockets were occupied by clip pens and various scribbled notes. But I was not supposed to have breast pockets. At all. In either blouse or jacket.

"We don't want you to have pockets like the men have. Because when you stuff pens or pencils in your breast pocket, it looks . . . you look . . . they don't lie flat. They stick out funny."

"Funny?"

"Well . . . We don't want anything drawing attention to the fact that you have a female figure. Attractive and feminine is one thing, but there's no need to—well, there's no need to have breast pockets."

Nonetheless, the company was very accommodating. Bill Copeman kept on writing letters and I kept on being measured, and finally I had pockets in my pants and in my jacket —but none above the waist. The blouse was fitted for epaulets, and in fairly short order I was able to go to work with my epaulets on my blouse and my keys in my pants pocket.

I was still without a proper airline hat, because all the ones we'd tried were either too severely military or looked like something one might wear for grouse-hunting or reveling with Robin Hood.

There were other ways in which I was not precisely standard issue. I wore the black shoes, as required, and the reliable watch, and I had my hair neatly trimmed but not above the collar. Tied back in a pony tail, it hung well below my shoulders. I offered to cut it, so that I'd look a bit more like a regulation pilot, but the company said No, no, we like your hair the way it is. We want you to look like a woman.

Hmm. Okay. Except between the waist and shoulders?

Neither did I have a uniform overcoat. Until midwinter, when I'd have to get something heavier, I would use my small men's navy blue London Fog. Not very feminine.

But of course my shoes had dainty little heels.

In all of my problems with clothes and concern with a neat but not gaudy personal appearance, the company—usually in the persons of Captains Melden and Copeman—was helpful and deeply interested. It was as if we were equally committed to trying to do something new together—which, indeed, we were—and the smallest details could not be overlooked. Image was important.

The one individual who did not seem to share our sense of venture was the P.R. man who had laid down the rules for my conduct outside working hours. Rightly, he was also concerned with image, but I could never determine what image he wanted me to present. After a while I began to get the impression that, ideally, I should be both unseen and unheard, although available for display to the public on carefully selected occasions. Careful to preserve the airline's conservative image, he screened virtually all requests for my presence that had anything to do with my role as a woman pilot.

The spate of mail that had begun shortly after I started training turned into a flood. Fortunately, neither the incoming letters nor my replies needed P.R. clearance, so I could really enjoy my correspondence.

Cards and letters came from Mexico City, Jamaica, Bangladesh, Australia, New Zealand, Nigeria, Egypt, Finland, Italy, Pakistan, Alabama, Alaska, Maine, Miami and Bob the Mailman. Congratulations from Emily Howell, Frontier's pioneer woman pilot. Good wishes from pilots on the line and from pilots who had flown with my father. Surprised notes from out-of-touch friends and friends of the family. A telegram from an old boyfriend who had never been too thrilled about my aspirations: DEAR BONNIE CONGRATULATIONS I HOPE THAT YOU ARE HAPPY NOW. Best wishes from Bella Abzug: "Your entry into this previously all-male field is one which has been too long in coming. Maybe now we will see some advertisements in which women are not saying 'Fly me,' but 'I'll fly you.' "

A letter in Spanish from José in Venezuela. A request for a photograph from Carlos of Colombia. Pleas for advice on how to become an airline pilot, from Maria, Lois, Heidi, Pia, Karen, Janet and John and Kenneth: "I am currently taking flying lessons. Would it be possible to visit with you regarding my career?" "The question is, how to go about getting started. How, if I may ask, did you get into the business?" "There is such a tremendous sum of money involved. I wonder if there is an easier way."

Then there were magnificently illustrated missives from Birdman Art Bean, a near-legendary hang glider pilot, addressed to Birdlady. And mash notes, as for example: "Dear Bonnie, Being single myself and thinking you are a most attractive girl . . ." And raps over the knuckles: "Miss Tiburzi, There is nothing more pretty in the world than a very feminine woman. . . . Male jobs should not be taken by young ladies like you. The persons who taught you to fly did a big mistake."

I answered all the letters, gratified and astonished at how many young people all over the world wanted to know how I had become an airline pilot and how they could, too. I began to believe, in dispensing my small store of advice, that I might be something of a spokeswoman for aviation in general and women pilots in particular. At the same time, I was unsure how to handle all the inquiries. There were so many, and with so many different questions, that I began to wish there was a book or information service I could recommend. I know I could have used something of the sort myself, when I was starting out.

It was about then that the idea of an information center began to enter my head, but it was a germ of an idea that took years to develop. Until it did, I could only offer the benefit of my own limited experience, and I would say, when asked, that the way I got into the airline business was the *worst way*. Sure, I got a lot of all-round experience, and much of it was both useful and enjoyable. But I wasted a lot of time. Today's guidance counselors might point out, I think, that women are employable in every branch of aviation and that there are a great many colleges offering appropriate courses and degrees.

For those of us who are not really interested in the academic approach, there is—for women—a relatively new and excellent way to prepare for airline flying, and that is to take the military route. My flight plan was completely without structure. What I did was spend a lot of time and money experimenting with different ways to reach a goal that wasn't all that hard to reach, had I only known the way, and one that is more easily reachable now because a number of determined women have done it. People need structure, it seems to me, and the military is extremely well structured. Too much so for me, but the training is unsurpassable. On the other hand, it isn't absolutely necessary; in addition to which, the armed services naturally want the fliers they train to fly for *them,* and require a commitment of at least several years of service.

When the first appeals for advice came in the mail, I didn't know all the answers, and I still don't because what is right for today might be wrong for tomorrow, but at that time I was starting to make some pretty good guesses on the basis of my own mistakes. Find out the FAA requirements, I urged my correspondents. Write to the airlines and find out theirs. Go to college, if you can, or at least take courses in basic mechanics, electronics and aeronautics. Start flying right away, even before you've brushed up on your arithmetic, and get your private license. Fly anything, anywhere. Go on and get your commercial license, and again fly anything, anywhere, anytime. Get your multiengine and instrument ratings and keep on flying—but while you're doing that, apply for and grab a job with a corporation or an air taxi line or any small firm with a plane for you to fly. Skip instructing. Every minute of corporate or commuter flying is high-quality time toward your airline ticket. Instructing is great experience and can be an extremely rewarding permanent career, but if you don't want it to be permanent there's no point in giving it a whole lot of your time. Get multiengine time. Get jet time, even a little. With a corporate or commuter job, you'll be pretty well qualified for an airline in a couple years—surely a short enough time in which to mold a career.

Mulling over what I myself had learned and what I was still finding out, I sat in crew lounges and hotel rooms and labored over my replies. I knew as little as anyone about the future of women in the airline business, but at least I could tell the little I knew about the past and present and I could tell about my own experiences. Sometimes I even managed to meet young hopefuls at airports before my trips, and on layovers, sometimes I spent hours on the telephone, but most often I wrote out what I had to say in longhand. I liked doing it. It seemed to me that that was part of what I was there for, and what I was all about.

11

The Most Junior Pilot on the Line

"What *is* this?" said a woman's voice.

Flight time was approaching. Passengers were boarding. The captain had reviewed the maintenance write-ups in the E-6 logbook as well as the special equipment list. We had gone over our instrument check, received departure clearance and were getting on with the before-starting-engines checklist.

I was as busy as I knew how, getting the feel of the pace and intent on calling out the list, hunched over my panel in the manner so carefully taught me by Boyd Dollar, when I felt as much as saw someone pausing at the cockpit door. And then came the high, strident voice.

There was a break in the rhythm as we all looked around. A well-dressed woman passenger was looking in on us, ignoring a flight attendant's pleas to proceed to the cabin.

"*What* is *that?*" She was pointing a finger at me and looking at the captain, a curiously mixed expression of revulsion and anger on her face.

The temperature in the cockpit dropped several degrees.

The captain opened his mouth, closed it, opened it.

"Why, madam, that's a—that's our—that's—" He stopped sputtering and tried again, this time polite but authoritative.

"Ma'am, that's our flight engineer, Bonnie Tiburzi. She's a pilot, and a highly qualified professional. An essential member of the crew."

Our visitor flicked her eyes back over at me and pursed her mouth. Then, with a wrinkling of her nose that dismissed me as a negligible if unpleasant object, she turned around and walked away.

I don't know when I have felt so diminished.

The three of us in the cockpit raised eyebrows at one another, not quite able to smile.

"Whew!" I said weakly, totally at a loss for a snappy comment.

The captain shrugged. "Guess it takes all kinds," he observed. "Don't let it get to you."

At least I was getting the support of my captain. On one of Emily Howell's first trips, or so I had heard, the captain had turned to her and snapped, "Don't touch a thing in this cockpit!" and ignored her thereafter.

I was kind of waiting for something like that to happen to me.

My budding career as an airline pilot had reached its most challenging stage: the will I make it or won't I phase. The trips were a thrilling kind of drudgery—thrilling because I was getting into the swing of a job I had dreamed of for years, and yet was now finding to be unfamiliar territory, full of surprises: drudgery because of the nature of the flights. They were all-nighters, or they were weekend trips or they started at four o'clock in the morning at JFK and ended up at La Guardia late at night or they had some other dreadful drawback common to beginning airline careers. When it came to being dealt choice trips, I was the low person on the totem pole.

A senior captain can get virtually any trip he wants. So can a senior copilot. But the seniority system is so rigidly observed, and rightly so, that it might take me ten to fifteen years or even longer to move up to the left seat and several more years to become senior enough to bid for the most desirable or convenient trips. Even a couple of years or so as flight engineer would put me in line to bid for the trips of my choice, and possibly even get them. But at this point I was the most junior crew member not only in New York but in the whole seniority system. With about 3,600 hires ahead of me, I wasn't expecting to be a senior anything for a very long time.

Seniority is based on the date of hire, not on superior performance or jockeying for position. There is no rapid rising through the ranks to become a star. All hires are regarded as similarly skilled. Obviously there are degrees of difference, but these are usually minor and tend to become apparent only when a second officer fails to upgrade to copilot, or a copilot to captain. For the most part, what separates the men from the boys and the women from the girls is time. It's waiting for people ahead of you to retire from the top of the ladder or remove themselves from their various rungs to change jobs or careers or grow roses in the country. You move up when people leave. And moving up has its privileges, one of them being a good crack at getting the bid you want.

Fortunately, not everybody wants the same thing. All pilots bid for different reasons. Some bid maximum flying hours for maximum pay, others minimum hours if they have compelling outside interests. Some bid for San Francisco or Phoenix because they like the layovers. Some bid for weekends off, or near the weekends so they can wind up spending time in a favorite place. One pilot I know arranges his schedule so that he can play Sunday golf with his pals in Los Angeles. Some bid to spend more time with their kids, and some to avoid all-day flights or all-nighters. A captain I flew with during my first few weeks had deliberately chosen a truly awful schedule because he was dating a lovely gal in New Jersey and he wanted to be with her every night. Then he married her and continued bidding for maximum time at home.

If someone senior to you bids the trip you want, you're obviously not going to get it. Nor is it usually possible to remonstrate, if you're so disposed, with some individual who gave you the worst of the pick, and say, "Hey! You can't do this to me. There must be some mistake!" because the bid selections are basically made up by computer pairing and flight schedules, a method made absolutely necessary by the great number of flights and flight employees. Fortunately, the crew schedulers are human, and it is sometimes possible to juggle your schedule to get particular days off by trading trips with other crew members.

Mainly, though, what bidding boils down to is that the most senior person at a base is going to get his number one choice while the most junior is likely to get the last thing anybody wants. For me, in the first months, it made no difference whether I bid or not. What I got was what nobody wanted.

Except me.

I was so happy to be working for an airline that I was content to do anything that was asked of me, even putting up with flak from insulting women passengers . . . although I wasn't sure how much of that I'd care to take.

My major concern during those first months of flying was getting settled in Manhattan so that I could concentrate on the job. Before the summer got much hotter I found myself an apartment on Seventy-third and Third—which to my delight was pronounced Seventy-t'oid and T'oid by my neighbors—right over a Chinese restaurant. At last, at the age of twenty-four, I had my own place. The only trouble was that, right after I found it, I was posted TDY to Buffalo for a month on reserve.

So instead of fixing up the apartment and hunting for bargain furniture, I lived out of a suitcase at the Williamsville Inn.

Such are the vagaries of the business for a brand-new airline pilot that I spent almost the entire month waiting for calls to duty that never came, speeding the passing hours by studying a bagful of flight manuals. It was rather like being back at the Inn of the Six Flags. On weekends, when I was not on call, I darted back to my bare and rather grimy new home to slosh paint on the walls and hang curtains.

The study time was valuable, because there is always a mass of technical material for flight engineers to keep abreast of, but it concerned me that I was neither establishing my own base nor getting much cockpit time. There were still elements that hadn't quite clicked into place. I was a transient, a bird of passage temporarily grounded in a city I'd first flown into from Pompano Beach for Tony Riccio, and I wanted my own nest. And I was a very green flight officer, with perhaps twenty flights behind me, and while I had the sense of knowing my job and doing it pretty smoothly, I felt I hadn't quite shaken down as an unexceptionable cog in the machinery.

And then came the flight from La Guardia into Buffalo, when the air whooshed out of the plane and cabin pressure dropped like a rock. Okay! Now I was definitely a fully functioning and integrated part of the team.

At the end of the month I went back to New York feeling lighthearted and ready for anything

I decorated the apartment with bright sunny colors and the barest minimum of furniture, choosing everything with as much care as if I'd been shopping for Chippendale at Sotheby's. Although I still felt rich on my probation pay of $650, soon to be raised to $675, I didn't have enough money to splash around.

I had been phenomenally lucky with the apartment. The rent was actually less than a third of my pay, a mere $175 a month—incredible for New York even then. With all my bills paid, I could actually afford to buy a few groceries.

The flight attendant on the Boston TDY had been right. Now that I'd gotten over feeling that I didn't have time to eat on the job or even drink a cup of coffee before it got cold, I was always hungry, ready to eat anything in sight. Perpetual hunger was a common joke about new flight engineers, I'd been told, and we were constantly being teased about eating everything on the airplane. And it was true. We didn't get paid enough, or perhaps just didn't budget well enough, to eat properly at home, so we ate any meal that was offered us. I have no complaints about airline food—I happily stuffed myself with it. I was glad to get to work so I could eat.

I was still checking in at an abominably early hour. (It became a habit—I've never been able to sleep late since.) Lacking a car or taxi fare, I'd leave the apartment at Seventy-t'oid and T'oid and walk down the street at three in the morning to catch the Second Avenue bus to the East Side terminal on Thirty-eighth Street, where I'd hop a Carey bus to the airport. Sometimes I'd have to step over someone sleeping in the hallway—there was one very attractive young streetperson, a latter-day flower child, who used to take advantage of the lockless front door quite a lot—before walking through the deathly quiet shadowy streets to the bus stop, and more often than not I'd be struck by the surreal quality of the people who seemed to be out at that time of the morning. They slid by in dark cars, or reeled or skulked or flitted about furtively with sinister looks on their lamplit faces, the lot of them obviously up to no good. The strange thing is that none of them ever bothered me. It may have been because I was wearing my uniform, but I'm sure it wasn't because I looked like a pilot and they happened to have inordinate respect for my profession. There was no way anyone would have assumed me to be a female airline pilot, the breed being virtually nonexistent, so I figured people must think I was a policewoman on late duty.

But whatever they thought, I walked through those predawn New York streets without ever feeling threatened.

I'd arrive at the airport, have a cup of coffee with the mechanics and leap into my work. I was beginning to speed it up. Things were falling into place. I had an hour to do my preflight before the passengers boarded, and on my first few trips I used every second of that hour to open up the airplane, to turn the lights and air conditioning on, to preflight the cockpit, to walk through the cabin, to go outside the airplane and do the walk-around check—I was exhausted. I didn't know how I was going to get everything done. And then, after a week or two on the line, I was done in forty-five minutes. I'd get back in the plane and, if I felt like it, read a magazine until the guys came, and we'd start the checklists together as the passengers began to board. All of a sudden everything was easy.

But the flight attendants were wary. I discovered this gradually, as I accepted their offers of food and eagerly wolfed it down instead of saying, "Oh, God no, I've no time for that!" There was even time to talk, and I found them very leery of me. The combination of "new hire" and "woman" made them quite nervous. I think that, with the best will in the world, they must have looked at me and thought, This has got to be a token woman. What does she know? Bet she hasn't had much aviation training. Bet she doesn't have the training the guys have.

I did get a lot of good responses, right away, from a number of the gals. "Wow, this is terrific! It's about time," they'd say. "I've always wanted to do that." But many did not like it. They were all pleasant to me, and as they came to the cockpit in spare moments and saw three flight officers at work, you would never have thought they were harboring deep reservations. Secretly, later, they would ask the captain or the copilot, "Is she qualified? What kind of job does she do? What sort of training does she have? Does she know what she's doing?"

It was an unfamiliar and sometimes awkward situation for the women. Should they talk to me as a woman primarily, or as one of the officers? In terms of the job, was I an equal or a superior? Should they come to me with cabin problems, or should they go to the guys? At first, when they wanted something done in the back, they'd ask the men. The men knew how to do things and the men were the authority figures. I'd say, "I'll go! It's my job, I'll do it!" And it *is* the flight engineer's job to field any problems in the back, from faulty equipment to unhappy passengers.

But from the men the women learned the kind of experience and training I had gone through, and after a little while they'd come up and sit on the jump seat and ask questions directly of me. How did I get interested in flying? Did I have a boyfriend? Did I cook? Did I sew? And how did I get along with the guys? That was a big question for the flight attendants. "Do they treat you the way they treat us?"

"Gee, I dunno . . . how *do* they treat you?"

In a rather cavalier fashion for the most part, I discovered,

Generally speaking, without sufficient respect or consideration. As trusted subordinates, yes, some of them agreed, if they'd been with the line for some time, but certainly not as equals.

That made me feel a little strange, because I was already—so far as I could see—being treated as very much of an equal by other flight officers.

With a difference. Other officers did not get pebbles tossed at their windows on layovers and have guys calling out, "Hey, come on down! We want to see the lady pilot!" Other flight officers did not get phone calls from fellow pilots saying, "Hi, Bonnie, my copilot's got a question for you," and hear the next voice on the line saying, "Hey! I just want to know, is the zipper in your uniform pants in the front or at the side?"

And other flight officers were not treated like women drivers by ground personnel, although I can think of only one occasion when that happened. We had had a hydraulic problem and I'd had to hand-crank the gear down. The normal procedure upon landing would be for a maintenance crew to come out and put the gear pins in the wheel wells before we taxied off the runway, so as to lock a joint in the gear assembly and prevent the gear from collapsing when we turned. But in Houston, where we landed that night in the dark, we had no maintenance crew of our own, so we requested nonengineering ground crew personnel to come out to the runway with a tug and tow us to the gate. The tow was necessary because, with the hydraulic problem to the gear, we didn't have maximum steering capability of the nose gear.

But before we went anywhere we had to put the gear pins in, as an extra safety precaution, and in the absence of mechanics it was my job to do it. I gathered my gear pins from my gear pouch beneath my engineer's desk and went outside. With the main gear, it's pretty obvious and instantly visible where the pins belong, so I popped them in quickly and moved along. But with the nose gear, it is not so obvious where the gear pin goes. I reached way up into the nose, sticking my head up into the wheel well and twisting my body as I did so, and thrust the pin into place out of sight of the ground crew.

One of them said, "No, no, that's not where it goes, that's not where it goes!"

"I assure you, it is," I retorted.

"No, it's not," he insisted. "Sure isn't," said another guy.

Then I started feeling insecure, and I thought, Oh, gee, maybe it's not. So, rather than do battle with a majority, I took the pin out and went back to the cockpit. "I'm having a problem with that nose gear pin," I announced, "and the guys down below say it's not where it's supposed to be."

So the copilot went down with me and put the gear pin in exactly where I had put it. And they didn't question him. Didn't even give him a doubting look.

I gnashed my teeth all the way back to the cockpit. It's perfectly okay to ask for a second opinion, and there was no reason to feel bad about that—only maybe I should have been more authoritative.

"Excuse *me,*" I should have said haughtily, "but this *is* where it goes."

This insignificant episode, happening not long after the incident with the woman passenger who seemed to think I was some kind of cockroach, gave me a gnawing feeling inside. I must *not* let anything so small make me feel insecure. If I think I can do the job, I must go ahead and do it—never mind who gives me funny looks.

Then something happened that made me feel better.

We landed at Albany one day on the first leg of a through flight to Chicago. As is usual on such trips, the captain and copilot went into Operations to recheck the weather for the next leg, get the flight plan and talk to the dispatchers. As flight engineer, I stayed with the airplane along with the flight attendants and through passengers to be on hand in case anything happened. We were parked a short distance from the terminal, with a truck-mounted stair reaching up into the forward entry door instead of the more common jet bridge that connects the airplane to the terminal, and I was outside doing my postflight.

If it hadn't been for the open stairway I would not have noticed the smoke so soon.

But as it was, I must have seen the very first cascade of wispy smoke as it tumbled gracefully down the stairway. From a slow walkaround I burst into a run and galloped up the steps two or three at a time through suddenly formed foglike billows, losing a shoe on the way, with the thought flashing through my mind that on a stationary, virtually shut-down plane there could only be one cause for the smoke. I knew it wasn't the APU, the auxiliary power unit, because I had just been walking around the main wheel area where it was located and there hadn't been the slightest whiff of trouble there, so it took no detective work to determine the source.

I had left on one of the air-conditioning packs to keep the cabin cool. That had to be it.

The cabin was beginning to look like a convention of exceptionally heavy smokers as I flung myself into the cockpit through the murk and reached for my panel. What must have happened—and what I saw proved it—was that the single operating pack fan, an essential part of the cooling system, had kicked off so that the air was no longer circulating and cooling, causing the air-conditioning pack to overheat. Thus the smoke.

My fingers automatically tripped switches, turning off the pack, resetting the air-conditioning system and reenergizing to ensure the cooling fan operation and blow out the smoke. Within about forty-five seconds from the time I had leapt back onto the airplane, the smoke began to disperse. When I walked back through the cabin the passengers were sitting bolt upright in their seats, unpanicked but ready for reassurance.

"Little foggy back here," I observed. "We just had an air-conditioning malfunction, slightly messy but minor, and it's all over. This'll be cleared up in just a minute."

The passengers nodded and went comfortably back to their reading. Clean air wafted through the cabin.

Any flight officer will realize that this was no desperately exciting, resourceful, nick-of-time save worthy of a medal. It was the only thing to do, it was my job to do it and I had been trained to do it instinctively. But smoke in a cabin is very frightening, and the chances were that people would pretty soon have started evacuating the airplane in some degree of confusion. I felt kind of heroic, not in the sense of having been brave, but of having been able to do what was necessary. Those passengers had been literally at my mercy, dependent on *me!* I was the only one who could have corrected the problem, unless the guys had suddenly come out of Operations, and it was my panel, my problem and I'd known what to do. I felt really good.

The smoke cleared, the guys came back and sniffed the air, we told them what had happened, passengers chattered away as if they'd had a little pleasurable excitement, people smiled at me . . . the whole world smiled at me.

Up and out again at 3 A.M. Down the dimly lit stairs, over the sleeping form in the hallway, over to Second Avenue for the downtown bus, onto the Carey bus and out to the airport. Same routine. One morning it varied.

I was standing at the bus stop shortly after three when a taxi pulled and the back door opened. A youngish guy in a tuxedo leaned out and said, "Hi. You want a ride?"

This is it, I thought. Wicked old New York. I'm about to be abducted.

But he was completely disarming as he went on. "Where're you going? To the Carey bus?"

"Yeah, as a matter of fact, I am," I said, delighted that he'd spotted my uniform for what it was.

"Great. I live down in that area. Hop in—I'll drop you off."

I hopped in and away we went.

His name was Ed Allen, he told me, and he'd just come from a terrific party. He was a businessman. He gave me his card. And what airline was I with?

I told him I flew for American and had only recently been hired.

By the end of the short ride we were chattering away like shipboard acquaintances and he had asked me out. I tucked away his card and said I'd call him sometime.

Which I did. Bob Lilly, a copilot with the company, invited me to a big party he was giving on the rooftop of the apartment building in which he lived. His studio apartment, he explained, couldn't accommodate the crowd but there was plenty of room on the roof and would I please bring a friend. So I asked Ed Allen to come along.

It was a pleasant late-summer evening and the rooftop was an elegant place for a big bash—almost the first party I'd been to in a New York full of strangers. Ed seemed to be enjoying the experience of being surrounded by airline people—generally speaking, a very attractive lot—and I felt happy to be partying with my own kind. To add to my simple pleasure, people kept coming up and congratulating me on being hired.

"Gee, that's really amazing," Ed said at length, as conversation swirled around us.

"What is?"

"Well, that so many people are coming up to congratulate you. I think that's terrific. I mean that so many people know—and they all seem to be so pleased—that you're a brand-new flight attendant."

Oh, Ed! That's why you thought I wanted the Carey bus.

I offered him a gentle smile.

"Wrong, Ed, I'm not," I said. And broke the news to him.

He took it very well.

But that was the beginning of a kind of avalanche. From then on, I kept meeting people who took me for a flight attendant. Or a purser, because of my stripes. Or a bus driver, because of my uniform. Other early-hires had the same experience. In one case a woman pilot in a hotel lobby was taken for a bellhop and instructed by a guest to take some bags out to the cab. She did it, too—the sport. In another case, a female passenger looked into the cockpit at the new flight engineer, Beverley Bass, and said, "*I* didn't know the captain had a secretary."

Look. Don't get me wrong. We respect secretaries, flight attendants, bellhops and bus drivers. But that's not what we are!

Shortly after Barbara Barrett got on the line for Eastern, she was doing her preflight check at the Miami airport when a security guard approached with a truculent air and asked her what she thought she was doing. Just doing her flight engineer's job, she assured him. Unconvinced, the guard got on his walkie-talkie and asked another security employee if there were any female pilots flying out of Miami for Eastern. Never heard of one, was the reply.

The guard got tough. Leaping to the conclusion that Barbara was trying to plant a bomb on the plane, he started swearing and threatening her. Understandably becoming apprehensive, Barbara ran up the stairway and locked herself inside the plane. The guard followed. "You come outa there!" he hollered, and hammered furiously on the cabin door. "Come on out!" Bang, bang.

Finally, the captain came out on the field and started walking toward his plane. There was this guard banging on the door.

"Hey, what's going on?"

"There's a woman in there who's dressed up as a pilot," yelled the guard.

"Y'crazy?" the captain shouted back, almost bursting with anger. "That's not a woman—that's our flight engineer!"

Some years later, Lynn Rippelmeyer, 5 feet 4 with pretty dimples, was sitting in the jump seat behind the captain with her arm resting on the back of his seat. Chatting away while passengers boarded, the two of them turned around at a sound in the doorway and saw a passenger look in.

"Oh, isn't that cute!" the woman cooed to the captain. "You brought your daughter along, dressed up just like you!"

"I'm not old enough to be her father!" the captain snarled.

It simply didn't occur to people that we could possibly have anything to do with flying the plane. They were unaware that there were such things as female airline pilots or even that there ever might be any. How *could* they cope with the reality of us, when we almost didn't exist? By the end of 1973 there were, in this equality-conscious land of opportunity, exactly four of us. And one in Canada.

But sometimes . . . sometimes there is recognition, and sometimes it can be great. I forgave every woman passenger in the world for the meanness of the one who jabbed a finger at me when I had to go back in the cabin one day and do a routine if rather conspicuous job.

We had one of those minor hydraulic failures which required us to get the gear down manually. I remember the copilot offering to help me, and the captain saying, "It's her job. She asked for it. Let her do it." So, after doing it, I had to go back into the cabin to check the gear doors by simply pulling up the carpet over the main landing gear and peering down through the viewer. That day, we had aboard a tour group of predominantly older women, and the captain announced to them that the flight engineer was going to come back and pull up the carpet and look down as a matter of routine to check on a minor gear problem.

So they were all expecting to see the flight engineer emerge from the cockpit and make his genial, confident way down the aisle.

When I appeared, they raised their eyebrows, stared, broke into beaming smiles, craned their necks to watch my progress, nudged each other and chuckled.

Regrettably, checking the gear is a task altogether lacking in dignity. To visually check the alignment of the gear with the red lines showing it to be in down position and locked in place, it is necessary, after pulling up the carpet, to bend way, way down and put your nose right up against the floor so that you can actually see those alignment lines through the viewer. I kneeled there, rear end sticking roundly up into the air, hearing a few muffled giggles and feeling quite embarrassed by the spectacle I presented.

Job done, I got up, dusted off my hands and felt the need to say something to the absorbed spectators.

"Well, no problem at all here," I said brightly, and waved a hand in a vaguely triumphant gesture.

The cabin broke into a stampede of applause—claps, bravos, hoorahs, a veritable standing ovation.

I felt my face bursting into a variety of rosy colors, and I should like to be able to say that I scuttled meekly back to the cockpit. But I didn't. They got a kick out of it—I got a kick out of it. Blushing merrily, and feeling warm all over, I strutted purposefully back to my place on the flight deck.

12

Strangers on a Plane

A whole new world was opening before my eyes. It was enormous, and it was awesome. Try to get a pilot to explain the wonder of flying. The answers range from offhand stammers and shy shuffling of feet to eloquent but not completely coherent rhapsodies. They all mean the same thing. There may be the rare pilot who flies just because he wants to show tough and tame that mechanical beast, the plane. But to the majority of pilots, the plane is not the Beast—it's Beauty.

It's a sweet, high-flying, responsive bird . . . some bird, that flies at thirty-seven thousand feet! Some bird, that takes off in the early morning before the sun is up and flies high over pastel clouds to see the sunrise from above. Some wonderful man-made bird, soaring and skimming between the sculptured cloud forms of an even more wondrous nature.

Awe-inspiring beauties seen from thirty-seven thousand feet. . . . Below, at the bottom of the ocean of air, a canyon bathed in moonlight, its rims and ravines carved out more subtly yet emphatically than if they had been awash in noonday sun, harsh and almost malevolent in the flat white light . . . and, days later, the same massive gorge looking soft and benign in the pink glow of an early morning. And then again, a black night, relieved at last by a sliver of light that turns into a moon, dark clouds rolling back like gigantic curtains to reveal an infinity of stars. Slowly the moonlight changes, the clouds drift softly downward, taking on the colors of the horizon as they meet land or sea, and the sky turns orange and blue.

The nights were long but sublime, a sequence of leaving a silent city to skim through splendor and land in the same silence at a different place, of getting to know New York as a carpet of pinpoint lights that suddenly burst into a dazzling, warmly enveloping blaze. We, the crew, came down to earth after long, quiet hours together, punctuated by exchanges with each other and informal chats with the traffic controllers. Nobody knew the companionable silences we had shared or the changing lights of the night and the breathtaking scenes that we had witnessed.

The nights were long—*but long*—so long that, sometimes after a trip, I might fall asleep without even knowing it. Once I was on a layover in Los Angeles, when the casual boyfriend of the moment gave me a call some time after I'd checked in. A friend, Gloria Joubert of the business staff of the Flight Academy, had met me at the airport and was staying over for a day's shopping in L.A., so she was in the room when the phone rang.

I reached out automatically and scooped it up.

"Hello," I said.

Next morning, over coffee, Gloria said, "Don't forget to return your call."

"Huh? What call?"

"I knew it!" Gloria chuckled. She was a bright, bouncy, wonderful person who had helped to shepherd hundreds of trainees through their more difficult days at the Flight Academy.

"Knew what?"

"You slept through it. The phone rang last night, you answered, said 'Hello.' I was half asleep and kinda waiting for you to go on talking. But you didn't. I turned on the bedside light and I looked across at you, and there you were lying with the receiver on your pillow. You were sound asleep, and there was a little voice on the other end of the phone yelling, 'Bonnie! Wake up, wake up!' So I woke you up."

"You did?" I couldn't remember at all.

"Yeah, and you said, 'Oh, thanks so much for calling. I'll talk to you later.' And you hung up the phone."

Little incidents like that brought home to me the fact that, while I was leading a wonderful life, it was one-sided. I'd started on the flying career of my dreams, but I had very few friends. I was meeting people in cockpits, but after a sequence of trips with them I never saw them again. Anyway, they were nearly all married.

I'd go home to my apartment, sleep a while, clean it up and then look around and wonder whom I could invite to a candlelit dinner. People asked me out once in a while, almost without exception people who had heard of me through newspaper interviews or some other branch of the publicity grapevine, and I went to their parties and dinners and discos because New York is a lonely town and I was lonely.

From the moment I got aboard the Carey bus to the airport, I felt secure and among my own kind. But when I looked around the apartment, alone, I felt alone, and when I went to parties, I felt strange. I was a novelty—a real live woman airline pilot! People would crowd around and I'd strut my stuff, tell them my father had taught me to fly and I'd been an instructor in Florida and that the guys were all terrific, and then I'd stand around for the rest of the evening feeling like a tattooed lady at a sideshow who, having shown off her tattoos and given a brief discourse on the art of tattooing, has nothing else to say.

And I didn't have anything else to say. Was there a person in the group who cared about my little problem with the left gear light? Why should there be? Anyone interested in a spirited discussion of one of my flight manuals? I thought not. Had I read anything provocative lately? Well, sure, *Aviation Week* always makes me think.

I didn't know what was on the best-seller lists, or even what the good books were. I knew nothing about art, or about theater, or about music, or the latest of the *in* restaurants or clubs. I could drop in a word or two about tennis or water-skiing, but I didn't know the Jets from the Mets. I could talk about flying, the use of new equipment, eating on the airplane, sleeping on the telephone, but not much else.

The New York crowd I met was too sophisticated for me. They overwhelmed me with their knowledgeable talk about the lively arts and the more dangerous sports, such as driving too fast while stoned or making illicit-sounding deals with high-powered people. I didn't like the low-lying fumes of pot, and I couldn't take another and another and yet another drink. I could always plead the company rule of twenty-four hours between the bottle and the throttle, and imply that the rule for grass was even more strict—like *none*—but in fact I simply didn't care much for anything that was served. Including the heavy passes that were proffered casually around like snacks between the drinks. I mean, those people were openly after my bod! I was astounded. By the blatancy, mainly, and by the fact that the sexual games, intermingled with the lofty conversation, seemed an inextricable part of the evening's entertainment. I really was the odd person out—I was just not in that league. Sure, I knew it was time to grow up, but was this really it? And if I'd only had more of a clue what they were talking about most of the time, I would have felt better. Maybe. Why should I give a damn about their therapy? Or what their shrink thought about *Deep Throat?*

I read the *New York Times* between chapters of new flight manuals and tried to sophisticate myself. But nothing I read could disguise the fact that I was, plainly and simply, lonesome. New York was even farther from Pompano Beach than I had thought it would be. I tried to bridge the gap by flying down to Florida to visit family and friends whenever I could. Bob and I saw each other once in a while but we were, inevitably, drifting apart.

Other relationships were also changing. Old friendships

were now touched with a curiosity that in some cases turned to envy. Debbie Gary was a rock, my best friend. And Judy Lee, an advanced student of mine at Pompano when I got hired, was an absolute gem. But the guys were kind of leery of me. They seemed not terribly happy that I was an airline pilot. It was only a little more than six months, now, since I'd gone away for training, and already I was separated from my old rough-and-tumble life by an enormous chasm.

I began to think seriously about the incompatibility of career and marriage. Never, in all my thoughts of a life plan, had I excluded marriage and children. If I were not to have a full home life as wife and mother and homemaker, I would be missing more than half a life. Yes, I wanted to be able to support myself always, if need be, by doing the thing that I loved doing and knew how to do. But my emotional self needed more out of life, and could give more to life, than the single-minded pursuit of a career.

At this stage I realized for the first time just how difficult it would be to combine my particular career with the role of wife. Bob and I had talked about some of the possible complications, but the future had seemed distant then. When the job itself was still only a dream, it had seemed unreal to anticipate personal conflicts.

It still seemed premature to worry, when there was no conceivable job-versus-domestic bliss collision anywhere on the horizon. Nor did I relish the prospect of the kind of conflict that might arise from my traveling-salesman lifestyle. I was perfectly happy to postpone it for a while. However, I wanted to keep all my options open. I'd always expected to get married someday, but right now the prospects were zero. I had dated a lot of guys in the past. Now I wasn't seeing anybody on any more than a fleeting basis. I wanted somebody permanent, but right then I didn't even have anybody temporary to joke and laugh with.

Okay, so that's the way it was going to be. I'd go on gobbling up the never-ending supply of technical bulletins and advisories designed for the continuing education of flight engineers, master my job, enjoy the people I happened to meet, learn to dodge when necessary and make the most of every day as it presented itself. Pretty soon I'd get my whole act together, and enjoy my private moments as much as my time on the airplane.

Meanwhile, guess I'll fly home for a weekend with Mother and Dad.

October 31, 1973. Halloween.

I was flying back to New York after visiting my parents and Bob, who was as interested as ever in my work and aspirations but—I rather sadly admitted to myself—less interested in me.

The flight attendant had taken my name, recognized it since she was attuned to female pilots because another woman was flying for her airline, and seated me in 2A, the very first seat in first class. There was no luggage compartment between the first row of seats and the cockpit, which is significant only in that there was an unobstructed view between cockpit and first class.

I vaguely noticed the flight attendant going into the cockpit but gave it no thought because flight attendants are always going into cockpits for one reason or another.

"Hey, fellas," she reportedly said, "there's an American pilot back there who'd like to sit up in the cockpit."

"Yeah? Is he in uniform?" said the captain.

"Well, I'll let you look for yourself," she said coyly. "The pilot's in Two-A."

She opened the cockpit door wide and they all looked out. And then stared. I was not in uniform.

I was reading a magazine and didn't see them, but they saw me.

"Hey, is that Bonnie Tiburzi?" said the copilot, as the F.A. shut the door. "I know her!"

"Oh, sure you do." That was the engineer, being skeptical.

"Yeah yeah yeah, I do," the copilot insisted. "She knows my dad."

He sent his card back with the flight attendant. I squinted at it. The name just didn't ring a bell. In the past few months I'd met so many people so briefly that I couldn't remember all the names. He knew me? I felt bad about it.

"Gosh, I really don't know," I told the flight attendant. "But could you just say hello from me?"

Off she went.

And, a little while later, back he came.

Tall and blond, neatly uniformed, impossibly good-looking, he stopped with an arm on my chair and smiled down at me.

"Hi. I'm Mike. I think you know my dad. He's often spoken of the smorgasbord Christmases he had with the Tiburzis." His smile widened. It knocked me out. "Including you. Glad to meet you, Bonnie. Welcome to the airlines."

"Mike! Of course I know your dad! How nice to see you!" I gazed up at him, flashing exclamation points with my eyes. This guy was adorable. Terrific looking—his voice carried authority—his manner was gentle—there was a crinkly humor in his face.

We exchanged phone numbers. When the trip was over, he walked me to the terminal.

On our first date we went out to New Jersey for his father's birthday party. It was a homey occasion, small and intimate . . . his father and mother, Mike and me. The year was cooling off but it was the best of times to be outdoors. We walked, smelling the autumn leaves, we barbecued steaks, we exchanged anecdotes and we laughed immoderately.

It was great to be with his family. All of a sudden I had friends in the New York area, down-to-earth people who could understand my passion for flying and yet treat me as a whole person rather than some sort of oddity.

Mike and I started dating steadily.

From the beginning, he made an enormous difference to my life. He was not like the New Yorkers I had met and felt a little afraid of. He was a *pilot.* Nice and normal, attractive, proper, well-mannered without overdoing it, fond of sports, incredibly clean-cut and wholesome after some of the open-toed, hairy-chested, chain-wearing caricatures I had met. So he didn't quote Proust and Gertrude Stein. Neither did I. So he preferred being out on an open boat to choking his last in a smoky club, and he was looking forward to the ski season in Vermont. So did I, so was I. I was only a neophyte skier, but I was yearning to learn.

As the weather got colder in New York I thought how much fun it would be to go out on the ski slopes with Mike. Shivering on a ramp at La Guardia at 4 A.M., I'd walk around a throbbing 727, its engines warming up while I shriveled in the bite of little snow-bearing gusts, thinking about how a little warmth in life made everything look better. What I'd loved before, I loved even more—the wonderful thrill of takeoff into the heights, the concentration and precision of the work, the rare double rainbows in the sky, the teamwork, the small problems to be solved, the camaraderie. . . .

By an incredible stroke of luck, I'd found the ideal man. Mike and I were seeing each other constantly—as constantly as our various trips would allow.

He was really special, so friendly and accommodating. Nothing seemed to throw him. He just rolled with the punches and came up laughing. There was nothing about my schedule that struck him as at all abnormal, nothing about my chosen way of life that he thought peculiar for a woman. At last I had met someone, other than my father and brother, with whom I could talk about flying on some level other than a change of flight plan or a maintenance squawk. Someday we would go flying together. We'd rent a plane, or buy one. And fly up to Vermont, where Mike had a condominium, and I would practice on the baby slopes while Mike gave me some pointers. I knew he had to be an excellent skier because he was on the airlines ski team.

I brushed snow out of my eyes and shivered my way into

the cockpit. We had already spoken about getting married some time in the future. The fact that we were both pilots was a more than a happy coincidence. We understood each other's job demands. As an eight-year airline pilot, Mike had enough seniority to bid trips that would give us a chance to be together, and when I got off probation in a few months I would also have an opportunity to be more accommodating. To me, enchanted by the prospect of a real-life solid relationship, Mike seemed the answer to a maiden's prayer—a Bob with wings, a flexible, understanding guy with dreams that dovetailed with my own.

The guys came into the cockpit with wintry noses and cheerful smiles. "Brrr! Let's have some more heat in here."

Cold weather always demanded extra care, especially when accompanied by rain or snow. The job is more than thawing out the crew and making things comfortable for passengers on the red-eye express. It's meticulously double-checking every item on our multiple checklists, and forestalling any problems caused or compounded by the weather, including, and especially, icing of the wings and fuselage.

I worked away contentedly. My world had miraculously become whole. Who could ask for anything more?

That was just before Christmas.

On December 31, the 214 of us who had been hired in the previous spring were given an unwelcome New Year's surprise: an indefinite furlough.

We no longer had our wonderful, sought-after jobs, and there was no telling when—or even if—we might be rehired.

The tough part was not knowing how long the furlough would last. All I did know was that, without any means of support, I could no longer afford to live in New York. I needed a new job, with any luck a temporary one, but I also needed a little time to think about what to do next.

Mike and I were pretty conventional, I guess. Maybe even

American Airlines photograph by Bill Winfrey, Dallas, Texas

It's official! I'm an American Airlines pilot and proud to look the part.

Doug McKenzie

(Right) Competition turns to friendship: Debbie Garry Collier and I stand in front of the Pitts in which she taught aerobatics during our flight instructing days. *(Below)* Like father, like daughter. Captain Gus was the major influence on my career.

(Above) Captain "Gus" Tiburzi's FBO at Danbury Airport, where I started to fly in the Cessnas seen far left. *(Below)* "Gunny" and "Gus," my Swedish mother and Italian father, taken in the early 1940s when my dad, Gus, flew with Air Transport Command.

American Airlines photograph by Ken N

(Above) Graduation of Class 73-9 at American Airlines Flight Academy. I'm the one without the hat. *(Below)* My first press conference. I sit under the glare of the lights while Captain Ted Melden, standing beneath the clock, keeps a watchful eye upon me.

American Airlines photograph by Bill Winfrey, Dallas,

Sunny South Florida charter-flying, Fort Lauderdale Airport.

Pictorial Magazine

Fort Worth Star Telegram

Taking my turn in the right seat of the Boeing 727 simulator during initial flight engineer training.

The 1980 meeting of I.S.A. in Denver, Colorado. *(Row one, left to right)* Molly Flanagan, United; Beverley Bass Harber, American; Linda Morley-Wells, United; Pat Toher, Continental; Elena Folch, Mexicana; Jane Bony, Braniff. *(Row two)* Maggie Rose, Piedmont; Jeanne Krosse, United; Claudia Jones, Continental; Tangela Masson Tricoli, American; *(Row three)* Sharon Kilgers Krask, Delta; Becky Rose, Piedmont; Emily Warner, Frontier; *(Row four)* Lynn Evans, United; Dorothy "Carat" Vallée, Republic; Emily Warner, Frontier; *(Row five)* Laurie S. Reeves, United; Jean Haley Harper, United; Cyd Fougner, Western; Terry London Rinehart, Western; *(Row six)* Bonnie Tiburzi, American; Judy Lee Buttgenbach, United; Sydney Andrews Hale, Republic; Lennie Sorenson, Continental; *(Row seven)* Norah O'Neill, Flying Tigers; Karen Kahn, Continental; Gail Gorski Schlight, United; Julie Clark, Republic; *(Row eight)* Denise Brown, Western; Karen Church Bland, United; Holly Fulton, Braniff; Susan Hytinen, United; *(Row nine)* Diane Hixson, United; Debbie Harvey, Braniff; Judy Cameron, Air Canada; *(Row ten)* Susan Arthurs, United; Gretchen Sanderson, Braniff; Maria Ziadie, Air Jamaica; Danielle Decuré, Air France; *(Row eleven)* Susan Horstman, Pan Am; Conchita Barnard, Mexicana; Julia Abston, Alaska Airlines; Cindy Morgan, Frontier.

The stages of outfitting a woman airline pilot: We'll keep trying until we get it right!

"Captain Bonnie," as she's dubbed by friends, in the co-pilot's seat of her favorite Boeing 727.

a touch old-fashioned, like our parents. He was living in a pretty little house on Long Island, but it barely occurred to either of us that I might move in with him. Unbelievable, really, but there it is. After all, we weren't even engaged.

I relinquished my apartment in Manhattan and went home to Mother.

Mike came down to Pompano Beach every other week and stayed for a day or two. After the first couple of visits it became obvious that it would be impractical for me to look for a job in Florida so long as Mike was based in New York. We started making concrete plans.

We were married on April 20, 1974. As a magnificent wedding present, friends chartered a boat for the occasion. It had been President Truman's old yacht, *El Presidente,* and we felt very festive and adventurous as we tied the knot on board.

With the suddenness of the furlough telegram, everything was changed. We would no longer be the flying career couple. Mike was the one with the career. But that was okay. I'd gotten over the first and worst hurdles of my own job, and now it was temporarily shelved. This was our big chance—time together, right at the important beginning of our marriage, to establish our home and our roots. I'd have the little nest that always figured somewhere in my fantasies. I could settle down and make a home for the two of us.

One major cloud marred an otherwise joyous occasion. That was the death of Mike's dad, a legendary pilot and great friend.

After the funeral, we went to Mike's house on Long Island. Our house. Home.

In small ways, I started infiltrating a little of myself into what had been very much a man's domain. It was a rented house, and we planned to buy something of our own as soon as we found the right place, but meanwhile I was looking forward to practicing my new domesticity. Now was my chance to try my hand at decorating to please us both and learning to cook for two.

Looked at in the light of a new marriage, the furlough—if it had to come—was neither a bad break nor badly timed for me. It never crossed my mind that better times might not be coming, and once I'd gotten over the immediate shock of an unexpected vacation I could see it as a blessing in disguise.

That, unfortunately, was not the case for many furloughed pilots. While it gave me a chance to catch up with my personal life, other jobless pilots were anxiously looking for ways to keep up with their mortgages, car payments, school bills and installment plans. It wasn't easy for pilots to find new jobs. When one airline furloughs, the chances are that others are also feeling the economic pinch. If they do happen to be hiring, they want to be certain that their new pilots won't go back to their old airline jobs when conditions change, so they generally require new hires to give up their seniority with previous companies. Corporations are equally cautious about hiring executive pilots they might soon lose. As for the various flying jobs that pilots take on their way up, such as piloting frozen turkeys and giving lessons, they scarcely pay the rent for even the most parsimonious of bachelors.

So a lot of pilots look outside the aviation field for jobs. Trouble is, a lot of pilots don't have skills for anything else, the reason being that most of us work so single-mindedly to reach our goals, either academically or in a branch of the service, or at an FBO doing the whole bit from sweeping the floors through selling the tickets to gassing up the plane and flying it, that there is no time to develop any sidelines. Many pilots go into real estate, only to discover that that is also a field requiring specialized knowledge and skill.

Fliers turn their hands to pumping gas, doing maintenance at airports, clerking in stores, driving buses, waiting tables, jockeying for jobs for which other people are far more qualified.

On the other hand, a few manage to turn hobbies into jobs and some are just plain lucky.

I was one of the just plain lucky ones.

Immediately upon being furloughed I had the usual Oh-God-What-Am-I-Going-to-Do unemployment blues. I didn't for a moment think of trying to get on with another airline. At that point my major concern was not to lose my number, such as it was, and to keep myself available for rehire. I was attached to American—proud of it as a company and proud of my association with it. Sooner or later I was going to get back with it.

Such stubborn determination to stick with what I thought of as the finest airline in the nation might very well have kept me out of the job market for an awkwardly long time. If I had known how long it would be before I was recalled, I might have made other choices, and then perhaps a lot of things might have turned out differently . . . but nobody knew.

We had expenses. There was the house rent, the upkeep of the car and Mike's place in Vermont. Soon, we hoped, we would buy a house, and that would be another major obligation. It would be necessary for me to make a contribution.

I wanted to. As soon as we were settled in a house of our own I would look for work commensurate with my career hopes.

I had the impression that it didn't matter much what I did as long as it was *something*. But this was the guy who had, I thought, admired my achievements and understood my career hopes. Obviously, I wasn't hearing straight. Or else he didn't realize that, given a little time, I could pursue some of the leads that had come my way during the winter and get on the track of some new ones, and work my way into something that would be worthwhile for both of us.

"You know, Mike," I tried to explain, "I don't really have to be a waitress or a clerk to make my financial contribution. I could probably get a pretty good job if I set my mind to it. I didn't come this far to all of a sudden regress dramatically to some sort of desperate choice. There are other things I can do —work for a corporation, demonstrate airplanes, do television commercials, do ground school instruction, whatever. I know I'm capable of doing more than just humdrum stuff. All it takes is a little time to land something."

We were in the midst of these discussions when General Electric offered me a job as a flight operations engineer, which would involve my becoming an expert on their CF-6 engine and its function in the DC-10. I would have to fly around quite a lot, much like a technical representative, going along in the jump seat of various DC-10s and advising the respective pilots on how to improve engine performance. I liked the idea of flying around a lot. Then there was the pay—$18,000 a year, more than twice what I had been making on my real job. Very nice. Trouble is, I'd have to move to Ohio, and commute home on the weekends.

No problem, Mike said.

No problem?

Lots of flying couples, other couples in business, did that sort of thing—

On their *honeymoon?*

And the best part was, the job was available right away and it was exactly the right kind of job—

How could it be right when we'll be apart five days a week and maybe more, and we only just got married?—It's a terrific opportunity—It's too far—The pay's pretty good—It's too soon—You'll be doing what you want to do.

Okay. There were elements of the offer that were enticing. To me, it was an almighty drawback that the job was on the fringes of Cincinnati. A career was one thing, but a commute between New York and Ohio was ridiculous.

I felt pressured. With that kind of pay, I'd really be pulling my weight. Mike was eight years older than I, more mature, more knowledgeable about financial matters. He seemed to want me to go, and maybe he was right. I didn't want to go.

But somehow I failed to communicate to him what it was that I did want. The right words wouldn't come.

So I went.

Afterward, Mike insisted it was a unilateral decision. Mine. But it wasn't. If he did not urge it, he condoned it. If I couldn't express my feeling that I should stay home with him, neither could he. "Well, we do want to buy a house," I remember him saying, "and we do need the money. So, yeah, why don't you give it a whirl? We can put the money aside, save it for the house."

I gave it a whirl. No sooner decided upon than done. Off I went to Evandale, Ohio, rented upstairs quarters from a German family and spent the first weeks of my married life taking apart and reassembling the CF-6 engine at ground school. After I had mastered that, I was to be sent out to Long Beach, California, to learn the DC-10 from a tech rep's point of view. But I couldn't even begin to think of California for a while. I was too sorry for myself, alone in Evandale.

Here I was, married yet single, living in part of someone else's home, spending my evenings by myself, eating takeout food in front of the tube instead of cooking gourmet meals for my handsome husband. In Fantasyland I could see myself whipping up a delicate pasta dish with a crisp green salad, ready to pour a simple Italian red for the two of us—if he was not flying in the morning.

Better than tasteless frozen food or grease-fried pizza or whatever it was I was eating. I wiped my fingers and reached for the phone.

Most weekends, I went home. Some, I couldn't get away, either because I had to work late on Friday or because I had to report in on Saturday. Mike couldn't make it down to see me because he had a boat he loved, and his sailing time was precious. There were so few days to sail, those few summer days when he was not working, and he'd rather not spend them flying passenger to Cincinnati.

I was not yet a sailing buff myself, but I could understand

his passion for a water sport. Certainly I'd rather go sailing with Mike than spend any leisure time without him.

There were times when I simply had to go home. Being grounded—as I literally had been by the company, and as I still was in my new job—was no fun and it was getting to me. The loneliness of the long-distance bride was grinding me down, making me weary and depressed. Between present job and absentee marriage, I was beginning to feel crushed.

One weekend I had been missing my husband, and I was tired and sad. That Friday, as soon as I found out what time I'd be getting out of work, I called Mike.

"I'm coming home," I said, on the verge of sniffles. "I'm really sort of miserable and lonely. Can you pick me up at the airport? I'd just love it if you could. I feel terrible."

Sure he could. He'd love to. He'd be there. What time?

I told him. We looked forward to seeing each other.

When I arrived at the airport that night, there was no sign of Mike. Must be delayed by traffic. I waited. And waited.

And waited.

There was no answer when I called the house.

I went home by Long Island limo, which was apparently what I should have done in the first place. Mike had called the airline and left a message asking for me to be paged and told that I was to take the limo because he couldn't make it to the airport.

Well, these things happen. I didn't get the message. I spent a couple of hours wondering what might have happened to him, ending up with a mental picture of him lying mangled on the side of the highway after some dreadful accident.

Nothing at all was wrong. After talking to me, Mike remembered that he'd planned to pull the sailboat out of the water that day, and since the weather and other conditions were so perfect, he decided to go ahead and do it. He had little enough time for the boat—might as well use it while he had it.

I knew that lots of pilots had boats and were devoted to them, and I knew they needed care. I'd have been happy to help. But I was devastated that the boat had taken priority over me when I'd called my husband and said please pick me up, I'm sad and lonely and he had said he would, and hadn't—just one lousy, casual message for me while he was pulling the goddamn boat out of the water . . . !

Obviously, pilots were an independent lot, particularly yesterday's bachelors. They get accustomed to doing what they want.

I went back to Cincinnati and my engines, but my heart was not in it. The job was not my kind of job nor the travel my kind of travel. I took it as long as I could, but after DC-10 familiarization school in Long Beach I threw in the towel and went home. There had to be a better way to make a life. Never mind an interim career. I'd take any job I could get if it gave me time to be at home.

We bought a house on Long Island, I got a job as a flight instructor at MacArthur Airport not far away. That worked out pretty well. Then we decided to move to Vermont, where Mike had his condo, so we rented out the Long Island place and moved to Sugarbush. There, too, I found work as a flight instructor at the local airport.

The condo was fine for weekends and vacations but we needed something more than a playhouse. So we bought some land, and lived in a couple of short-term rentals while deciding what to build. We bought a condo and we sold it. Then we bought a farm house.

I went on instructing at Sugarbush whenever the weather permitted. Ski season was when it didn't, and that was when Mike was in his element. He was magic on the slopes. During our first winter in Vermont I managed to demonstrate that I could scarcely ski at all, so Mike, dashing off to join his ski team, advised me gently that I was not an ideal skiing partner and couldn't go with him. "When you're good enough," he said, and zoomed off with his fellow champions.

There were times when I felt insecure and insufficient. This was one of them. That first year, I went by myself to the baby slopes of Sugarbush, snug in the Green Mountains, and fell over my skis until I almost knew what I was doing.

The next year I took lessons. Mike and I went skiing together once in a while.

I see us speeding almost together down the slopes, he ahead of me and superb in his skill, his body crouched in the classic lines of a downhill racer at his athletic, exultant best, and I plowing along close behind with waves of white spray on both sides of me, hesitant still but feeling the glow of confidence that everything would turn out all right.

13

I Am an Experiment

The May 1976 issue of the union newsletter put it in a nutshell:

"In response to many inquiries—Yes, Bonnie is back!"

Who wouldn't get a kick out of that? "In response to many inquiries . . .!" Some of the guys had cared. Some of them had actually missed me.

I was back and happy as a lark.

The telegram had come two or three weeks earlier, asking if I wished to accept recall. Or words to that effect. "Are you kidding?" I queried the telegram silently, and shot an answer back so fast I must have burned the wires up. I myself followed shortly thereafter, winging down to Dallas for retraining.

It was like a kind of homecoming or a class reunion. There were many of the familiar faces of Class 73–9, and the less familiar but still recognizable faces of the scores of others who had been going through original training at the same time, all of us there to plunge back into our manuals, brush up on our techniques, catch up with whatever was new. This is a process that every crew member goes through regularly, but of course it is particularly important after a long layoff. Almost two and a half years! I would never have believed it was going to be so long.

In the give-and-take of renewed companionship, there was a lot to talk about. Various marriages, new babies, the jobs and problems of the past couple of years and how great it was to be on familiar turf. Plus gossip, of course.

Some pilots, or so it was rumored—and certainly none of those present was among them, they said—were surprised that I had come back. Supposedly, I had made my point by getting hired and flying until furloughed. The theory was that I had intended to use my brief airline experience as a stepping-stone . . . to what, the theorists didn't say.

Sure, I wanted to use it as a stepping-stone—to captain.

My mentor, Leroy Leddon, told me something that raised my eyebrows. We talked about my job with G.E., for which he had given me a recommendation when they had called the airline, and about the flight instructing jobs I'd held after that. Then he said, "There were several guys that said, 'Well, Bonnie's going to work for G.E. we heard. Well, she won't ever come back. Ah'll bet you, she won't ever come back. She's done her thing, and she won't ever make pilot with the airlines again.' I made a coupla bets that you would come back."

Well, Leroy'd won his bets, and I was glad he'd made them.

A couple of other comments made me realize that there were pilots who might still have reservations about me and perhaps even some reason for resentment. I'd done a couple of print ads and commercial promotions while on furlough, partly because they were fun to do but mostly because I had nothing against the extra money, and while most of my fellow pilots indicated that these activities were acceptable to terrific there was just a little suggestion in some quarters that I wouldn't have engaged in them if I had been a serious pilot.

Well, I was a serious pilot—without a serious job. And I needed the fun and the money.

But there were little pockets of resentment in unexpected places, giving me the impression that there were some male pilots on one airline or another who just did not want women pilots to succeed and tried to fantasize us out of work. Mike told me a story about an exchange he'd had with a fellow pilot after I'd been back on the line for a while.

Mike was flying copilot, and the flight engineer on the trip began the conversation.

F.E.: "Y'hear about the gal with Eastern? And that broad with American?"

Mike: "No, I didn't. What about 'em?"

F.E.: "Well, they both got fired. One got fired for falsifying her flight records, and the broad with American got fired for doing a commercial."

Mike: "Oh, yeah? I didn't hear that, and I'm really close to that broad with American."

F.E. (*skeptically*): "No kidding, how come you're so close to her?"

Mike: "Well, she happens to be my wife."

For the record, the other gal had not been fired any more than I had, and had certainly not falsified her flight records. But a few guys seemed to get some sort of satisfaction out of tossing little barbs at the women fliers who had the audacity to invade the cockpit. It always rather amused me that they gossiped about us as women are reputed to gossip about them—which, of course, we do—but rumors reflecting on our professionalism are no more amusing than they are true. I still hear stories about how So-and-so couldn't take time out to do the landing because she was so busy fussing over her fingernails, or how the gal at Nameless Airlines had gotten her job by sleeping her way up. Who do you sleep with? We've never figured that one out. Or how the blond broad rolled up late at the airport one morning after layover because she'd spent the night carousing.

Man talk! Forty-year-old five-year-olds! Threatened by a handful of women who'd somehow gotten into the men's room. We have our own cliché about some of the guys: when they're on the ground they talk about nothing but flying, and when they're in the air they talk about nothing but women.

There is another side to the resentment coin, and that is a kind of unwilling admiration. At least, I think that's what it is. Perhaps . . . reluctant recognition? I caught echoes of it when

I went back to the academy, where we'd all studied our brains out to make it to the line. And we had made it, but by golly it was tough! That Bonnie, she really had to work hard, but boy, she did it. I mean, would you believe a woman could get through *this?* She has got to be an exceptional person, or she would never have made it!

And then when I had gone out on the line, I'd actually done my job the way I was supposed to. Amazing! Well, it could only be because I was Wonder Woman, or how else could I handle such incredibly specialized, terribly difficult man's work?

I accepted their compliments with enthusiasm and refrained from pointing out how they were complimenting—and reinforcing—themselves.

Anyway, here I was again, unexceptional as ever, back on my stepping-stone and, to mix a metaphor, floating on air.

The bad news was that I was assigned to be based in Boston, and not on TDY. With Mike based in New York, that meant I would have to commute, and the commute wasn't going to be an easy one. But the good news was that I would be doing my real job, and with me in my proper career place Mike and I could finally try out that two-pilot marriage we'd talked about when we'd first dreamed of a life together.

One of things a woman working with men finds out in the course of time is that she has to watch her language. Another thing is that she can't get too uptight about sexist jokes, especially when she leads right into them, because mostly they're no more than good-natured ribbing between guys and gals.

My first checkride after getting back to work was with Dutch Schultz, a check airman of about Leroy's vintage and one of the nicest guys in the world—very knowledgeable, very thorough and very calm. For part of the checkout, the captain was Tony Felder and the copilot Spike Holden, both experienced and highly professional pilots. It was the first time I'd met any of them.

The captain was taxiing with one engine shut down and I was going through what seemed like three or four checklists at once, rather slowly, and bumbling around a bit after the long layoff. It must have been apparent to all that I was having a little trouble getting things down smoothly. After a while, I broke through the rust and got back into a pretty good semblance of the old rhythm, but not without feeling somewhat embarrassed about my labored performance.

Engines started up to the accompaniment of the appropriate checklist, we took off and climbed. I sighed with relief.

"Thank God that's over," I said to Dutch. "Sorry I was so slow. Boy, you were really lucky to draw me!"

"Oh, no, you're doing just fine," he said. The conversation turned briefly to the draw, and then he added, "Anyway, I'm the chief engineer here, so I get my choice.

"Well," I said, "you really got the booby prize, didn't you?"

And they all, in unison, said, "Did he ever!" I didn't get it. Captain Tony Felder, laughing, turned to me. "Bonnie," he said, "do you know what a pun that was?"

Not thinking for a moment that I was the only woman doing checkrides, I felt baffled and kind of silly. Then I caught on, and laughed, too.

Point is, there was nothing mean about their laughter. Nothing brilliant about our wit, either, but we enjoyed it. I have, I think, learned to be a little more aware of what I say. I still come out with bloopers—like "busy little beaver"—but I'm no longer surprised at the gales of laughter. And the guys don't miss a trick.

Oops! There goes another!

The occasional practical joke is also to be expected, and only once in a great while does it go over the border into nastiness. Usually it's just a picture of a nude male tucked into the pages of the special equipment list. Sometimes it's more subtle. Once it was so subtle I didn't realize I'd been had until the joker called attention to his joke.

Some captain or copilot I had flown with had planted a ten-pound flat weight in the bottom of my flight bag. It was well concealed by my usual fifteen- to twenty-pound load of manuals and folders, collection of tools, including flashlight, two screwdrivers and pair of pliers, a notebook and a computer, a fistful of spare pens and pencils, a fold-up raincoat, earplugs, an emery board and a candy bar or two, and I was only subliminally aware of something not quite right. Sure the bag was heavy, but it was always heavy and I just thought I must be getting old and weak before my time.

One day, sitting near the end of the runway at Detroit waiting to take off, I called the tower and said the usual, something like, "Tower, American 235 ready on Runway Three," and the tower came back and said, "American 235, hold short for company traffic." There was another American on final, and as we waited a pilot's voice came over the radio and said, "Hey, Tiburzi, have you checked your flight bag lately! Isn't it getting rather heavy?"

And then I knew.

The gag was only mildly funny, but I liked it because it was playful. As for the weight, I kept it as a souvenir.

Thus, the men on the line. Funny, klutzy, friendly, warm, eternally curious about the more intimate details of my uniform, interested in my marriage to another pilot, complimentary about my work, my clothes and the length of my hair. "Don't cut it, don't cut it!" I didn't cut it. It never got in the way.

Except once. Even then, it didn't get in the way of my work, but of what someone thought of as my pilot's image.

There is a rule that a pilot's hair is to be cut short of his collar. *His.* I didn't follow it, and was never asked to. In fact, I was urged to disregard it as inappropriate to me.

Toward the end of my probation year I was called down from Vermont between trips to go before my probationary board in New York. This board, consisting of several chief pilots, reviews the various captains' reports of the individual's performance, submitted in the form of probationary slips, and brings in a few flight engineers to add their comments and ask a number of Leroy-type questions. My reports were all okay to glowing, none critical of my work, and I checked out satisfactorily on the review questions designed to make sure I had maintained my proficiency. Everything was fine, and I was very happy.

One of the captains asked me if I had had any problems with the men.

"Oh, no," I said emphatically.

"No hassle with the checklists or responses? They answering you all right?"

"Oh, sure, absolutely."

"No personal conflicts, harassment of any sort?"

"Gosh, no, nothing—no problems at all."

Then it was over. We all relaxed, and I was congratulated on my record.

As the meeting broke up, a chief pilot took me aside and said quietly, "Can I see you in my office for a minute?"

I nodded, and followed him, not worried but wondering.

We sat down.

"Um . . ." he began uncomfortably. "I have a comment from Mrs. Er . . ." and he mentioned the wife of our Chief Pilot in New York at that time. "Apparently she was on one of your flights recently, and she had a comment about the length of your hair." For the first time, he looked at me directly. "It is, of course, longer than anyone else's."

It happened to be very, very long right then. I wore it in a pony tail that I pulled back very severely, but nonetheless it was obviously long.

"Oh. She complained?"

"She did. She said the men have to wear their hair according to our regulations, above the collar, and she thought that probably you ought to do the same thing."

"Gosh . . . I don't look good with my hair that short." I thought of her. She had one of those beehive hairdos, hair way above the collar and certainly neatly groomed, but really no neater than mine. "You want me to cut it?"

"No, I do not," he said firmly. "I'm telling you about it because I think you ought to know. I'm embarrassed to tell you, but there it is. She made her comment, now you've heard it and I don't expect you to do anything about it. Your hair looks fine."

That was the finale of my probationary board. I hopped on Allegheny and went home to Vermont, thinking about how I'd been urged by the men to keep my hair long and then been criticized by a woman.

But I did, later, cut off a few inches.

Nothing had changed during my prolonged absence from the line. The work was as hard and rewarding, the jokes and complaints as trivial, the cloud forms as spectacular. I filled my duty days with concentration and light relief. Off-duty times were less easy to manage and were sometimes exceedingly difficult. The two-way commute was the problem. Mike had to commute between New York and Vermont, and I between Vermont and Boston.

Theoretically, airline pilots can live wherever they want, commuting to work by hopping airplanes. For some, that works out very well, but most of us don't exactly live in the shadows of the hangars. There's nearly always some driving to do. And Mike and I both had that.

To complicate the normal problems of getting back and forth to work, I had a rather awkward schedule of paired trips, or back-to-backs. I'd fly a two-day trip out of Boston and back, have about sixteen hours off, then fly another two-day trip. The guys who lived in the Boston area obviously went home after two days, then back to work. For me, that was impractical; I'd have to spend about seven of my sixteen hours in a car, driving all the way up to Vermont and back. So I'd stay in a hotel. In effect, I was gone from home for five days at a stretch.

Once in a while I couldn't even get to a hotel. On those few occasions I could be very glad I was married to a guy who was able to understand—with very little explanation—when some guy got up in the morning and yelled to his buddies, "Hey, everybody, I just slept with Tiburzi!" That happened when I tried to leave the airport at ten o'clock one night and couldn't get out of the parking lot because of a blizzard. I'd gone back into the terminal and fallen asleep on a recliner in the crew lounge, one of a number of sardines unexpectedly packed in for the night, and risen at the crack of dawn to hear my captain's jovial cry as he rose from a recliner alongside of me. "Hey, fellas . . .!"

There was a laugh all around and I chuckled, too. It had been said in fun, a kind of comfortable wisecrack in a comradely setting, and there was no way I could take it amiss. But I did think to myself, Here I am, twenty-seven years old, going on twenty-eight, and I'm sleeping in a recliner in a Boston crew lounge when I really should be home somewhere—or have a home to miss.

Because there was no emotional core to my life, even then. Only a nagging worry that I didn't know how to make a marriage work, whether I was with my husband or without him.

Deep in work and slightly amusing trivia, I could shunt aside the growing realization that Mike and I were not achieving the partnership we'd hoped for. Alone inside my head, I had to face it.

My flight instructing jobs, first at MacArthur and then at Sugarbush, had required me to work when my students were available, which, as usual, meant early in the mornings, after five in the evenings, on weekends, and scattered hours throughout the weekdays. Once the appointments were made I was expected to keep them, no matter what changes were made in my flier-husband's schedule.

But when Mike came home, he wanted me to be there.

It was a wish that I shared, but my candlelight-wine-crackling-fire-gourmet-dinner fantasy was only rarely a possibility. If I had been able to get dinner ready on time, I wouldn't have been able to stay for it myself . . . but it wasn't simply a question of dinnertime. It was Mike-time and Bonnie-time that mattered, and these times were hard to bring together. On a nine-to-five job it probably would have worked out better. Mike didn't necessarily want me to be waiting with the table set and the wine cooling when he arrived, but he did want me to be there when he was. *I* could take time off, because I didn't have a meaningful job.

I tried to arrange and readjust my teaching commitments to match Mike's shifting schedule, but I couldn't take many days off without inconveniencing numbers of other people. This made for some awkwardness with Mike. I accused him of being unreasonable. He wanted me to continue to work, and yet he also wanted me to be the typical wife.

He tended to laugh at that, pointing out that what I was doing was not exactly career-type work. It wouldn't hurt my job future if I took time off to attend to my personal life.

That *did* seem reasonable, because personal relationships are more important than bringing home a few extra dollars. On the other hand, since I had undertaken to do a job, then I felt I must do it. And he wanted me to work—here we go on the roundabout again—even though we weren't in desperate need of the money. It was something I had to do for the sake of our financial planning, but it was also something I could drop at his convenience.

I had to admit to myself that I found it hard to work and be a wife. Did other women have this difficulty? We had known that ours would be an unconventional marriage, but it had seemed so right. The problem had to be with my work—and my hours. It was because of my inconvenient schedule that we got irritated with each other. Now if I were to get back to my real job, with its promise of advancement and prestige, we would surely be able to rise above petty disagreements and get on with our two-career marriage.

I convinced myself that things would be better when I was recalled.

I was wrong.

There was no longer any question of my canceling work appointments to slip swiftly into my housewife role. We airline pilots knew our job rules and abided by them. That issue, at least, could no longer spark an argument. Just as well, too, because we had no time to argue. Fate had dealt me a tricky hand, with its Boston back-to-backs. If we managed to have a weekend together, we were lucky. Whenever our schedules meshed, Mike would take Allegheny to Burlington and drive home from there. I would drive up from Boston, which took about three and a half hours. When we could not coordinate, which was often, Mike stayed over at his mother's house in Long Island, because we were still renting out our house there, and I stayed in a Boston hotel room between trips.

We both complained about the commute. It allowed us so little time together that we seldom saw each other for breakfast or dinner, and the between-trips travel was more tiring than our work. We both loved Vermont, but I thought it was impractical to maintain our home base there as long as it meant that both of us had to commute. Why didn't we both move back to New York? But Mike was not really attuned to the city. He liked the country life and the skiing and hunting in Vermont.

Perhaps we could keep a place there, just as he'd had for years, and find a place that was close to the New York airports, so that we could have dinners and overnights together. Or maybe Mike could ask for a temporary transfer to Boston, until my own requested transfer to New York came through? No, that really would be unsatisfactory. Possibly a compromise place in Rhode Island or New Hampshire or Massachusetts might be the answer . . . or, if I could get my transfer, maybe Connecticut or New Jersey . . .? Sure, all those were possibilities. I should go ahead and look around.

In my sixteen hours between the back-to-backs, I house-hunted, scouring one state after another to find a place we both liked that was close enough to the airports so that we would waste little time traveling. Mike looked, too.

It seemed to me that Mike had been perfectly content before we were married. He had had his property, his sports, his various routines, and somehow I had thrown him out of gear. I prayed for my transfer, or his. I prayed to find the right house in the right place, and I searched for it relentlessly. Increasingly, I thought that any incompatibility between us was not rooted in our jobs but in our lack of focus, and to me that focus was a home of our own that would be ours forever. And I was the one who had to work hardest to find it, because I had created the need.

We could not agree on what we wanted or where it should be. I went back and forth like a paddle ball, searching for some magic solution, trying to get some sort of stability into our relationship without really knowing how to do it. Both of us, I think, began to realize that the basic problem was not in the housing any more than it was in our jobs—it was in us. We were getting on each other's nerves when we met, outdoing each other in complaints about our commutes, incapable of discussing our future on any concrete terms. It was obvious that it would take more than a rose-covered cottage halfway between Logan Airport and LaGuardia to bring us together.

What had gone wrong? We had seemed so ideally suited.

I was stricken with guilt.

We met, argued, fell silent and went back to work.

At home, such as it was, I could do nothing right. At work, I was getting compliments and companionship. If there was any joy in life, it was in the job. Work got to be more and more important as a source of gratification and a means of fulfillment. To me, anyway. I didn't know how it was for Mike, because we were not explaining things to each other very well.

"Say, Bonnie! News! You coming to Dallas one of these days?"

"Sure, got a sitaround coming up. What's happening?"

It was Captain "Bud" Ehmann's office—Captain Ehmann having succeeded Captain Ted Melden as Vice-President of Flight—calling with exciting news.

"We've hired another woman! Yeah, you heard me. Her name is Angela Mason. Thought you'd be pleased."

I was thrilled. My mind conjured up visions of someone exactly like me, who'd share all my hopes and aspirations. We would understand each other perfectly—we would surely have so much in common, so much to talk about.

"Great! Terrific! She started school?"

"Yup. Want you to come and meet her, talk to her about uniforms and stuff like that. See you when?"

I told him when, made arrangements to meet Gloria Joubert at the academy and hung up feeling positively exultant. It was as if the lone female at the space station, after three and a half years of being the only one of her kind, were to clap eyes at last upon another woman. It was, of course, remotely possible that we would loathe each other on sight, but I did not seriously entertain that possibility. If she was a pilot, she had to be okay.

My sitaround in Dallas gave me four hours between planes. I took the limo from the airport to the academy and met Gloria at the service center.

"Isn't this fun?" I said excitedly. "I'm really looking forward to meeting her. Gee, another woman hire at last! What's she like?"

Gloria gave me an enormous smile.

"Not at all like you," she said cheerfully. "Taller, blond,

blue eyes. Terribly well educated. Started flying as a kid, been cross-country air racing since she was twenty-one, has a bachelor's degree in design and architecture—designed space ships, I believe—um, let's see, two master's degrees, one in political science and one in public administration—"

"Wow!"

"—and a Ph.D with a special in areospace and systems management, dissertation entitled 'Women as Military Pilots,' published in nineteen seventy-six, presented to the Congressional Committee on the Armed Forces that summer. And what else . . ."

"No flight instructing? No odd jobs?"

"Oh, yes. At Santa Monica Airport, for the Claire Walters Flight Academy, mainly teaching ROTC cadets to fly, Air Force and Navy. And some other instruction, I forget where, classy place. She also flew for the Navy as a civilian contract pilot ferrying airplane parts, lived at the barracks, wore Navy flight gear—really hot stuff. *And* she had a corporate job, company pilot, for a land investment outfit. I think, for a hobby"—Gloria was enjoying herself hugely—"she dabbles in aerospace medicine."

"You're kidding!"

"No, I believe she's written some quite important papers. Well, let's go meet her, shall we?"

On our way up to the ivory tower Gloria regaled me with other little fragments of information about Angela . . . fluent in four languages . . . hundreds of hours air racing . . . coast-to-coast record . . . prizes . . . flights over the North and South Poles . . . applied for flight training with the Air Force . . . passed all their tests . . .

Dr. Angela Mason was chatting quietly with some top-management types as we entered the office. I had an immediate impression of a glorious mass of blond hair pulled back in a loose chignon, of sculptured, almost delicate features with *Four College Degrees* written all over them and a pile of formidable looking books on the desk beside her. In that instant I thought,

This is just like a blind date. You come down expecting some freckle-faced graduate of a small town FBO, and it turns out to be Marilyn Monroe with a Ph.D.

Nonetheless, I told myself, I just know I'm going to like her.

And I did.

Angela spoke very little. She was cool, quiet and serene, very receptive to what the rest of us were saying. Yes, she had gone through the strength test and it had been no problem. Yes, she planned to wear her hair in that big braid. Yes, the uniform was fine. Yes, the men in her class were extremely accepting and cooperative.

Since Angela spoke only in answer to direct questions, I—show me a vacuum, and I'll fill it—talked a blue streak. When I came away, I felt I knew myself very well indeed, while Angela remained sedate, demure, introspective and aloof.

Well! Gloria told me afterward that, as soon as I left, Angela opened up and became very outgoing and chatty, just bubbling with enthusiasm about everything to do with flying and the airlines.

And that's the way I came to know her: as a vibrant individualist, smart and funny, intellectual and frivolous, fascinatingly contradictory and very much herself . . . not like the stereotype of a female airline pilot I'd created in my mind, based solely on myself. She was different. That astounded me.

There was no way Angela could be stereotyped. Next time I heard of her, she was on the line, doing her flight engineer's job to perfection. As scuttlebutt had it, there was only one problem: hair. Ordinarily she wore it tucked under her hat or pinned back in a braid. But one day she let it loose. Somebody saw her with her hair swirling around her waist, and told somebody else.

According to Leroy, he was the one who told her she would have to cut her hair. She was not happy about it, Leroy said, but she had it cut. Says Leroy, "She put it in an envelope, and she put a copy of a bill in with it and she sent it to me!"

But that haircut wasn't really quite right for Angela. She had a picture taken of herself and sent it to Vidal Sassoon with a covering letter explaining that she was an airline pilot who needed a hairstyling that would look good with her uniform hat. Sassoon wrote back to say that he himself did not do hair anymore but that he would arrange for one of his stylists in New York or Los Angeles to give her a style-cut. She took him up on his offer.

A few months later I met the company's third female hire. Snapped to reality by my meeting with Angela, I did not presume to think that Beverley Bass would be anything like me.

And of course she wasn't, but she still surprised me. And made me surprise myself. "Oh, Beverley," I squealed, "you look so cute in your uniform!" I heard myself, and I was appalled. That was what the guys were always saying, and I found it so condescending that I was about ready to chew their buttons off. And now, here was I, doing it myself. To a fellow-professional, another serious woman flier!

Actually, she did—and does—look terrific. Small, blond, petite and bubbly, she seems like a coed for whom life is one long exciting date. But she can fly! It's not every male pilot who can appreciate, in another pilot, a combination of almost frilly femininity, high exuberance and steely expertise, but Captain Tony Felder got her number right away and raves about her. "She's a sweetheart, she's a good gal, high-spirited, bouncy after she's been flying—bouncing right off the ceiling, she's just feeling so great. Even when the guys fuss at her and give her a hard time, she still loves it. She loves flying so much."

Now that there were three women on the airline, conversation obviously veered toward clothes. The Adolfo hat—an inexpensive riding-cap affair—that Gloria and I had chosen and bought for us, was not a great success. Some of the guys loved it, some hated it, and neither Angela nor Beverley thought it was the type of hat that would look good on every woman pilot. And that was what we were looking for: something that might become a standard, at least in our airline, and maybe throughout the industry. The design that I had developed, based on another airline's flight attendants' hat, had never been satisfactorily executed, so we were still wearing makeshifts.

Then one day, home in Vermont, I got a call from Beverley. "Come on down to New York! I've just seen a great hat in Josephine's that looks a lot like the one you designed, except it's straw and has a little feather. You'll love it!"

I went down to Josephine's, and dear little seventy-seven-year-old Josephine put this silly hat on me. "You know," she said, fussily tucking in stray strands of hair, "I've got this wonderful dark-blue felt—it's Navy surplus, and it's very durable—and I can make this hat for you in that felt. You'll see, dear. It'll look just lovely. And so practical, too. There isn't a woman who wouldn't look good in it."

So she made it, and it looked terrific in blue felt without the feather. And that's the hat we wear today, the one that's being adapted—consciously or not—by other airlines for their women pilots. Even our guys like it. Tony Felder says he likes it better than his own hat, which, he says, "is shaped like a damn Frisbee."

We still needed a uniform coat. That came to us when I was browsing around in a Waitsfield, Vermont, boutique managed by Rachel Trahern, a dear friend of mine. At last, after years of looking, I stumbled on this rack hung with navy blue polo coats, pretty-looking, double-breasted, blue-buttoned, warm as horse blankets, that had been the same design for the last fifty years and weren't about to go out of style or production. Through Rachel, we got them at cost from the manufacturer.

And that concludes the saga of the outfitting of three woman airline pilots: jacket and pants (both with pockets) created down in Dallas, completed by a tailor named Cy out at La Guardia Airport; blouse and epaulets by d'Armigene of Bay Shore, Long Island; winter overcoat from the Troll Shop in Vermont; hat from Josephine's in New York City; and comfortable black shoes wherever we can find them.

Uniformed as we were, we were still not uniform, and I think it took all three of us a while to put our expectations of each other into perspective. We liked and appreciated each other. I know it took me a while to realize that it was perfectly reasonable—in fact, inevitable—that we should be three completely different people with little in common aside from being women pilots employed by the same airline. It was a revelation to see that we were not carbon copies, and a relief to have living proof of our gut feeling that there is no such thing as a pilot personality. Contrary to expectation, we did not become bosom buddies—another favorite expression of the guys—but we did become friends and representatives of a new breed.

At about the time the company made its fourth female hire, Leslie Rasberry—a young woman who was hired with more flying hours than most guys get in several years with the airlines, and who raises black Labradors with her husband on the side—a check airman from my hiring group of 214 told me that I had been hired as an experiment.

Experiment?

Well, yeah, that's what he'd heard, and it made sense to him. If I hadn't worked out, if I hadn't gotten along with the crews and passengers, and if I hadn't done my job as well as the fellows, the company would not have hired another woman. As it was, we were about to hire even more, other companies were hiring, too, and I only had myself to thank. Or blame, whichever I preferred.

I did not believe this. If I hadn't made it, I was sure the company would have tried again. There were plenty of qualified women who were beginning to realize that they were qualified, and as long as airlines were hiring they were going to have their chance.

Still, it was a novel idea to me. *I am an experiment.*

Am I really a successful one? I wondered.

Some ways I was, some ways I wasn't.

All I knew was, I was more comfortable on the job than I was at home.

The job of flight engineer combines the roles of technician, second officer, third pilot, odd-jobber and general all-round troubleshooter. It's a testing ground of small experiences that are novel at first and gradually assume the familiarity of routine.

A bell in the cockpit dings twice. The flight engineer answers. Often he says, "Engine Room"; if he's feeling good and kind of silly, he'll say "Joe's Bar and Grill"; other times, when there's no time for kidding around or he's feeling a bit growly, he'll just say, "Yeah, cockpit." Generally, I just say "Hello."

The bell ding-dinged.

"Hello?"

It was Jesse, a very competent, well-muscled male flight attendant.

"Bonnie? We've got a badly stuck drawer in the galley here, y'know, one of the carrier trays? I've been wrestling with it, I can't get it unstuck. You've gotta get one of the guys that's very strong to come back and fix this thing for me."

Well, okay, I was that guy. I picked up my trusty screwdriver, without which I hardly go anywhere on an airplane, and I went back to the aft galley where Jesse was trying to get the retainer bar in place to keep the carrier trays from sliding out.

He looked at me in some alarm. "Oh, Bonnie, no, you really have to get one of the guys. We need somebody very, very strong here. See, this thing is jammed, the door won't close, the retainer bar won't come down—the whole thing is really stuck. Brute force is what it needs."

"Well, let's just have a look first." I looked. I saw immediately what the problem was. One of the food carrier trays was off its track. It just needed recentering on its runners. Jesse and several interested passengers watched as I tickled the drawer out, recentered it with my screwdriver, slid it back on its tracks and put the retainer bar down. No problem at all.

Jesse was mortified.

"Jesse, look, it didn't take any strength. We've been trained for this. I'm supposed to know how to do this."

I apologized all the way back to the cockpit, feeling worse than he did for having done something he thought he or some other really tough guy should have been able to do.

Just doing my job, that's all.

Other times have been trickier. Fact is, I had been trained to fix anything mechanically fixable on the airplane, but no amount of training could have prepared me for some of the more personal issues that quite often arise back in the cabin. From them, I learned the true magic of a uniform hat and stripes—symbols of a little authority.

Ding-ding.

"Hello."

"Bonnie?" comes a call from a flight attendant, trained to call the flight engineer as soon as anything goes wrong in the back. "Look, we have a problem. Two guys are squaring up to each other in first class, about to start a fight. Would you please come out and do something about it?"

Reluctantly, I buttoned up my jacket, put on my hat, and walked back wondering what on earth I was going to do: talk to them like their mother? Grab each by the collar and hold them off?

There they were, standing up in the aisle nose-to-nose, like a baseball manager and an umpire, hands bunching, shoulders twitching, cords straining in their necks.

I walked toward them, silently rehearsing. Gentlemen, I must ask you to return to your seats. (Be courteous but firm.) I know you wouldn't want to do anything that might jeopardize the safety of the aircraft. (If there's any trouble, I have three flight attendants and a copilot to stand by and hold my coat.)

They took one look at me and stopped growling before I even reached them. Then they huffed and puffed a few times, averted their eyes from each other and from me and sat down in their respective seats.

I had not even opened my mouth.

I eyed them for a moment as one picked up a magazine and the other stared out a window. Amazing, what a uniform hat will do!

They were as docile as they could be for the rest of the flight.

We were all relieved. Any situation involving our human cargo is of great concern to us, and there is always a slight twinge of tension when a passenger behaves in a belligerent or irrational manner. It could be a signal of danger. Is the person's threatening behavior or excessive drinking a preliminary to some aggressive act? We can't be paranoid about it—an obstreperous passenger may simply be momentarily annoyed about something, or genuinely afraid of flying. But what if he's scared or putting up a smokescreen because of something he's planning to do? Perhaps set off an explosion, or hijack the airplane?

Airlines have been scrupulous about training their personnel in antihijack procedures. Those of us aboard the planes are convinced that the best procedure is prevention. Crews I've traveled with have been lucky enough to avoid dangerous in-air confrontations, and it may be that only luck is involved. But constant awareness helps, too. If anybody looks suspicious, we like to know it before the doors close, and on a number of occasions flight attendants have blown the whistle on erratic passengers while the plane is still at the gate. The agent gets the airport police, and they take over.

Sometimes, only a little diplomatic handholding is required, and the flight can go on its way. But at other times the decision is made not only to detain the passenger but to scour the baggage compartment for anything he might have checked through—in case he had left something lethal aboard as a blackmail tool or a means of blowing up his mother-in-law.

Once I had thought that skiing would help to strengthen the bond between my husband and me. We had fun one winter, and then I got on American's B Ski Team and won a couple of races. After that, Mike didn't seem to want us to go skiing together anymore. He was still a much better skier than I, but I think he thought I was being too competitive.

It seemed to be increasingly difficult to coordinate our schedules or agree on anything. Even at the farmhouse in Vermont I felt temporary, rootless, because it was inconvenient for both of us. We felt that we should find a permanent place, but we couldn't decide where to live. Maybe the West Coast, maybe Chicago, maybe the Hamptons, maybe Marblehead. We couldn't decide which of us should stop commuting, when we should have children, whether we should winterize the house or wait until we found something else. Everything was always so complicated, and there never seemed to be any solutions. All we ever did together was eat, rake the driveway, wash the cars and chop wood for winter—all very useful activities, no doubt, but nothing to stimulate zest for life and togetherness, and all a kind of smokescreen for our lack of real stability.

Then, one day, Mike breezed home full of excitement. He had found a 1941 Waco UPF-7, a beautiful open-cockpit biplane, at the Oshkosh airshow—great condition, price kind of steep but the plane was worth it. He was sure he could swing it if we got our finances together and watched our budget on other things.

I saw pictures of the plane and loved it, a big red-and-white beauty of a taildragger, getting on in years but the more desirable for it, a sweet-running old-timer that could be the perfect grown-up toy for two people who lived to fly. Oh, yes, I wanted us to buy it! If we bought it and flew it together, we would at last be sharing an experience that we enjoyed above all else.

"Mike, I love it. Let's get it."

We grinned at each other like a couple of kids, and began to work out the economics of it.

We bought it.

Mike didn't want to let me fly it.

It wasn't because he wanted all the fun for himself. It was because he figured that one of us should learn to master the airplane before the other tried it, so as to be sure that there was one expert Waco-flier aboard. I think he always felt more confident when he was in command of any vehicle we occupied together, but I couldn't think of any good reason why he should be unduly concerned about my flying.

In vain I pointed out that, while he had far more experience in airline flying than I, my expertise was in general aviation. Though he, too, had a solid background in small-plane flying, most of his flight time was heavy jet. Most of mine was in smaller aircraft, and a wide variety of them. I'd flown a lot of old taildraggers, I had my seaplane rating, I had towed gliders, I had taught in all kinds of little training planes—and, for that matter, I knew the local airfields like the driveway to the house because I'd flown out of them with students many a time.

Nevertheless, he felt it was better for him to be at the controls. The man of the household is, after all, the captain of the ship. And I didn't like to press the issue too mercilessly, because sometimes our discussions would flare into arguments in front of other people, and that was no way for us to enjoy our Waco.

The standoff went on for a long, long time. I thought it was ridiculous. I knew how to fly that plane. All I needed was one chance to try it out. Then we could really enjoy it together. But I couldn't break through Mike's reluctance.

One day, I was home while he was off on a trip. I looked at that lovely plane tucked neatly into its hangar in Mike's meticulous way: tied down with knots just so, oilpans under the engine, sheets of parachute cloth draped over it to keep it clean

. . . and I said, damn it, this plane is partly mine, and I am going to fly it.

I called up a girlfriend, Barbara Pearce, and asked her to come along with me. Not knowing any better, she wasn't the least bit nervous. We hopped into the airplane and flew across the valley for lunch in Vergennes, chugging down onto the airstrip, smooth as could be, attracting little groups of people who clustered around the handsome red-and-white Waco and oohed and aahed. Just dropped in for lunch? What fun!

We got back safely, cleaned up the plane, tied it down, covered it. When Mike came home, I told him about our trip—a happy little flight, and never a problem.

Okay. He realized I could fly the plane.

But he never relaxed. The issue of the Waco was still a challenge, still a problem. I was always, it seemed, on the verge of doing something wrong. I couldn't figure out how I'd suddenly gotten so klutzy . . . don't put your fingers here—don't do this—don't do that.

It still boiled down to the simple fact that he felt better doing it himself.

I think, perhaps, that what we were going through was symptomatic of many marriages of the seventies. For women, hopes and expectations had been changed by the liberation movement of the previous decade. For men, there was an effort to understand and accept women's aspirations. Fine, let us have a partnership, and at the same time let us each be independent.

But in practice, it didn't always work out so well. Enlightened young couples, consciousness raised, plunged earnestly into the equal-partnership marriage and found it as complicated by emotion and tradition as ever. A woman should have her career, but a man should still be the ultimate decision-maker. Someone has to be in charge around here.

We two who had seemed so compatible, so understanding of each other, were not.

The Waco hadn't solved any problems. It had exposed another one.

My transfer notice to New York finally came through. From the beginning of the month—January 1979—I would no longer be flying out of Boston. Thus one decision had been made for me, bringing up another.

I loved that last month of flying out of Boston. The flight team was Captain Tony Felder, First Officer Tom Preston and myself, and we hit it off as if we'd been born for it.

Tony had been leery of a woman flight engineer, even though we'd liked each other when I'd done my checkride with him and Dutch Schultz. It was all strange and new to him, he said as we got to know each other. He had been in college in the fifties, and had gone through the civil rights turmoil with mixed feelings. Then came rights for women, and then a female in the cockpit.

But Tony is a special guy, and one of the things that makes him special is his philosophy of flying and of working together. He expounded once: "Everybody in the airline business, every pilot in the world, likes to have somebody fly with him that he can get along with. The best people to be with are those who can do their jobs in a very professional manner and can still be nice and easygoing. Believe it or not, there are a few people in this business who actually work at making this a hard job, when it's really such a delightful and easy thing to do. And whoever can do this job that way is okay with me."

So we did our jobs and got along, and ultimately Tony paid me a high compliment. "You know," he said, "you've kind of turned my head around as far as women in the cockpit are concerned. If we get any more like you, it'll be all right."

When a few more came along, and they weren't a bit like me, it was still all right.

None of us on that crew felt we had any really pressing commitments at home right then, so we were flying all the holidays and not minding it very much. All of us, including a terrific group of flight attendants, spent Christmas in Omaha with a husband-and-wife team who worked for the company. We had a good dinner with nice people, exchanged small gifts and were taken back to our hotel, where we retired to our several rooms. It had been a family—even perhaps a tribal—celebration, enjoyed by people who shared a common framework of experience and a common language. The bonds of understanding companionship were strong, and helped immeasurably to make up for whoever else they might be missing.

On New Year's Eve Tony, Tom and I were in New York staying at the Americana with the rest of our crew. We got together with another crew, had a marvelous French dinner, then walked down to Times Square and watched the ball falling off the building. We linked arms and just marveled at how many people could be crammed into a small space. We kissed and felt a little sad. Tom was not long divorced, Tony was seriously thinking about a separation and I could scarcely bear to think about the state of my own marriage. We hadn't talked much about it, because, as Tony says, "You can't get bogged down with personal things when you're doing something like flying an airplane." But each of us knew what was on the others' minds, and we felt very close.

The next day was our last trip—down to Dallas, back to New York and that was it. We were quiet on the way back.

At thirty-something thousand feet, we had a cockpit party for the three of us. Surprise! We were no longer quiet.

It's company policy that only two of us eat at a time, to guard against the possibility of food poisoning. But it was late, not much was going on and the captain decided that we should have our farewell meal together.

Tony and Tom had prepared by buying a huge can of Welch's grape juice and a parting gift. At the appointed hour, Number One Flight Attendant brought in three meals and some wineglasses. Tony and Tom turned the cockpit lights down low so that we were bathed in soft light and the red glow of the instrument panels. Wineglasses filled, we merrily toasted each other in grape juice—the champagne of the skies when you are working.

It was a cheerful party, although the guys kept bugging me to stay in Boston and making bitter-funny jokes about marriage. They were knocking themselves out to be nice to me, trying to make me feel better about . . . about whatever was going to happen.

So that was my send-off party. I wouldn't be flying with the two of them again. But didn't I look forward to settling down somewhere!

The gift was a T-shirt, a very cute one. It had a message.

"Nobody's Perfect," it read.

I don't know what they meant by that. When I asked them, they just leered.

When the trip was over and we had finished our farewells, I went to the place I had decided to consider home.

Mike wasn't there. He was still in Vermont. I dumped my bags in the house on Long Island. We had stopped renting it out, and I was going to use it as my base for a new round of househunting. I didn't know if this was the beginning of the end, way past the beginning or the beginning of a new try.

14

A Flying Pilot at Last

During the next several weeks I must have looked at every empty or about-to-be-empty house in Connecticut and New Jersey to find a compromise between urban New York and rural Vermont. Either my husband didn't like it or I didn't like it, or neither of us liked it.

Any one of several of the houses would have been fine. It was the marriage that was on the rocks. Both Mike and I were forever looking for something else, trying to decide where and how we should live and moving restlessly from place to place to find a home and hearth where we could be happy together. Gradually, I came to think that there probably was no such place, but we both kept trying to salvage what we had and keep our lives together wherever we happened to be living at the time.

I couldn't believe this was happening to us. Similar backgrounds, similar interests and strong mutual attraction seemed, in our case, not to be the basis for a good marriage. Even flying turned out not to be a binding factor. We enjoyed a certain amount of hangar flying, but a little shop talk goes a long way. We had to be able to do better.

But we didn't know how. It seemed that Mike resented me for the very things I thought he had married me for. My guilt ballooned into a huge, solid thing inside me. Perhaps I should have given more thought to what a two-pilot marriage would be like in practice. Probably I wanted too much: career, travel, divine husband, warm home life, antique airplane with flying privileges, skiing companion, tennis partner, gourmet meals and cosy chats about children-to-be. I was simply not a success as a wife, and that was the whole problem. It was my fault. I had to hang in there and make it work.

My transfer, as a measure of my seniority as a flight engineer, made my trip schedule a little easier. I didn't have to fly back-to-backs or all-nighters anymore, and I was getting bid selections to the West Indies and other comparatively exotic areas that were really fun.

Or would have been, if home had been happy.

I went off on my trips thinking to myself that since I knew how to do my job, why couldn't I learn how to be married? The personal part of one's life is far more important than just work.

But this isn't "just" work. It's a very big part of me.

As soon as I reached the departure gate and saw the airplane, I put everything but the job out of my mind. A lot of crew members go through what I was going through—as Tony Felder says, "That's the story of most people in the cockpit"—and they manage to override it while they are working. Unless the trip is very, very long and altogether lacking in event, there's no opportunity to sit around and brood. The job, for the time being, is everything. Far more so than most jobs.

But underneath it all, I was miserable.

I would arrive at the hotel with the rest of the guys, laughing at some gruesomely bad joke told by the copilot, and walk into my hotel room full of a residue of professionalism from my day's work. I'd close the door and I'd be alone.

Then my shoulders would slump while I put down my bag, took off my hat, kicked off my shoes, plopped down in the easy chair and remembered . . . oh God, what's happening? And the tears, unnoticed at first, would stream down my cheeks. The sobs remained inside.

I sat there in silence, virtually motionless, wrapped in a cocoon of unhappiness and not even realizing that I was crying until I felt the warmth of the tears on my cheeks and the little wet droplets dripping down my neck. Only then would I know I was weeping again. That's when I'd pick myself up, go into the bathroom, slosh water all over my face and brush my hair so vigorously that it shone and my scalp almost hurt. Then the carefully applied makeup, the crisp blouse and Levi's, a last going-over with a comb and I'd head for the lobby to join the rest of the crew for dinner. By the time I met them I was one of the gang again, ready to discuss the virtues of Chinese or Mexican food, or perhaps the choices offered by the local movies.

So far as I was concerned—in fact, as far as I knew—I was the only woman in the world with my particular marital problems. Many male pilots with either stay-at-home or working wives seemed to have considerable difficulty keeping their marriages intact, but I couldn't exactly put myself in their shoes. Mike, maybe, but not myself. Besides, how many of them were married to women pilots? None of the guys I knew. Furthermore, I was only slightly acquainted with other married women pilots, so there was no one with whom I could compare my situation. Did all or most or some other women pilots have similar domestic problems? And if so, were they directly career-related, or would they have occurred no matter what the job? I could scarcely call them up and say, "Uh, Emily, er, Barbara, how's your marriage?" It is not always rewarding to be a pioneer, especially if what you're pioneering is the breakup of a two-pilot marriage.

The fact that there were hundreds, maybe thousands, of married flight attendants, many of them with children, who managed both their jobs and personal lives with apparent success was of no help to me in trying to get at the root of my problem. Their situation was different from mine, in terms of possible career conflicts and competitiveness.

Misery would have loved some company. *Was there anybody like me out there?*

A year or two later, when I began to enlarge my small circle of women airline pilot friends and find out about some others, I was fascinated to discover how many were married, had been married, were about to be married for the first, second or third time and how many had children. Some were or had been or were about to be married to other airline pilots. Once again I had that curious and wonderful sensation of the world opening up, this time to reveal that there were more than a few women who, although in many ways quite different from me, shared my most basic concerns and must have gone through very much what I had gone through.

Those who had married or were to marry nonpilots included Captain Emily Howell Warner, Sandra Simmons of Braniff, Norah O'Neill of Flying Tigers, Beverley Bass Harber and Leslie Rasberry of American, Judy Lee of United, Becky Rose of Piedmont, whose naval officer husband had been one of her flight students, and Claudia Jones of Continental, whose stepdaughter had become a pilot. Sharon Griggs of Delta falls into a special category by virtue of having been married first to a dentist and then to a pilot.

Among the women who have married airline pilots are Joy Walker of Delta, wedded to another Delta pilot; Barbara Barrett Kruger of Eastern, who got married at about the same time I did; Jane Bonny, a Braniff pilot like her husband and the mother of a son; Valerie Walker Petrie, married to a pilot on another airline; Jean Haley Harper of United, hitched to a Frontier pilot; Terry London Rinehart of Western, mother of three, whose incredibly attractive husband flies for United; and Susan King Horstman of Pan American, wife of a pilot on another airline and stepmother of four. For such couples, the way to arrange maximum time together has generally been for the partner with less seniority to bid for his or her flight first, enabling the senior partner to bid for matching schedules. Had I only known about this wealth of experience among women of my own kind, I might have been able to accept my own situation as less than unique, and even, perhaps, have found a way to ease it. Not knowing, I found no solace anywhere but in my work.

Even through the tears I could plainly see that Band-Aid solutions were doing nothing to help patch up my failing marriage. It was perplexing and saddening for me to look at the kind of life I had shaped for myself as a liberated woman. I was not a crusading feminist; I had simply picked up the options that were available. I wondered: Is this what it's like to liberated? Are we supposed to be superwomen, to handle a home life and a career? Do we have to give up one for the other? If I had a different kind of career, if I were a different person, could I do a better job of safeguarding—with or without my partner's help—what we were apparently about to lose?

We made one more try.

Some six years after I had joined the airline, including the long furlough, I was promoted to copilot. That meant going down to the academy for four weeks of upgrade training. It also meant that, if I got through pilot training successfully, I would be starting at the bottom of a new ladder as the junior copilot on the line, once again drawing the least desirable of the bid selections. But I would be *flying.* At last, I would be sitting in one of the two front seats of the airplane, doing what I'd spent much of my life learning how to do, doing what I yearned to do.

I went down to Dallas thinking that it was time for something to give, that if I didn't see Mike for a while I would have the courage to make a decision to stay with the marriage or move along. Instead of going home for weekends I'd stay down at the school or nearby with friends, studying some and playing a little tennis.

By the end of that time it was clear that my husband and I

had made our final approach. I took my copilot checkrides, disposed of the Long Island house and moved to a studio apartment in Manhattan. I started flying all-nighters again.

It was like taking a step back in time. But some things had changed. I was older, more experienced in one way or another, earning enough to make a pleasant home for myself and decorate it in all the sunny colors I loved, and I was taking my turns at flying the airplane. When it was all over, I knew the marriage should have ended some time before. We who had seemed so right together just weren't. The last tears were not for what happened, but for what hadn't.

"Ladies and gentlemen, this is your copilot, Bonnie Tiburzi. We are now cruising at thirty-one thousand feet and estimate Cincinnati on schedule. The weather is good, eighty-two degrees and clear. We request that you please remain in your seats while your seat belts are fastened."

The flight engineer snickered. The captain said, "Huh?"

It was my very first P.A. announcement on my first flight as first officer, and I had a touch of mike fright.

"What'd I say wrong? Oh, I get it."

But who could care? I was happier than I had been in a long time, just elated to be doing the job I'd been hired for. In the flight engineer's seat you are not a flying pilot, no matter what your training may be. In the flight engineer's seat you can't really hear the dialogue between captain and the copilot. You're a third wheel in the back seat, to mix a metaphor. You don't have a corner office with a window.

I looked out my little window at the side, holding the yoke with a light and loving touch. Pretty soon I would be making my first landing. I would glide down like a feather. . . .

The flying was wonderful. As a copilot I had become an intimate, active part of the operation of moving the aircraft from land through air to land. It responded to my fingers and my feet. For half of each trip the bird was mine and the captain

FIRST OFFICER (CO-pilot)
FIRST Female pilot FOR American Airlin
FIRST TRip FOR American.
(BONNIE TIBURZI)

```
- FLT 649/27 LGA DTW  RTE 1 CAB SEGMENT
 PLAN 1 OF 1
 FAA PREF
ZCN
AAL2101113 FP AA649 B727/A 0469 LGA P2230 310
LGA. SLOAT1. DKK. J36. . HL36. . J36. . V2. RHYME.  DTW/0116
```

TO	FL	I	TD	TP	WIND	WCP	GS	MK	SD	TTLD	ST	TTLT	SB	TTLB	
													259		58
SLOA	13	0	P15	41	27019	M010	391		038	0038	007	0007			
HUO	20	0	P15	40	27020	M014	387		027	0065	005	0012			
DARB	30	0	P15	40	27032	M030	371		068	0133	009	0021			
TOC	31	0	P15	40	27038	M035	366		017	0150	002	0023	067	0067	21
DKK	31	0	P11	39	27047	M044	425	780	134	0284	019	0042	192 025	0092	40
BOD	31	0	P11	38	27053	M053	416	780	107	0391	016	0058	167 021	0113	56
RHYM	13	0	P13	38	27041	M041	277		049	0440	010	0108	146		
DTW	00	0	P13	38	27030	M024	294		038	0478	008	0116	126 020	0133	14

```
RAMP WT P05000 TIME P01 FUEL P0296 COST P024 FL 310   OUT 1839     ETA 201
RAMP WT M05000 TIME P00 FUEL M0253 COST M020 FL 310   OFF 1858     SKD 201

7271 D02302 RWT137713 PL021000 GND17/04 Q00 S3 M78 SKD2230/0011

ENROUTE013293 RES04872 ALTN03933 HLD02215 ADD01000 TTL025313
RLS IFR    649/27 ACFT N969 LGA DTW ALTN CLE FL090
RNWY CNDS 1
RLS FUEL LGA 25313 FUBO 13293
RMKS
DISP NYCE G. DOWNEY
CAPTAIN DICKERSON GJ          RESTRD YES NO    CREW CAT II YES NO   272100
F/O TIBURZI BL               F/E BLAIR RT

AUZD SGNTRS CAPT G J Dickerson         AGT W. Fudurich      DATE 7/27/79
////// APPENDED MESSAGES //////
ACFT RESTR -
   969 MEL    7-1072 NR 1 ENG FIRE WRNG GROUND DET LIGHT.
              THIS A/C IS EQUIPED WITH JT8D-9 ENG.

END
```

Congratulation to Bonnie Tiburzi!
The air is for women too!
Hugh L. Carey
Governor of New York
Aug 24, 1979

Flight plan of my first trip as co-pilot for American Airlines. Congratulations from Governor Carey were added.

was my copilot. For the other half, I was the new copilot, engaged in a quiet dialogue with the captain. It was a role change I enjoyed almost as much as the flying.

What added to my already almost boundless pleasure was the spontaneous response generated by my satisfactory job. As a flight engineer, you don't have people turning around and saying to you, "Hey, Bonnie, that was great pressurization!" or, "Wow, that was the best air conditioning I ever felt." But when you've actually been flying the airplane, the guys do say things like "Nice landing!" and, "Gee, that was a really smooth approach." It was heady stuff. Makes you proud as a peacock. The captain looks at you, and you look back at your miniature reflection in his aviator's glasses and he says, "You did a nice job." You love it, of course. And one day you'll be saying it to someone else, maybe another woman in the cockpit.

There was one thing I found rather odd and slightly ego-diminishing. Moving up to copilot meant that I wasn't the new kid on the block anymore. There were brand-new flight engineers, fresh out of junior high it seemed like, maybe twenty-two, twenty-three years old, going on twelve. By this time I was six or seven years older than these kids. And I hadn't really thought of myself as being that much older than the new crop of hires until I got into that copilot's seat and these respectful youngsters said "Yes, sir," to the captain and "Yes, ma'am," to me. I thought, Ma'am? *Ma'am?* I mean, that really sounded like "Yes, Mother."

Furthermore, these babies looked at me differently. I've never been too delighted when fellows undress me with their eyes, but neither have I ever really objected to admiring or even slightly suggestive glances. However, I could plainly see that what the new young engineers had on their minds was not healthy lust but deference, consideration and respect for the aging female copilot. Oh, God! Who needs that? I thought.

All of a sudden I was a seasoned airline pilot getting more respect from some quarters than I bargained for.

I had also gone into a new sequence of flight attendant and

passenger reactions. The flight attendants were terrific, male as well as female. Those with whom I had flown as engineer accepted me as copilot without question and helped to pave my way toward acceptance by the rest. Captains also helped, providing reassurance, whenever necessary, that I was a qualified copilot.

But the passengers were a little harder to read or predict. I knew that, while I was flight engineer, several passengers had on various occasions asked another officer or an attendant whether I was actually going to fly the airplane. When the answer was in the negative, the questioner seemed relieved. Now that I was flying, I was half expecting someone with cold feet to get out and walk.

That never happened. But some time later, Leslie Rasberry actually had a passenger get off her flight when she found out that Leslie was going to be the flight engineer. And when Norah O'Neill started flying copilot on Flying Tigers' international flights, women frequently came up to the cockpit and said such things as, "I just can't believe you're doing this—*you're* not going to fly, are you?" One woman said that, if she had known, she would have gone on some other airline. But she didn't get off.

Just once, as copilot, did I come close to the humiliating "What's *that?*" episode of my early flight-engineering days.

I had brought the plane into La Guardia at the end of my leg that day. We in the cockpit were standing near the open door to beam our farewells upon the debarking passengers when one of them looked at me, gave a double-take and addressed the air in a penetrating undertone: "Who's that woman? What does she do in there?"

The question was fielded by Number One Flight Attendant.

"That lady, madam," he said, "is our pilot. Have a nice day."

Undoubtedly, what some women miss in women airline pilots is that aura of quiet but nonetheless macho authority surrounding the more traditional cockpit figure. Many passengers are worried enough about being up in an airplane without having to cope with an additional unfamiliar element—a member of the "weaker" sex with her hands on the controls and her voice coming over the P.A. system. They pay keen attention to announcements, listening for words between the words and nuances of expression to explain sudden bumps and vibrations that strike them as out of the ordinary and possibly dangerous. Appropriate reassurance is of the utmost importance.

There was the time when the captain said, "Well, Bonnie, on your leg, so long as you're flying, why don't you make all the announcements? And I'll make them on mine."

So I flew the plane cross-country, making a few announcements as they suggested themselves. "Ladies and gentlemen, we're flying over the Mississippi River . . . Now we're over the Rocky Mountains, and if you look down on your left you'll see . . ." and so forth.

In the normal sequence of events, an airplane passed in front of us. We expected it to, we knew where it was, it knew where we were and we had so much room that we could barely see each other except as specks in the sky. At that point we were at an altitude of about five miles, where there was little if any wind, so the vortices of the other aircraft, corresponding to the wake thrown by a boat, sort of stagnated in the thin air rather than diminishing to gentle, peripheral ripples. In effect, though the plane was long gone, its kinetic energy remained.

As we went through its flight path, our airplane shook from nose to tail.

I made an announcement. "We are feeling a slight turbulence at the moment because an airplane flew in front of us several minutes ago and left behind it a pattern of its vortices, much like the wake of a boat, and we are currently crossing that wake. We'll be through it shortly." And a few more words to that effect, which I intended to be both explanatory and soothing. From my years as flight engineer, I knew that people were likely to be disturbed by what they didn't understand.

No sooner had we cleared the turbulence than a flight attendant came up and said that our passengers were upset because they'd understood us to have had a near-miss.

"Oh, no no no," I said. "It wasn't anything like that!"

"Well, no, sure, but when they heard you say something about a plane passing in front of us, they immediately thought we must have had a near-miss. And then, with those bumps, they figured you must have made some sort of erratic movement to avoid it . . . and of course they're not used to hearing a woman's voice coming from the cockpit."

I was already reaching for the microphone, searching my mind for better words to explain what had happened. Near-misses and erratic movements obviously make passengers nervous. I fell over myself trying to make up for not having explained things properly the first time. ". . . Just like to say once again that it was not a near-miss but a perfectly normal procedure. We apologize for any discomfort and . . ."

It was not my finest hour, in terms of customer relations. As we came in for a landing at the end of my leg I thought that, under other circumstances I, too, might have worried about the combination of "a plane passed in front of us," a wave of turbulence and a woman's voice making the announcements.

Probably thought the real pilot was incapacitated, I mused to myself as we taxied to the gate. What if the captain, in his nice big masculine voice, had been making the announcements? Like as not, no problem.

Then we have these occasional little differences regarding landings. In my experience, male pilots tend to thud the plane in—to make good, firm, by-the-book landings—whereas women tend to float gracefully in as if they were making chiffon pie or something. There's no need to do that; it's just something we like to do. But passengers can't know this. Once when I was flying copilot with Reggie Heard he made a very firm—*very firm*—but good safe landing, nothing fancy and none of that grease-it-in-stuff, just the kind of neat, no-nonsense landing the company would commend. Featherlight, it wasn't. A bit of a jolt, it was.

A debarking male passenger stuck his head in the cockpit and said accusingly, "Did the girl make that landing?"

Captain Heard stiffened defensively. "No, sir, *I* made that landing," he said coldly. "And it was a good landing, at that."

The passenger went off without another word.

During one of her flights with Hughes Airwest, Mary Bush was flying in the copilot's seat when the captain made a hard landing. "Don't worry," Mary said reassuringly as they bounced along the strip. "The passengers'll just think, Isn't that cute—she's learning."

There isn't a member of the crew, cockpit or cabin, who doesn't indulge in some form of Monday-morning quarter-backing. Critiques of performance are the order of the day. It is common, and desirable, practice for the flight crew to review a faulty flight and try to pinpoint just what went wrong and why, and it is also one of the hazards of the business that every pilot must be subjected to the criticism not only of his fellow fliers but also of the rest of the crew. Flight attendants can be merciless, especially the women. Hard landings come under particularly pitiless scrutiny.

Mickey, one of everybody's favorite flight attendants, is a great Italian gal who looks like Sophia Loren. All the guys have a crush on her because she is both gorgeous and funny. One day the captain made one of those fine, firm landings that feel—and are—okay in the cockpit and first class but can really be felt back in the tail where the wheels are. Mickey was in the jump seat way in the back when the airplane came thumping down. I've heard of landings that have been so solid that the oxygen masks have come barreling down, but this one wasn't like that. It was just a little too firm for Mickey.

She waited until the plane was parked and the passengers had disembarked before racing to the front of the airplane and banging on the cockpit door. Ordinarily the flight crew would have been there at the open doorway taking their bows after another wonderful performance, but this time the captain and copilot were too shy to come out and take credit.

Mickey flung the door open and stumbled in, her hair disheveled and her pantyhose apparently fallen down around her ankles.

"Don't worry about a thing," she panted. "Everybody survived!"

"Oh, Mickey, gid ouda here, that's not funny!" they huffed.

Then there was the time when a flight attendant much like Mickey in her zest for life was flying with another flight attendant who happened to be pregnant. *Thump! thump! ouch!* came one of those wonderful textbook-hard landings. The pregnant flight attendant calmly attended to her usual postlanding tasks. The other went bounding into the cockpit shrieking joyously, "It's a boy! It's a boy!"

I think the guys secretly like to smack in the airplane as if they were landing on the deck of an aircraft carrier, but they also like to demonstrate that they can slide in gracefully anytime they feel like it. Captain Mitch Engels and I had something of a private competition one time, on a New York–Toronto–New York turnaround, both of us trying, with studied nonchalance, to do our most highly polished stuff.

Mitch was a brand-new captain and I was still a brand-new first officer. I had known him before being paired with him on the trip. His girlfriend was a friend of mine, the three of us had played tennis together and Mitch and I had become friends. I knew he was a bit curious about my flying. So here we were, sharing the front of the airplane for the first time: the big macho airline captain, product of the military service, and the distinctly nonmacho female copilot, strictly a civilian flier.

We had drawn an evening flight because of our low seniority, and the light was fading as we approached Toronto. Mitch, the absolute epitome of supercool pilot, was flying the airplane. The captain usually takes the first leg of the trip, pretty much to show the copilot how he likes things done. Ninety-nine percent of an airline pilot's technique is dictated by the company, but each captain stamps his own personality on his flights by way of little refinements and nuances of style. So, in taking the first lap, he sets his own subtle guidelines, which the alert copilot will duly note . . . preferably with admiration.

The outbound trip had been a better than textbook flight. Nothing had marred the soaring takeoff, the navigation had been perfect and the approach was lovely. We came in through the last rays of the sun and down onto the runway with an absolutely superb landing, gentle as a snowflake.

"Oh, Mitch, that's a *nice* one!" I said warmly.

He gave a relieved little sigh and remarked, "Boy, if I ever wanted to make a good landing, tonight was the night."

We both laughed appreciatively.

With a new load of passengers, we turned around at about nine o'clock and headed for La Guardia Airport. I was flying the leg, and Mitch wasn't saying a word.

It was a crystal-clear night. Coming in from the north, we could see the city and its surroundings as one huge, shimmering carpet of light. Long Island, Manhattan, Yonkers and New Jersey seemed to merge together. Yet every single light was distinguishable, and there were patterns within the shining mass discernible to anyone who had flown in and out of LGA for the better part of a couple of years.

We were to land on Runway Thirty-one, which requires a rather odd approach if you're coming in from the north: south toward the city, then a left turn to come around into a left-hand pattern for the landing. But since the sky was clear of all other traffic, I suggested to Mitch that we ask for a right turn in. Agreeably, he reached for the mike—because the one who's not flying usually does the talking on the radio—and called Approach Control for approval. Granted.

So we were now embarking on a slightly nonstandard approach, which meant that we had a different perspective on our land references and our orientation had shifted. Things just don't look quite the same when you change your approach pattern.

But I had more than a basic idea where we were. I could see the Long Island Expressway feeding into the city, so I used that as a guideline. Then I saw the big red sign of the Tastee Bakery, and I started slowing the airplane down.

"Okay, I'm on a right base," I said.

Mitch gave me a sideways glance, got the wind direction and velocity from the tower and we were cleared to land.

We got to about two hundred knots, and I called for flaps two.

Mitch gave me two degrees of flaps, and green lights appeared on the panel. "Green light, flaps five," I called. Mitch gave me five degrees of flaps. I continued to slow down . . . 180 knots . . . called for flaps 15 . . . got flaps 15 . . . down to about 160 knots . . . called for gear down. . .

Mitch put the gear down. *Wham-bump,* we heard it go, and three green lights appeared on the panel.

"Down three green, no red," Mitch called out.

I made a nice, even, slow right turn at the Tastee sign and lined up on the runway. We could not see it yet, but I knew exactly where it was. Mitch wasn't saying a word.

"Flaps twenty-five, one thousand feet . . . flaps thirty . . . landing flaps selected. . ."

"Before-landing is complete," said the flight engineer.

The runway lights came into focus.

We skimmed down between them and came in for the landing.

As we turned off the runway, Mitch let his breath out explosively and said, "*God,* that was a good job. Y'know, I didn't know where the heck we were, but I sure didn't want to say anything to interrupt a perfect job!" Of course he had known, and so had the tower, but I didn't want to interrupt his compliment. "That was a beautiful approach and touchdown," he finished, giving me his most appreciative smile.

I grinned back at him and said, "If I ever wanted to make a good approach and landing, this was the time!"

For both of us, and I believe for our passengers, too, it had been a most satisfying flight.

Although sometimes I do wonder what passengers might think if they knew that, in these days of high technology and sophisticated equipment, the way we find the airport is to follow the expressway and make a right turn at the bakery.

For the better part of a year I continued to draw late flights, overnighters and back-to-back trips. At one time I had three months of all-nighters, flying New York to Cleveland, Cleveland to Los Angeles, and Los Angeles to Cleveland and back to New York. Once in a while, instead of doing a turnaround at L.A., the flight crew might have a thirty-six-hour layover before heading back to New York.

Two-night layovers were not wildly popular with the pilots' spouses. Rumor had it that the wives had actually complained that they didn't want pilots and flight attendants laying over in the same place, especially after flying together for a whole month and getting to know each other pretty well, so it had become customary for the flight attendants to either pick up another flight out of LAX or to lay over in the city of Los Angeles while the male crew members—ha!—spent their nights in the town of Ontario several miles away.

Barry Frank and I had flown together quite a bit when we drew the thirty-six-hour L.A.-Ontario layover and were reasonably sure that we were not going to be bored in each other's company. When we landed very late that first night, the flight attendants duly went off to their various destinations, the young flight engineer was picked up by his parents and Barry and I went off in the limo which was to take us to a sprawling, moderately luxurious hotel in Ontario.

We laughed like guilty kids along the way.

As soon as we had checked into our separate—yes, separate—rooms, we went right into the Jacuzzi and sat there for a while with the energizing yet relaxing water bubbling up around us. Feeling cheerfully smug and altogether comfortable, we chuckled over what we thought of as a kind of coup. Whoever had separated the girls from the boys had overlooked something. Just he and I alone, man and woman, flung together by fate. Not a flight attendant or engineer around to keep an inquisitive eye on us—no doubt just the sort of situation envisioned by the people who most wanted us separated. We thought this was very funny.

We talked and enjoyed the fake hot springs and then we went chastely to our respective beds.

Up early the next morning, we swam in the pool, went running for awhile, then sat at the poolside baking in the sun and slowly turning pink. As lunchtime approached, we decided to skip the formality of a restaurant or the dreariness of a fast food joint and get something we could eat by the pool. So we went across the street to the shopping center to buy some fruit and cheese and a few other odds and ends.

The cashier apparently realized from our conversation that we weren't from around there. As Barry picked up the bag of groceries and she gave us our change, she said, "Where are you people from?"

"New York," we answered.

"Oh, wonderful. So you're visiting here?"

"Not exactly," I said shyly. "We're on our honeymoon."

Barry dropped the groceries on the counter, turning red—"Oh, lovely," she said—picked them up, dropped his change, cleared his throat and thanked her nicely.

We both giggled about it as we went back across the street and settled ourselves at the poolside, but for a moment there I was the only one who thought it was funny.

The rest of our stay was as respectable as the start, but there's no denying that opportunities for less respectable behavior were rampant.

If one has absolutely no strings attached and two or three

days off at a stretch, one might let down the hair a little. I wouldn't know. Or tell.

On the way home Barry kept trying to get back at me with practical jokes which he thought were hysterically funny, but as far as I was concerned never quite made it.

We'd had a splendid minivacation, and it might be thought that we'd have many another laugh together or maybe even pursue a sort of office flirtation. But, such is the nature of the airline business, Barry and I have not flown together since that sequence of trips or even seen each other except around Operations or on the crew bus.

15

Life Is Full of Ups and Downs

The silly and rather wonderful fun we enjoyed on and off the job was only a small part of what was becoming a richly satisfying working life. So was the ego-gratification of having a front-row seat in the airplane. The major part was the sheer joy of flying, coupled with an added responsibility for the safety and comfort of our passengers.

Sounds stuffy, but it's true. Because when you're flying for an airline—and we all know this—you're not just flying a plane. You're flying the people on it. And you have to understand their anxieties and needs. The closer you get to command position, the more likely you are to identify with the people whose lives are in your hands.

We know that comfort, such as it is on an airplane, is more than a cushy seat, hot and cold drinks, a lap rug and enough room to stretch the legs. Comfort is also peace of mind, which involves a sense that one's flight is going to be reasonably punctual and that it is going to be perfectly safe. And sometimes, of course, there is a conflict between punctuality and safety, which must be resolved in favor of the safety factor.

As I became more and more at ease as a copilot, I became increasingly aware of the relationship between comfort and safety, between the fear of being late for an important appointment and the fear of flying under less than optimal conditions and between one person's pleasurable thrill and another one's nightmare.

We were delayed one evening out of La Guardia by a snowfall that kept ebbing and flowing, one moment seeming to let up and the next to whip itself into a storm. The forecast was for momentarily clearing weather, but we kept on having to postpone departure while the snow persisted in defying the weatherman, and after a while there were murmurs from our passengers. Some were apprehensive, some impatient, some merely bored.

Finally the snow stopped and we took off for Rochester, assured that the weather and landing conditions there were well within our recommended safety limits. By the time we got there we were getting reports that it had snowed quite heavily, but that the runways were usable and the braking action was fair to good.

We couldn't see much as we came down, because residual snow flurries turned the airport lighting into a blur, but as we made our final approach our landing lights lit the surface of the runway and showed it to be covered with snow. At this point there was nothing to do but complete the landing with as much care as humanly possible.

The captain made a crisp, firm touchdown, exactly as recommended for conditions of that sort, and put the engines into reverse. Instantly upon touchdown we realized that the braking action, rather than fair to good, was poor to nil. As we went into reverse, we started to slide. Manipulating his engine levers like organ stops, the captain orchestrated the reverse thrust—a little more out of engine one, a little less out of two and three, then less out of one and more out of the others, in a meticulous balancing act to keep the airplane in directional control. With his feet firmly on the brakes, his hands playing the reverse levers, he kept us gradually decelerating and more or less straight. I, meanwhile, had shoved the yoke full forward and was holding it there to keep weight on the nose wheel.

Slowly, slowly, agonizingly slowly, we decelerated. At no time did we lose control of the airplane . . . but we didn't have complete control. The slide we'd begun on landing straightened out, started again and built into a slow but alarming pivot. I felt my eyes rounding out like golf balls. Our very new and young flight engineer, on about his second or third trip, was looking pale and firm-jawed. Through our side windows we could see something of what the passengers must have been seeing through theirs: a carnival effect of snow kicked up by the landing, the reverse thrust and the incipient swivel, swirling up and driving past the windows in the blaze of our landing lights.

Beautiful, if you like that sort of thing, in what was basically not the most comfortable of situations.

We came to a slightly crooked stop, heaved sighs of relief and rather crossly reported the condition of the runway. If we had known we probably would not have landed, for even though the captain had done an excellent job, we knew it had been no treat for our precious cargo.

We taxied very slowly to the gate area and parked. All the debarking passengers were subdued, and got off rather hurriedly.

Another time, when we were to make an early flight to Chicago from La Guardia, we were informed that the runways had been cleared but the ramp area was still icy. We were moving very slowly away from the gate when we received the advisory that the runways were not in as good condition as had been thought and were to be regarded with extreme caution, because a slushy residue of snow had melted and refrozen over the blacktop, creating areas of slickness that were difficult to see but must somehow be avoided. To make matters just a little more tricky, gusty crosswinds were slapping at the airfield and everything on it.

As if on thin ice already, we crept toward Runway Four, the most favorable from the point of view of the winds. Before we reached it, another air carrier slid slightly on its landing rollout, and came to rest off the runway with part of its body still straddling the strip. Damage was minimal, but the mishap temporarily put the runway out of action. We trundled cautiously over to Runway Thirteen and stopped again. Eddies of windborne snow swirled past our windows. We begged our passengers' indulgence, and we waited.

Time ticked by. It was a business flight, and passengers were restive. Looking down the rows, we could see them glancing at their watches, tapping their feet, tapping their fingers, shuffling their *Wall Street Journal*s, peering over the tops of their glasses, glowering at the flight attendants. Their whole attitude said, Come on, let's get on with it, I gotta get to Chicago, I've got a business meeting at nine and a whole day of appointments, time is money, you said eight o'clock departure so let's have those wheels up in the wheel well and get going! They must have known, and probably appreciated, that they were flying with an extremely safety-conscious airline, but the glinting sunlight outside probably fooled them into thinking we were being far too conservative. I won't say there was a murmur of mutiny, but they definitely wanted to get going.

So we had a cockpit conference. We were acutely aware of the crosswind and the icy conditions on the runway, both of which caused us concern. But everything was well within our limits and recommended procedures. We should try it, we agreed.

And it was a question of agreeing. No captain flies alone. Every flight crew member has the right and the obligation to express an opinion on available options, and reservations, if any, on a proposed course of action. On occasion—very rare —I have said firmly, "No, I really don't think we ought to go ahead with this takeoff," and even if I was in the minority and got some "Oh, Bonnie . . .!" grumbles in return, we would turn around and go back to the gate. Each of us is a safety valve and sounding board for the others, and we do listen. The captain is the ultimate decision-maker and doesn't always permit a crew member to sway him, but part of his executive duty in the cockpit is to accept the assistance of the crew.

Thus we agreed to attempt a takeoff.

At about five hundred feet along the runway and a speed of about seventy knots, we realized as one that the wind was nudging us too hard and the runway wanted to get rid of us.

We slowed, stopped, made an announcement to the effect that we had decided to abort the takeoff, turned around and taxied back. What we planned to do was go back to the gate until the winds subsided a little or shifted direction in a manner more favorable to Runway Thirteen. But while we were heading back to the gate, the winds picked up briskly and scooped the snow out of its banks, swirling it up and around in a sort of low-ceiling blizzard.

More and more it blew, until the passengers could scarcely see out of the windows. They no longer looked impatient.

We were at the gate when we were informed that the airport was being closed. Wind, slick runways and icing conditions made it advisable for flights to be curtailed indefinitely.

The passengers getting off were completely different from the passengers getting on. It was no more, "Well, Captain, I hope you're going to get me to Chicago on time. I've got an important business deal today." It was, "Great decision, Captain . . . Liked that command decision to abort the takeoff . . . Glad you were prudent—appreciate it . . . Better safe than sorry, right? . . . No business is more important than life and limb . . . I can do all my business through a conference call . . . Might as well just get on the Teletype . . . Thank you, thank you, no problem, no problem."

And they were exuberant. The little excitement of the aborted takeoff had really set them up. Like kids whose schools had been closed because of a blizzard, they knew that no one could blame them for not showing up in Chicago. They had skirted danger and survived. Now they were relieved and jolly. And most of them hadn't really needed to take that plane at all. Their business, they agreed, could wait or be handled by mail or over the telephone. Some said they had enjoyed the aborted takeoff as a sort of adventure. Others admitted that the last few minutes had thoroughly scared them. Whatever they thought individually, off they all went, not knowing or caring about the brainstorming that had gone on in the cockpit before we had attempted and then aborted the takeoff.

The cockpit crew rarely gets to observe passenger reaction to uncomfortable or potentially dangerous situations—or even to situations which only seem dangerous. The little things we take for granted may be worrying others unnecessarily. How can the pilots find their way through these thick clouds? How do they know what's down below? Why is that red light flashing on the wingtip? What's that grinding noise? Why did we make that sudden lurch? Why are we flying sideways? What are those little flames coming out of the wings? Is that ding-ding sound some kind of alarm signal? Aren't we coming awfully close to the water? Will somebody please tell me what's going on around here?

Glad to. Everything can be explained. But sometimes we have to be reminded that what's commonplace to us can be quite disturbing to an infrequent traveler. It's just that we're so used to those little bumps and grinds that we no longer think about them.

When there is a problem we don't hide it, unless it happens so quickly that there's no time to mention it. Nor does the pilot in command solve it with a snap decision. For us, the job is a matter of teamwork. There are very few prima donnas on the flight deck, and those few last only a short time before the company catches onto them. Even if convenience sometimes goes by the boards, there is no playing fast and loose with safety.

Things happen. Accidents do occur. Severe icing, wind shear, a sudden malfunction, pilot error—something tips the scales from a perfectly normal flight to a hair-raising and even tragic event.

I have never been in an airplane accident in all my years of flying. Once in a while my pulse has raced and my adrenaline has flowed like a millstream, but moments of apprehension have been brief and few. Commercial flights are not adventurous sagas but rather mundane sequences of getting from here to there. Neither I nor any of my friends in the airlines have any personal experience of flying catastrophes.

But, obviously, we are intensely aware of the terrible disasters that sometimes strike. And, obviously, we talk about them. The closer to home, the more poignant they are and the more deeply they affect us.

If there is one thing that gives us extremely serious concern, it is the unknowable, unpredictable deterioration of some part of a thoroughly inspected airplane. In a pilot's nightmare, the worst thing that can happen is an airplane falling apart in flight. It happens so seldom that the percentage must be a decimal point followed by a series of zeros. But once is enough. We mourn our losses, and the losses of the people who had loved ones aboard, and we resolve that such tragedies must never occur again.

One thing the disasters do not do is infect us with fear. We know that the stress, or structural, failure occurs far less frequently than other types of failure—human failure, for example. When we hear of such catastrophes we think, "There, but for the grace of God, go I." But it would be foolish for us to harbor the unnerving thought that we are likely to confront a mechanical breakdown. We are not. We are much more likely to encounter some aspect of human frailty. And we know that we cannot afford that either.

An accident occurs. Like other people, we think, "Oh, God, isn't that awful, isn't that tragic!" And like other people, we wonder what caused the accident. We can make educated guesses, but we don't pretend to know the cause until the FAA completes its investigation. That may take many months. In the meantime, we continue to wonder what happened.

But after we've said how sad it is, and even while we speculate about cause, we don't say to ourselves that we've got to be more careful. There's something more than just care involved, something more complex. Bearing in mind that there are things in life over which we have no control, no matter how much we wish we did, we have an attitude toward our work that includes what Tom Wolfe calls the "right stuff."

It is not a swaggering attitude. We know we aren't perfect, but we also know that we have what it takes to do our detail-packed, precisely timed and sometimes very demanding jobs. We expect optimal performance from ourselves.

We joke, we laugh, but we are very serious and self-critical. We don't blame instruments or mechanics or weathermen for flawed flights. Outside the area of freak mechanical malfunctions, hidden structural defects and bizarre, unpredictable tricks of the wind, most of what goes wrong on a flight can be traced to some form of pilot error. And in the vast majority of cases, the error has nothing to do with pushing the wrong button or pulling the wrong lever or ignoring warning lights or taking chances or—as some aviation fiction would have it—cockpit arguments about a two-timing woman or the state of the captain's psyche. It's an error of judgment: a matter of should we or shouldn't we?

In all reputable airlines, both pilots and planes are meticulously maintained . . . again, within the limits of human error. Ideally, the well-maintained pilot, who is repeatedly subjected to performance and health checks, will review the list of maintenance squawks and make a correct judgment about the reliability of the airplane. He will do the same with the weather information and all other data at his disposal. His crew members offer their input and their opinions. The same process holds true throughout the trip and upon landing: review available information, and make the judgment.

The judgment is sometimes wrong.

So it isn't simply a matter of being careful. It is a matter of using the trained mind, or minds, to absorb and analyze all pertinent data, then act upon it appropriately.

In very rare cases, there may not be time to deliberate before acting with the necessary speed. It is here that training, experience and keen reflexes come into play. Then again, in even rarer cases, there may be no time to do anything at all.

Yet, barring acts of God and truly unforeseeable circumstances, the pilot's judgment is the determining factor. When we talk about accidents and try to figure out what could have caused them, we don't blame the pilots but we tend to believe we would have avoided whatever mistake must have been made. Icing on the wings? Surely we would have checked again and again while we waited for takeoff. A report of possible wind-shear conditions at departure time? We would have waited until assured that the conditions no longer prevailed. A mechanical problem? It should have been observed, or predicted, on the basis of the maintenance log and the preflight check. A fuel emergency in midflight? A combination of ground and flight crew carelessness—scrupulous reading of the checklists would have revealed?

Sure, it's easier to second guess than to be right when you have to be, but when pilots make their assessments of what probably went wrong they are not criticizing but doing their homework. Instead of frightening us or putting us off flying, whatever goes wrong gives us an extra incentive to prove that we have the right stuff to make the correct decisions and avoid accidents. And that means thinking, getting our heads together and using our experience.

Without personal and professional problems to trouble my mind, I was having the time of my life. The flying was marvelous. Sitting in that front seat—no matter how far I had to pull it forward to feel comfortable with the yoke—made me feel content with life and thoroughly in tune with my job.

The fun of flying was enhanced not only by peace of mind but also by the exceptional fringe benefits of an airline career. Flexible hours and immediate financial considerations aside, we also had the advantage of huge discounts on personal trips in this country and overseas. I have never gotten over my love affair with Europe, and I have been able to take flights to my favorite European capitals at truly ridiculous prices. I have also been to the Orient at not much more than the cost of a hot ticket to Broadway. These privileges meant a lot to me, and I appreciated them.

I was still flying all-nighters, but the time would soon come when I could bid for easier hours—maybe the Caribbean flights I'd enjoyed as a charter pilot and flight engineer. Meanwhile, I was perfectly happy going to L.A., Salt Lake City, San Diego and other mainland destinations. I like those cities, and I loved living in New York.

By the time I'd been copilot for about a year I was starting to get even better trips. Some of my classmates, with about my seniority, were putting in their bids for B-707 copilot. Things looked good: the economy seemed healthy, our seniority was moving and things were happening. I liked the idea of putting in a bid on the 707. It would mean flying a four-engine jet, and the prospect was appealing.

There were certain things I'd miss. I'd become accustomed to being part of a 727 operation. The 727 had virtually been my place of work, my office, for the better part of eight years, and I had a deep affection for it. For me, that airplane will always be associated with some of the happiest experiences of my life, from the enormous thrill of being hired to fly it for the first time to the little incidents that add pleasure and spice to one's working days.

One favorite episode was a small celebration, not unlike the party in the sky organized by my fellow flight officers when I was leaving the Boston base, except that this one marked my birthday and left me with a written souvenir.

The party was organized by Billy Zendry and Chuck Easton at LGA Operations. We held it before an all-nighter to Cleveland and Los Angeles. We toasted each other in—of course—nonalcoholic sparkling apple juice "champagne," after which I was given a T-shirt with my picture on it. I don't know why the guys think I need T-shirts, but I guess they do. Billy and Chuck had one each printed up for themselves as well, causing considerable comment about what their girlfriends would think about it.

Coincidentally, my flight that night marked the end of a monthly sequence of flights with Captain Ralph Applegate. When we were well on our way, he gave me his birthday present. It was a Snoopy card, with Snoopy in his aviator's gear looking down at little Woodstock in his tiny scarf and goggles and saying, "I'm glad we've got each other." Inside was the line, "Everybody needs a copilot," followed by the expected HAPPY BIRTHDAY.

But there was also an original Applegate poem, signed "Apple," and that was my present. It may not be the world's greatest piece of verse, but it was written for me and I cherish it.

It is called "Ode to an August All-Nighter," and its deathless words are as follows:

Those nights we spent together
in our cabin in the sky,
We watched the constellations form
and shooting stars go by.
We followed the Venus to the East
and bade the moon farewell.
We greeted morning's sunrise
and the haze it would dispel.

In this romantic setting
our relationship grew deeper.

Your hand brushed mine on takeoff
as you evened up the EPR.
We skirted thunderstorms and lightning
and saw St. Elmo's Fire,
Whose reflections in the cockpit
intensified desire.

But this affair was doomed, my love,
to become a dying ember,
By the indisputable bid results
which emerged for the month of September.
And it's probably just as well, my friend,
this affair must indeed decline,
For my ego is bruised and abused because
your landings are better than mine!

Now *that's* a present from a pilot!

I haven't seen Ralph Applegate since then. Our bids never brought us together again, and it seems highly unlikely that they will in the foreseeable future. Last I heard, he was flying copilot on the 747. As for me, I never did make my bid for the 707.

There was another slump in the economy, affecting transportation and other industries. American was obliged to ground the B-707, furlough about seven hundred pilots and bump a couple of hundred of us back to flight engineer. I wouldn't have to feel nostalgic for the 727 because I'd still be on it, although farther away from the left seat. Captain Applegate's poem suddenly represented, for me, a memento of one of the happiest, most satisfying times of my life . . . unexpectedly curtailed.

No question, it was a blow. I'd been flying so high with those guys in the sky, and then suddenly—zap! Back into the corner. A disheartening setback in what had seemed to be a promising career. No more flying with the hands on the yoke and the feet on the rudder pedals. No more thrill of being in the front row. No more, "Nice landing, Bonnie." Nobody was going to turn to me and say, "Gee, Tiburzi, you did a terrific job of monitoring the fuel."

Sure, there's a question of ego involved. It's much more fun and more flattering to get compliments on a front-seat job than to regress to the engineer's slot you'd occupied for years. You feel out of the action, a third person in the back of the cockpit, much older than when you began and not even particularly senior.

Thinking about those furloughed, I was certainly glad I wasn't among them this time around. It was nice to have a job, but doggone it, I hired on as a pilot! That's what my expectations had been. And that's what they still were.

I had options. I could almost certainly have transferred to Dallas, which was becoming a much bigger base than New York though not an especially desirable location for Easterners like myself. I would have been pretty sure of being able to fly copilot from there. But at this stage of my life I didn't want to move again. I had my own base: a place to live, a neighborhood, firm friends in New York, much-loved relatives in the New York area, a life of my own that was not solely dependent on any satisfaction obtained from the job and a distinct aversion to moving away from what had become familiar and lovable. So the Dallas option was closed.

There were smaller airlines with bases in the New York area which, like smaller airlines with their headquarters in other parts of the country, might very well have hired me on as a copilot with the prospects of an upgrade to captain within perhaps a year or two. I'd heard that some quite recent hires with several of the regionals had already started flying copilot and had pretty good expectations of upgrading after a couple of years. But I'd never wanted to fly anything other than the majors. Furthermore, although there seemed to be employment risks involved in flying almost any airline at that time, I felt that the main risk of flying for a smaller airline was not knowing if the airline would exist from one month to the next.

Then there were questions regarding flight pay, office or ground school work between flights, scheduling and a number of greater or lesser considerations that made me feel that a small airline was not for me. I mean, I was a New Yorker!

I do want to make absolutely clear that pilot training on all airlines is excellent. Proficiency of possible teammates was positively not a factor in my decision to stay with the majors and, specifically, the airline that had hired me. Essentially, I wanted to stay with American and stay in New York and that was it.

But it was an odd feeling, stepping back out of the action and having to watch two other pilots exercise the know-how and skill I knew I, too, possessed.

The first few days were no fun. I felt dreadful about being bumped back. I sat at my engineer's panel and did my job but my hands itched to get at the controls. Every reflex strained to fly the plane.

But, as I got back into my old routine, I saw that nothing much had changed. The old camaraderie was still there, and the teamwork, and the shared wonder at the incredible beauty of flight and the occasional moments of excitement. The trips were a little more tiring because the controllers, who were also being affected by the economy and were threatening to strike, weren't working as closely with us as usual. For the first time there was tension between the people flying the airplanes and those in the towers, and there were times when we felt that our joint efforts to move the airplanes safely weren't as well coordinated as they should have been. A valuable partnership seemed to be dissolving.

Still, we were doing the flying, and even if the lack of harmony meant that we had to be even more than ordinarily careful about checking, cross-checking and rechecking, we knew that we could make it. The fact that the controllers seemed to have become adversaries rather than allies was just one more element we had to take into consideration when we flew.

Other than that aggravation the flying was great, back seat or not.

There is one trip I will always remember vividly.

We were coming into Detroit after a nice smooth flight marred only by some minor but irritating communications gaps between ourselves and ATC, and we were feeling good but slightly weary.

The scene up ahead was spectacular.

There had been thunderstorms that day. The air was still tremulous with fading energy as we approached Detroit on the track of the setting sun. Miles away, well clear of the airport and brilliantly backlit by the sunset, was a charcoal-gray mass of cumulus cloud. Slowly it retreated, its body churning and flashing with unspent electricity, sinister-looking as a wicked witch's castle.

At the edge of the darkness a rainbow was forming. Around and beneath us, everything gleamed. The sky was rain-washed and crystal clear, and we could see details of sparkling landscape way into the distance as well as down below.

Benign, wonderful weather. Everything breathtakingly beautiful. We didn't talk about it but we were all drinking it in.

Lining up on Runway 21-right at five or six miles out, we observed what the stormcloud had left in its wake: a sheen of moisture on the grassy fields between us and the airfield, glinting silver in the last rays of the sun, and a film of gleaming rainwater on the runway that made the blacktop look like a moonlit sheet of ice. Well, it wasn't, but it might still be a little slick.

We descend sedately.

We're on our approach. Harnesses buckled for landing. Conversation at a bare, businesslike minimum. Altitude fifteen hundred feet. Runway a narrow strip in the distance but dead ahead and waiting for us.

"Surface wind zero-four-zero degrees," reported Approach Control, "velocity three miles per hour."

Okay, that's almost a tailwind, and a very slight one. A nice easy landing.

"Ground speed one hundred thirty knots." That was the speed at which we were being tracked from below.

Hmm. Instruments indicated an airspeed of 148 knots. An 18-knot discrepancy.

Easily explained. We had a headwind at altitude, a trace of a tailwind below. We'd have to be prepared for a bit of a wind shift close in to the runway. All right, we were.

We reviewed our approach, as we always do. The captain briefed us on our landing and go-around procedures, also standard practice. All hands have to know what the other hands are doing.

At 148 knots we were 20 knots above our reference speed—and we wouldn't want to touch down too fast on that wet and slippery runway. But already we're bleeding off speed at the desired rate. And we're aware that there's a surface wind shift. If we find it's significant when we get closer down, we'll go around. Otherwise we're aiming for the thousand-foot mark. That should give us plenty of room to roll out to a nice gentle stop.

Gradually descending into the tranquil twilight, we reduced forward speed and rate of sink.

The copilot was at the controls, the captain on the radio.

Copilot: "One thousand feet, flaps thirty."

Captain: "One thousand feet, landing flaps selected."

Flight engineer: "Before-landing checklist complete."

We are momentarily silent. Engines throb smoothly.

Captain: "Five hundred feet plus ten, sink rate six hundred."

Altitude, five hundred feet, and ten knots above reference speed. Rate of descent's right on the button, six hundred feet per minute, less than a minute to touchdown. Clean, routine approach.

I cleaned up my panel and tuned all my senses into the landing. No matter how routine the approach, no matter how smooth and calm the weather, all attention must focus on the touchdown. You watch the flight instruments in front of the pilots, you tune your ears and your mind into the radio Nav aids, you maintain a traffic watch—you simply lock yourself into that final approach.

Our aim was right on for the mouth of the slot, an invisible tunnel leading down through the sky to our touchdown point.

Captain: "Four hundred feet . . . three hundred feet . . . two hundred feet . . ."

We're all of us watching the runway and the instruments

At two hundred feet we're in the slot, our glide path declining easily. Air speed acceptable, in view of the changing wind; we're homing right in on the touchdown target a thousand feet down the runway; we're right on the money with a perfectly aimed and controlled approach.

The middle marker identifier bleeped and an orange light flashed on the forward panel. We're at the midpoint in the approach slot. Glide path's just right. Speed's slowly dissipating along with the sink rate.

Three pairs of eyes kept flicking back and forth between instrument panels and runway. Terrific, a textbook landing into the sunset. What a team we are!

Runway 100 feet ahead. We're drawing a bead on the thousand-foot marker. Ten seconds to touchdown. Altitude 150 feet. Sink rate—

Oh, my God! My eyes were on the pilots' panel and in one chilling split second I knew we were losing forward speed and dropping too fast and I could sense the ground coming up to grab us and I heard myself say loudly in my most authoritative baritone rather than the squeal I felt inside: "Sinking seven hundred, reference minus five!"

Simultaneously, the captain's voice, loud and urgent: "More power, more power!"

But his hands were already on the throttles, thrusting hard.

The sink rate was over a thousand feet a minute and we had less than a hundred feet—eighty, seventy—of space between us and the rough ground.

Captain and copilot instinctively exchanged roles.

My eyes were glued to the instrument panels but still I could see the unpaved earth terrifyingly close beneath us and getting closer. Damn, damn this beautiful deceptive weather. Wind *shift?* This is a *goddamn wind shear,* and it's clawing us right down to the ground.

Up! Up! Get up!

I was willing that plane to rise.

The engines growled and roared.

My heart was pounding and there was ice in my spine. Suddenly, in the blink of an eye, the wind was no longer where it had been. We had dropped from one air current to an opposing one—we had dropped right out of the slot seconds short of the runway.

Power surged. I felt the control coming back as the aircraft responded. The noise of the engines was almost deafening, but by God it was welcome.

We were back at safe speed and gliding neatly within the invisible slot. Altitude a hundred, sink rate back to normal. . . .

There was an instant decision to be made, and the captain made it. We would not go around.

We're going a little faster than we would have preferred but we're on an appropriate glide path and rain slick or no slick we want to plant this airplane on the runway where it belongs. Ordinarily we would let the speed dissipate a bit more before touchdown, but this time we feel we can't afford that luxury. We want to get it down before we run out of room . . . and as it is we can still make our thousand-foot target.

So we came in hot and fast.

All this, within just a few seconds of "Sinking seven hundred!"

Whomp! A hard landing, but a nice healthy one.

We touched down right on the thousand-foot mark just as if we hadn't taken an unintentional dip.

Thank heaven.

But we weren't quite home yet.

The captain pulled the speed brakes and applied reverse thrust. The plane kept skimming along. The wheels weren't grabbing the pavement through the film of rainwater left by the departing thunderstorm. Sure, we'd allowed plenty of room, but we were sliding more than we'd figured we would.

Quite gracefully, yet with disconcerting speed, we hydroplaned toward the end of the runway.

Oh, no, no more of this, please.

Gradually, the spoilers on the wings helped to do their job of slowing us down. As the captain kept applying reverse thrust, the wheels began to grip the hard surface beneath the sheen of water . . . and then we were rolling rapidly but noticeably decelerating.

There wasn't much runway left by the time we turned off and trundled toward the ramp.

We heaved a joint sigh of relief.

We all knew how close we had come to having a very unpleasant landing. If the captain's response hadn't been so swift and correct, if the airplane hadn't responded, if . . .

The cockpit door opened and Number One Flight Attendant came in. She looked a little ruffled.

"Passengers didn't like that," she said.

"Neither did we," said the captain. "Our apologies to them. A shift of the wind."

"Wind?" She stared at him for a moment, and I think she turned pale but maybe I was projecting. "You mean wind shear? Good God. Nice landing, guys."

She gave us a small smile and went back into the cabin.

We had a couple of comments from debarking passengers. They were not complaints. "Bit bouncy there for a while, but great stuff, Captain."

Boy, you don't know how great it was.

We had been in a potentially life-threatening situation and we'd come through it with a couple of bounces and a long rollout.

The cockpit debriefing was not a self-congratulatory one. We'd let ourselves be fooled by the apparent benignancy of the weather. Of course, with the proximity of the thunderstorm there would be currents of energy still traveling through the air. We should have been more prepared for wind shear, instead of just a shift, and given more thought to the merits of going around instead of attempting the landing.

There's no point in playing that endless game called We Shoulda Done, so we didn't. But we knew we'd had a lesson, with a happy ending.

Afterward I realized that, for the first time in my flying career, I had been really scared.

It also occurred to me that my past had not flashed before my eyes, as is supposed to happen, but for one piercing instant I had looked into a future that held—what?

I'd been so intent on my job that I'd been shortchanging other areas of my life. It dawned on me that staying proficient in my work, whether as flight engineer or whatever, didn't mean eliminating everything else. I'd always thought I didn't have time. But now, even between going to refresher clinics, catching up on the new manuals and repeatedly reviewing all procedures under the eagle eyes of assorted instructors and chief pilots, I had time to think for the first time in years.

The first thing I thought was that I had scarcely read a book in years that wasn't a flight manual. Magazines, okay; newspapers, company and union newsletters, an occasional paperback, but a real book, no. I was tired of *Aviation Week.* For five years, I hadn't read a novel. I'd seen movies, hardly any plays, I'd scarcely been to a concert, I knew very little about politics and I didn't know my way around the museums of New York. Now I had an opportunity to start filling in the blanks. And I had a need. I'd been jolted into confronting myself as a one-track person, and I wanted more out of life.

I could start taking steps to bridge the culture gaps. I could become more active in the Wings Club, and organize meetings to bring together women of accomplishment in all fields of professional endeavor—sports, business, communications, entertainment, science, space. I could meet more people, men and women, in many walks of life. I could look at life with an altogether broader view. If I wanted to—having become an expert on packing a suitcase and living out of it—I could write a slim volume of travel tips. Perhaps I could establish some kind of information service for young people, especially women, who were interested in becoming pilots. I could . . .

There was no limit to what I could do.

I could even, perhaps, start working on my social life again.

16

Other Airwomen

Things were happening in 1979 and 1980 that were eye-opening for me. One of the big things was that, for the first time, I met other women airline pilots en masse. Throughout my years of airline flying, the only female commercial pilots I had gotten to know at all well were those who flew for American. I knew Judy Lee, whose friendship dated back to my flight instruction days in Florida and who had subsequently become a pilot with United. I'd met Stephanie Wallach of Braniff a time or two, corresponded with Emily Howell of Frontier and become acquainted with Barbara Barrett on a skiing trip, but I'd had very little contact with other women pilots. Now, at last, I did. I was literally struck dumb—an unusual experience for me—with surprise and admiration.

The occasion was the second annual meeting of the International Social Affiliation of Women Airline Pilots, held that year in Miami. For various reasons I'd been unable to attend the first gathering, which twenty-one women pilots attended, leading to the group's nickname: ISA + 21. Husbands and boyfriends were also there and established their own informal group irreverently called HALP, or Husbands of Airline Pilots. Several of the HALPers are airline pilots themselves, and one of their main occupations is to collect what they think of as hilarious anecdotes about the women in their male-dominated world.

The primary purpose of ISA + 21 is social. Since the likelihood of any woman pilot meeting up with another at an airport or anywhere else is exceedingly slim, most of us have felt pretty isolated. With the birth of ISA, we can at least meet once a year to swap stories, exchange addresses, show off pictures of husbands and babies and generally be supportive of each other.

When I went to the ISA meeting in Miami that year, I really didn't know what to expect. All I knew was that there were perhaps sixty or seventy members at that time and that probably only about half, maybe fewer, would be able to attend because of their work and personal schedules. I just knew I was going to be in the midst of a gaggle of female airline pilots for the first time, which would undoubtedly be a strange sensation. Getting to know a couple of women fliers—sister pilots? I did not even know how to refer to them—still had not wiped away my feeling that I was virtually one of a kind.

So there I was again, off on another blind date, with what turned out to be about thirty women. We few needed the reassurance of each other. And again I thought that the other women pilots would be a lot like me—would I never learn?—and that of course we would be bound to get along famously because we had so much in common.

As it turned out, we had two things in common. One, we were all women airline pilots. Two, we all expected to have a great deal in common.

As to the latter, we were wrong. The common denominator of our profession was a powerful bond, but the differences between us were incredible. Our backgrounds were different. We looked different—we were not the clones of the Flight Academy. We sounded different, not just in our accents but in our manner of speech. Some of us talked a lot, some were quiet and reserved. A few had done nothing but immerse themselves in aviation all their lives, and some had had several other careers. For some, flying was a hobby as much as a job; and for others, music or art was as important as aviation. For a number of the women, husband and family came first, with flying a very close but incomparable second.

I looked around and asked myself: How did all these women get to where they are when they're not at all like me? How did I get to where I am, when I'm not at all like them?

The physical differences alone astounded me. We came in all sizes and shapes. I thought that really amazing. We should have been stamped out of a particular mold, like uniformed Barbie dolls, but of course we were not. Quite a few of the women were really tall, which didn't really surprise me. What did surprise me was how many rather little gals there were.

Who would ever suspect them of being airline pilots? This must be some kind of chauvinism on my part. I just expected female pilots to be quite big, as people have always seemed to expect me to be some kind of outsize tomboy and are surprised to see I'm not. It was odd to find myself having the same feeling. No lady wrestlers here? Amazing.

But short, medium or tall, the women were a good-looking bunch. I could scarcely believe how pretty they were. Norah O'Neill, herself among the most striking of the group, said afterward that she thought she'd stumbled on a models' convention because virtually all of those present were unusually attractive and poised—but again, in very individual ways.

I first saw them together at an evening cocktail party. All wore elegant dresses, heels, varying degrees of makeup and nailpolish; all were beautifully groomed, exuding a modellike confidence and the self-assuredness of attractive, successful women. Staggering! The next day, when we gathered for business, I had another shock when I saw all these beauties in uniform. How stunningly trim they looked, how erectly they stood, how totally professional their appearance and manner. Under no circumstances would anyone give any of these obviously competent women the Hey, girlie! treatment. And yet, of course, some of us still get it.

We talked about that. We talked about people asking, "Are you the real pilot?" and others declaring flatly that they'd never travel on an airline with a woman in the cockpit. We agreed that in spite of the mainly petty but sometimes extreme displays of resentment that came our way, we had the greatest job in the world. "If we told Them how much we love it, They might not want to pay us."

And we did our share of girl-type chitchat—What kind of shoes do you wear when you're flying? Don't your heels get caught in the rudder? You fly *barefoot?* We just hate these hats. Where do you get yours?—as well as more personal things about boyfriends, husbands and babies.

But there was other talk, too. Airplane talk. Shop talk. It was the first time I had ever experienced airplane talk—hangar flying—with other women. It just seemed unreal to me, to be there with all those other females, talking shop with them: to discuss little nuances of flying technique, to compare airline procedures, airplane characteristics, bidding, approaches to various airports, mechanical problems, malfunctioning lights and instruments, stuck cargo doors, pressure drops, new type ratings. . . . You just checked out in the DC-9? What's it like? Love it, it's terrific. Lemme tell you . . . I was making an approach into Charlotte the other day and the weather was on the deck and . . . It was the oldest plane on the line I was flying that day, and everything bad happened except losing the engine—lost the APU, lost the weather, lost the screwdriver—every freaky little thing went wrong until we landed and we just greased it in. . . .

I was enchanted. I listened and talked as if in a dream, or as if having finally awakened. We were talking what is traditionally known as man talk, using highly technical terms and the lighthearted slang of the crew room and making it clear to each other that we knew exactly what we were talking about as well as any of the men we flew with. Only difference is, we larded our conversation with shades of nailpolish and comments about each other's uniforms.

It did strike me that these were all very tough ladies.

Not tough in the sense of being hard or thick-skinned or

ruthlessly ambitious, but in the sense of being tough-minded and determined. There were healthy egos here, conscientious and dedicated workers prepared to pull their weight and even *more* than their weight along with the best and the brightest, strong-fibered women who had rapped on closed doors and forced them to open, resilient, good-humored, well-balanced people who just hung in there as long as humanly possible and showed their particular brand of right stuff.

As the ice broke and we got to know each other, the conversation pretty soon got around to such questions as, What did you do before you joined the airline? And why did you want to be a pilot? Was someone in your family a flier?

The answers were wonderfully varied.

It isn't necessary to come from a flying family to become a pilot, but there's no doubt that having a flying parent or two does have some effect. Denise Blankenship's father is a pilot with Eastern Airlines. Just as in my case, it wasn't a question of following in Daddy's footsteps, because there seemed to be no possibility of women following that route, but something rubs off. What a parent does and loves is just as important to girls as it is to boys. Denise, in her mellow Southern accent, says she always wanted to be a pilot but was afraid to say so. "People woulda thought I was crazy," she claims. And I think she's probably right, because at the beginning of the 1970s it was a rare Southern woman indeed who looked to the airlines for a career.

So she took the traditional route expected of young women in those days. She went to the University of Georgia and studied interior design and home economics. But she also learned to fly. By the time Denise graduated with a design degree in 1973, she had logged 350 hours of flight time and earned both her commercial ticket and her instrument rating. And by graduation day of that year, both Emily Howell and I had started flying for the airlines.

Denise was still building her hours. It took her a lot of flying jobs and several years, but by the time she had over three thousand hours and superb qualifications, there were nine airline companies ready to interview her. She chose Piedmont Airlines of North Carolina and signed up on March 7, 1977.

Both parents of Terry London of Western Airlines were military pilots in World War II. Jack was an Air Force pilot who retired as a colonel; Barbara Erickson London was a WASP squadron commander who earned the Air Medal for her superlative service. Terry, a Californian, never considered a career outside of aviation. She soloed on her sixteenth birthday and has been flying seriously ever since. I guess it's not surprising that she married a flier, nor would it be a surprise if her babies grew up to be pilots, too.

Another flier born to the tradition of aviation is Jean Haley, who might yet choose a career in journalism as a secondary interest but who was drawn to the sky from childhood and likes it better up there. Her father was a professional cropduster pilot in central California. "Mom and Dad said I could be anything I wanted to be," says Jean. A high school teacher told her that her ambition to be an airline pilot was ridiculous because she probably wasn't even tall enough to be a stewardess. This dampened her spirits for a few years but she took flying lessons anyway. Her brother, a flier who at the time was a skydiver drop pilot, persuaded her to train for his line of work. She found herself warmly accepted by skydivers and fellow pilots, and launched herself on her flying career.

Mary Bush is another of us who was lured by family flying tradition. Mary's father had been a commercial pilot and flight instructor, and while Mary was growing up was operating an FBO at Fort Lauderdale–Hollywood International Airport.

"It's hard to tell exactly just when my first flight lesson was," she says. "There were six children in our family and we had to take turns. I remember waiting my turn to sit on my father's lap and steer his aircraft."

I had heard a lot about Mary Bush before I met her. She was a legend to me and to other female pilots because of her extraordinary expertise and experience. There can't be another woman in the business today who has flown what Mary has flown. Never mind the twenty-odd single- and twin-engine planes she has put through their paces, from every variety of Piper and Cessna known to man to the eccentric little Pitts Special to the Beechcraft D-18. Just as soon as she was qualified she was flying the Connie—the chunky L-1049H Constellation—down to Mexico for Sky-Truck International. She's also flown the DC-7-CF, the DC-6, the DC-3 (my old Gooney Bird pal), the C-46, the Mallard Grumman Amphibian . . . and she's flown these things and others throughout North, Central and South America. This woman, who went on to fly DC-9s for Republic, is an exceptional flier, the best in the business. I thought she'd be venerable with the weight of her experience and the years she'd taken to accumulate it. She isn't. She's my age, with a kind of small-boned aristocratic beauty not generally associated with people who fly sky trucks.

So a lot of women fliers do have flying in their genes or their environment, but it takes something more than parental inspiration to make a pilot's daughter yearn to be a pilot. Most women pilots do not have flying fathers, and they can't really explain why and how they got hooked on flying.

Beverley Bass is a Florida-born Texan whose family was raising quarter-horses while she was growing up. She loved horses, but she says, "For some unknown reason I was simply fascinated with airplanes. I suppose this happens to many children whose fathers were in the Air Force, but my father drove PT boats in the Navy."

When she was about eight years old, she woke up one morning having decided that her greatest wish in life was to land a jet in San Francisco at midnight. At midnight? Says Bev: "I think my parents just thought they had a strange child! For nine years I rode and trained and taught riding. And I'm an only child. So I think my Dad thought, if I started flying, I would lose interest in the horses.

"Eventually we sold the ranch and the horses, and I went to college and started flying right away. I just zipped right through all my licenses and ratings, because I'd been so serious about it right from the beginning."

Beverley's first part-time job was as pilot of an ancient Bonanza, flying corpses for the Fort Worth Mortician Service. She says that operating airborne hearses may not be a great deal of fun, but at least you don't get any backchat.

But landing a jet in San Francisco at midnight is worth what you have to go through to do it, and seventeen years after Beverley awoke with her dream, American offered her the opportunity to make it come true.

Judy Lee is another professional rider turned sky jockey.

Her life with horses began when she was three years old. Her parents put her on a pony and could hardly get her off. By the time she was ten she was showing and exercising horses as a professional, and she kept at it with scarcely a day off until she was twenty.

That indefinable something pointing to a future in aviation had surfaced a couple of years earlier. In the beginning it was nothing more than a sense that flying might be even more fun than riding. She played at flying while she worked with horses. Gradually, she became more and more serious about airplanes. Flying was an enormous pleasure and maybe even a way to earn a living. The money from her equestrian jobs began to flow into increasingly advanced flying courses and the inevitable business of picking up hours. For several years she continued to ride, galloping racehorses for various trainers in seven different states, loving the life and the horses but deciding eventually that what she really wanted to do was break into the airline business. I like to think she caught some of her airline fever from me when I was flight instructing in Florida. But if she ever needs some other line of work, she could easily go back to horse handling. She could also be the most terrific sportscaster in the world. And continue being a housewife.

In 1973 Norah O'Neill took her first small-plane ride while

modeling ski clothes on Mount McKinley, Alaska. She was not looking forward to it, nor to the next few days on location. An athletic, feisty redhead, Norah knew the mountains of her home state of Washington and the ski slopes of Sun Valley, but this was something altogether different. "A ski plane was to drop us on a glacier ten thousand feet up the side of the mountain," she says, "and pick us up five days later. That plane looked like a mosquito to me. Even as reckless and adventurous as I was in those days, I didn't want to get into it. It was a mind-boggling experience and it changed my life completely within days.

"We flew over canyons twice as deep as the Grand Canyon, over bottomless crevasses, and I knew the only way to keep experiencing this was to be a bird or a small-plane pilot. The day we got back to civilization I got a night job and started flying lessons on Kodiak Island, Alaska. Three weeks later I got my private license."

And so it went, onward and upward through flight instructing in Fairbanks, flying pipeline routes throughout Alaska and hiring on as Flying Tigers' first female pilot in December 1976.

I don't know why one young woman left home at fifteen, supported herself as a rock musician through high school and college, opened an advertising agency, then gave up everything to fly full time and join an airline. I just know she did. Another started work as a clerk-typist for an airline, went on to personnel clerk, took up flying as a hobby, became a secretary, then a trainee in the crew scheduling department, then a crew scheduler and then an applicant for a position as an airline pilot, which she won. Two or three other women started their flying careers as flight attendants and wound up as flight officers.

Beauticians, singers, models, editors, film-cutters, journalists, art directors, daughters of actors, mothers of small children, women who want to prove something to themselves or their boyfriends . . . it takes all kinds. You try the job for a multitude of reasons. You stick with it for one. Jeannie Haley says it very simply for all of us: "I am in love with my work."

For me, the result of that ISA meeting was a new sense of belonging. By our best count, those of us at the Miami gathering represented approximately 110 women flying for airlines throughout the free world. There were some thirty-five to forty thousand male pilots in the United States airline industry alone, never mind the rest of the world. I'm not sure how these figures compare today, because of recent discouraging events in the business, but I have heard it estimated that, nationwide, 25 percent of the positions in previously male-dominated professions such as law and medicine are currently held by women, whereas in the business of airline piloting the figure is a puny *0.25.* I can't begin to guess at the figures for the rest of the world, but it's obvious that we women are ridiculously outnumbered by the men. So it's still a little lonely up there.

But that's okay. We have ISA now, and it represents an attractive kind of positive feminism that may well, in time, extend its influence into areas of interest to women at large. Meanwhile, we have at last found out that we are not some kind of flaky persons demanding the impossible of the world. We've discovered that it doesn't matter where you're from or where you're at, what your parents do or did, what you look like or what your other interests are. You can be an airline pilot if you've got the makings and if you're prepared to work at it.

We know that we have, in these past few years, gained a degree of acceptance and confidence from all levels of airline personnel and the traveling public. What we want to do now, through ISA and individually, is to encourage more women to contemplate careers with the airlines, and we would like to help them avoid some of the pitfalls we blundered into. Being a flier in an industry that might not yet be completely ready for women does not mean that we have abandoned femininity or that we cannot enjoy extremely happy private lives. We are resented sometimes, and we are patronized and we may be made to feel less equal than our equals. Generally speaking, we can hack all this.

But the strength test . . . c'mon, guys! As Denise says, "The only thing you need strength for is to pick up your flight bags"—and that's with or without a ten-pound weight.

17

Cockpits and Layovers: Sex and Violence on the Job

Some years back there was a rash of purported news stories, told with a kind of self-righteous glee, about goings-on in the cockpit between the stewardesses and the all-male flight crew: lap-sitting, muffled giggles, the captain taking his hands off the wheel, the plane plunging a couple of thousand feet—that sort of thing. Well, maybe. I know that I've never seen anything like that. In my sadly limited experience, the closest approach to ribaldry in the cockpit was when a flight attendant, after delivering the captain's sandwich lunch, inquired, "Anything else?" He said, "Yeah, scratch my back." She uttered two censorable words and left.

Since I was hired to occupy a portion of the cockpit I've been periodically asked about sexual fun and frolic on the flight deck. The answer: it is minimal. There is little time for fun and games between crew members. Work has to be done on a programmed basis, the atmosphere is not conducive to shenanigans and there's no room to chase around the desks. Boring! Well, no. There is a lot of mild romancing on the job and after hours, just as there is in most jobs. Guys make advances. They flirt. I flirt. They have to make a pitch, and if they don't, I worry. It's an inevitable, necessary part of the male-female relationship. We know that, and we know we're friends.

In the beginning there was some minor sexual harassment,

usually in the form of lascivious looks and suggestive jokes. These were easily ignored or brushed aside. A couple of times I was furious. Now I forget why. The episodes were brief and not worthy of recall.

Most women pilots feel the same. Some attitudes were fleetingly expressed, and seldom memorably. You could feel as hurt as you wanted to feel, or be as blind as you wanted to be.

But there have been some very unpleasant exceptions. Lynn Rippelmeyer, who is now flying 737s for People Express, had an experience with a couple of boors at her previous airline that makes you wonder about the mentality of some allegedly adult males. They were captain and first officer, she was the first female flight engineer they had ever flown with, and they —men in their forties or early fifties—were juvenile enough to use her as the brunt of their extremely puerile jokes throughout the trip. Incredibly, they allowed their warped sense of fun to override their professionalism.

One of their favorite tricks was to interfere with communications. Lynn would make a radio call to ground control. One of the comedians would cut in on the interphone, as if responding, and foul up the interchange. Equally funny was their little trick of cutting out the flight attendants' P.A. announcement so that one of the air hostesses would have to come into the cockpit and tell the engineer that the P.A. was broken. That was just a little gambit to lure the flight attendant into the cockpit to become a second butt for their rich humor.

They knew Lynn was from St. Louis. One of the flight attendants was also from St. Louis. An ostensibly innocent conversation would develop, a setup for the humorists to slide in the query: "Oh, are all girls from St. Louis flat-chested?" Or something far more offensive. Then the F.A. would walk out, unsmiling, and they would wonder why.

At one stop the jokers bought masses of popcorn, and as soon as anybody walked into the cockpit—possibly Lynn, after checking something elsewhere in the aircraft, or one of the attendants—the boys let go with a bombardment generally seen only at Saturday afternoon movies attended by preteen delinquents. Funny! "Where's your sensayuma?"

After failing to get a lot of laughs with the popcorn, the boys got gross. They lit up fat, stinking cigars and puffed on them until the cockpit filled up with vile-smelling smoke. Smoking, within reason, is permitted in the cockpit, which is obviously a confined, not very well ventilated space. Usually a smoker asks, "Do you mind if I smoke?" and then lights up a relatively innocuous low-tar cigarette. Or he'll take a break to satisfy what are known in the trade as "physiological needs," and have a fast puff at the same time. Not these sweeties. When the atmosphere was truly disgusting, the captain turned to Lynn and said, "Oh, you don't mind, do you?"

"Yes, I do," she said. "But I really don't think it matters what I care about on this trip, because obviously you're doing everything you can to upset me."

"Aw, don't be upset, honey. Join us. We happen to have one of your brand." And he handed her a tampon.

The flight droned slowly to an end, all three horrible days of it. Unbelievably, when it was all over, the officers earnestly inquired how Lynn had enjoyed the trip.

She did not mince words. "It was the most horrible trip I've ever had," she said. "I hope I never have to fly with you two again."

"Now, Lynn, come on," they said. "Didn't you really have a good time?"

Lynn was astounded. Could they truly not realize how she must have felt? Wasn't that the way they had wanted her to feel?

"No, it was awful," she said bluntly. "You were nauseating."

They turned serious, putting on their stern old-boy looks. "Now, look," they said, alternating lines like some fourth-rate vaudeville team, "for your own good, we've got to tell you that if you're going to be in this job—"

"—if you're going to get along in this *world*—"

"—you better learn to take this sort of kidding around—"

"—and if you want to make it in a *man's* world—"

"—that's how it's going to be."

But it wasn't and it isn't. To Lynn, as to me, this episode is not an example of what goes on all the time. It is probably a one-in-a-thousand story. Those particular pilots typify the worst kind of aging, adolescent cowboy. The mentality is not unknown in the world of flying, but these lads just happened to have an extreme case of phony machismo. Or something. None of us has found it necessary to become accustomed to that kind of asinine horseplay in the real world of real men and women.

One young woman stumbled into a major career obstacle while training to upgrade, meeting her bête noire in the uncomfortably intimate quarters of the simulator. Ordinarily, there's plenty of room in a simulator for up to six people, but when one of them has a long and groping arm then two becomes a crowd.

The man was an instructor, and he was obnoxious. He was due to retire the following month to devote full time to his real estate business, so he had no fear of losing his job. Never mind teaching the girl to fly: his primary objective was to get her to bed. And he was not subtle about it. "I haven't arm-wrestled with anybody since I was a teenager," she recalls, suddenly looking much less low-key than usual. "And all of a sudden, at thirty, there I was doing it again!"

The usual procedure in simulator training is for two students to work together as a team under the eye of the instructor. That did not suit Casanova. After each of the scheduled sessions, during which he lavished unwanted attentions on the young woman and virtually ignored the male student, he told her that she needed an extra session. Her partner would not need to come along. In fact, her partner had better not come along.

"Oh, yes, he will," she insisted. "I get extra time, he gets extra time. I'm not coming alone."

Her simulator partner, like the rest of her classmates, was a protective and understanding fellow who quickly caught on to what was happening. He always went with her to the simulator—regular sessions, extra ones and overtime. In rebuttal, the instructor canceled some sessions on the spot and took a girlfriend along with him on others. The latter move turned out to be self-defeating, since he then had two people watching him try to paw his girl student. Once he managed to get the girl alone in his car, saying that he had to talk to her about setting up a makeup lesson and swearing he would take her straight home. He stopped at a railroad crossing, grabbed her, smothered her with moist kisses and told her he could teach her so much more than how to fly.

I don't quite know how she got out of that one, but she did. Karate, perhaps. She's tiny, but she's tough. The point of having her partner along whenever possible was not to use him as a bodyguard but as a buffer against senseless humiliation. She also thought she might learn more if permitted to concentrate on the main tasks at hand. As it was, both she and her simulator partner flunked checkrides because they simply were not taught the maneuvers they needed to know to pass their airplane tests.

Prince Charming was very soothing when he told her she had failed.

"If you feel like crying," he said softly, "just go ahead. I'll comfort you."

She avoided his reaching arms and said crisply, "I don't feel like crying. I think we'd better sit down and go over the things I just got shown on the checkride, things I've never seen before that I was supposed to know, and we'd better set up a time when we can do them."

The question arises: Why hadn't she blown the whistle? Surely there was some recourse.

"Sure, I could go to the company that had just hired me as

their first woman, and say, 'I'm not doing well in this course because of the instructor,' and they're either going to take the instructor's word for it, or mine. I can try to get through it in spite of him, I told myself, and I did try. Looking back on it, I know it was a mistake. My simulator partner and I were both being shortchanged. We were both negligent in not demanding another instructor. But we were new hires, and we didn't want to make waves. I especially. I just wanted to get through as smoothly and calmly and unnoticeably as possible. As a woman, you want to fit in, and just do everything normally. You don't want special attention. You don't want the extra time. And for me to go to them and say, 'I need extra sessions and an extra instructor!'—I was hoping we could do without all that. As it turned out, we ended up needing makeup time and a new instructor, and I had to explain why instead of having gotten it over with earlier. It turned out all right, but it was a very unfortunate circumstance."

It is even harder to point a finger of blame at superior officers when you're on the line. It's not easy, in any business, to complain about a supervisor, manager or vice-president. With pilots, about the only effective recourse is the union, or an informal talk with the chief pilot.

It seems to be an unfortunate fact of life that some captains in some airlines have used the pilot letter system to denigrate and damage their women pilots. Most pilots don't get letters written on them at all; a simple "shape up" is sufficient. And it is unthinkable for a captain to write a letter on a crew member without previously warning the offender. But one woman, whom I'll call Kelly Albright, was slapped with six letters in two months, and not one of the six captains said anything at all to her beforehand. The letters made various unfounded complaints: lateness when she had not been late, a bad landing when she had not been at the controls, unprofessional behavior on the ground or the way she was wearing her hair—"Hey, did he tell me he didn't like it? No, he didn't." Kelly's hair, a silky mane in genuine shades of autumn, falls luxuriantly onto her shoulders when she doesn't tie it back. "Had he told me he didn't like it, I would have said, 'Okay, how do you want it?' and I would've done it. A couple of times guys have said, 'We don't like your hair down. It looks unprofessional.' I say, 'Okay,' and I put it up in a bun. It takes me about two minutes to put it up in the bun. It's not that it dangles into the machinery. It never has. But I think they'd be glad if it did!"

Writing a letter on a pilot is a very, very serious step for a captain to take. It is only written when a crew member has for some reason become totally incompetent or recalcitrant. But when Kelly was up before the chief pilot for the sixth time, trying to figure out why she was there, that officer said, "You know, you won't believe it—we've gotten more letters on our women pilots than we've had on all the men, total, in this company." Considering that, at the time, there were only nine women and nine hundred male pilots in that company, the fact that the little group of females elicited more complaint letters than all the men in the airline's history meant one of two things: "Either we're grossly incompetent and shouldn't be here, or there's a lot of disguised prejudice at work out there and the men don't want to admit—maybe even to themselves—that that is what it is." Kelly adds: "And we get to live with this."

Fact is, we succeed in living with it.

An inevitable question arises and that is: *Are* women pilots grossly incompetent? And a second question: If we are, how does that speak for the airlines' hiring practices and training procedures?

In Kelly's airline: "The company has assured itself over and over again that we're competent. If you get a letter saying your flying is unsatisfactory, they pull you down to headquarters and throw you into a simulator and give you a very strenuous checkride to see where your weak points are. The women they've pulled in for checkrides because of complaints have all gone through the checkride with flying colors. And the check pilots say, 'Nothing wrong with this person. Must have been a personality difference out there on the line, or she musta had a bad day. Maybe she was in her period.' "

That old chestnut again! But let's just give it a rest this time.

I agree with Kelly. Nobody is really questioning anymore whether or not we're competent. "Except," Kelly adds, "that there are different levels of competency—and they presume we're at the lower end!"

No airline can afford to hire, or to keep on, a bad pilot. So far as I know, only one woman airline pilot has been released from her job for purported incompetence. My understanding of what happened there is that her qualifications, which looked impressive on paper and in the classroom, did not measure up to the real-life demands of an airliner cockpit. No, the record of the female fliers is good, the volume of complaining letters notwithstanding.

So why are the letters written? Clues creep reluctantly to mind. Several of my flying sisters have been called on the chief pilot's carpet because of these insidious little notes. One has, I think, been the subject of three or four complaints. Of her, a checkride pilot once said contemptuously, "I could teach a monkey to do what she can do." The woman in question is one of the finest fliers I know. She is superb. She is experienced, intelligent, an excellent team worker—a woman known and acknowledged for her skills. She does not have "bad days." An occasional mediocre day, perhaps, but fewer than most of us. Come to think of it, she's almost perfect. And come to think of *that,* being so near perfection must be exasperating to some of her colleagues. Maybe if she was less than terrific, she would not be the subject of complaints.

I think of other women who have uncomplimentary letters in their files. They are an amalgam of the intellectually brilliant, slightly bizarre, outspoken, unusually attractive and impossible to ignore: they stand out. They dazzle. That's bad. Mustn't be eccentric, mustn't be noticed. Mustn't make waves.

Kelly has a problem. She is tall, extremely attractive, funny and smart and one helluva pilot.

This is a problem? Yes. She stands out in every crowd. Among pilots, generally a conformist lot, that's a no-no, and in the cockpit it is very awkward. I think her visibility—and, by now, the chip that is beginning to appear on her elegant shoulder—is a major contributory factor to her collection of pilots' letters. She gets her back up; she gets sassy. But God knows she's had provocation.

Without exception, all the letters and all the hassle Kelly has received have come from youthful captains, whose brand of resentment is beyond her powers of analysis, and mine.

Some years back, Kelly flew copilot on a six-day charter with a guy named Jack. It's normal in the industry for the captain to fly the first leg of the flight, the copilot the second and so on. Pilots are so accustomed to this procedure that they simply get in the airplane and assume that they will be flying alternate legs. Not true in this case. Throughout the six days, Captain Jack never let his lady copilot fly the airplane.

And shortly after they got back, surprise! The chief pilot called Kelly in and said he'd had a letter from the captain saying that she was incompetent. In what way, he didn't say.

"Explain," said the chief pilot.

"Well, hell," said Kelly. "Pull the paperwork on the flight, because all I did was talk on the radio and do paperwork. If you don't like the paperwork, I'll do it over."

All the paperwork was in order and neatly done.

"Now," said the chief, "we've proved you can write and I know you can talk. So what's he complaining about?"

"I don't know."

"Well, did you have some problem, a personality conflict with him? Did he make a pass at you?"

"No." Nothing had happened.

And the meeting ended with nothing explained and nothing solved. Three years later, Kelly pulled another trip with Captain Jack. It was the first time she'd seen him since the business of the letter, which she had never mentioned to anyone. Nor did he or she mention it now. They took their seats on the New York to Chicago flight, captain on the left, copilot on the right, engineer to the rear, and the captain handled the takeoff.

A few minutes later, number one engine caught fire.

At the same time the New York weather, very poor on takeoff, became even worse. They turned and headed back into a deluge.

They missed the first approach and went around again.

The minutes in the air were jam-packed with things to do simultaneously: refer to checklists, review approach plates, talk to the tower and, primarily, fly the plane. Everybody was working.

It was an unpleasant few minutes during which the crew worked smoothly together and did an excellent job, with a few minor glitches that had no effect on the outcome. The fire trucks were waiting as the airplane touched down and trundled down the runway, the captain becoming so anxious about getting the thing stopped that he stood on the brakes and overheated them. No matter—it was a good, safe landing.

They reached the ramp. The captain turned to his cockpit crew and said to Kelly and the engineer, "I gotta thank you guys. We really needed all three of us, and you did a wonderful job."

No one was anxious to take another stab at it, but the company decided that the show must go on. While the crew waited, all the freight was offloaded from the damaged plane and reloaded onto another. The crew went back to work. When the flight finally arrived in Chicago many hours behind time, it was late, all the bars were closed and everybody felt like a drink.

Pausing in the hotel lobby, the captain said casually to Kelly, "I have enough Scotch for a couple of drinks—not enough for all of us, but if you wanta come by, I'll give you a drink."

She said, "Oh, great. Thanks."

Kelly dumped her suitcase in her room, went down the hall and tapped on the captain's door.

He flung it open, pulled her in and slammed it shut behind her. "It was incredible! He was a big guy—he picked me up, all five feet ten of me, threw me on the bed and jumped on top of me. I tried to be my diplomatic self. I said, 'Jack! What're you doing? Hey, I'm just not interested in this.' He was panting and giving me a bunch of baloney. I tried to say something he could handle without feeling put-down. I said, 'Jack, you're very attractive, but I don't have affairs with married men.'

"He didn't handle it at all. He said, 'We're not going to have an affair, we're just going to have one night.' Crude!

"So I said, 'Jack, I'm really in love with another man, and I'm not going to bed with you, whether you're married or not.'

"He said, "Ah, come on, what's wrong with you—can't you just take advantage of a little sexual excitement?' I said, 'Jack, I'm not sexually excited. I just came to your room for a drink, that's what you asked me for, and I've lost interest in that drink. Let me up. I'm leaving.'

"The whole time, this guy is still lying on me, fumbling around with me, my neck, my face. I finally realized that there was not going to be any reasoning with the fellow.

"I said, 'Jack, if you don't get off me this second, I'm going to start screaming *rape!* And you can explain why two people in airline pilot uniforms are in a room with one of them screaming rape! I *will* do it. I'm going to count to ten, and if you're not off me, I'm going to start doing it.'

"That got him up. I leapt off the bed, snapped an icy 'Goodnight' and walked to the door. As I opened it, he said, 'I think you ought to know that I don't think you did a good job tonight. It was a bad enough job so that I'm going to have to write a letter on you.'

"I stopped with my hand on the doorknob and turned to him. 'What's wrong?' I said, very politely. 'Won't your wife sleep with you anymore? Do you really have to blackmail a woman to get her into bed with you?'

"His face twisted up. 'That's it,'' he said. 'I'm writing a letter on you tomorrow and I'm going to get you fired.'

"By this time, I had had it. I said, 'Jack, let me tell you what's going to happen if you write a letter on me. I'm tired of this shit, I've taken ten years of this shit and I won't take this shit anymore. If you write a letter on me, I'm going to write a letter addressed to the whole pilot group. I'm going to make nine hundred copies and make sure that every single pilot gets one at his home address. And I'm going to make sure that the chairman of the board gets one, and the president of the company and every chief pilot, and it's going to say in detail exactly what happened tonight. And it's going to say in detail what mistakes you made in the airplane—because you were the one who made them, right? Never mind they worked out okay. We all know you made 'em. I'm going to say, in my letter, exactly what you said and did, and how you told your crew that they'd done a really good job. And how you changed your mind when I refused to sleep with you. I'm going to tell them in detail what was said in this room, how you approached me and how you threw me on the bed. And I'm going to make sure your wife gets a copy, too. And everybody on this line is going to find out that the only way Jack can get laid is by blackmailing and bludgeoning women into it. So you go ahead and write up that letter.'

"He just looked at me, said nothing. That was it. I left."

But that was not quite the end of the matter. On the return trip, Kelly was again not permitted to fly, and conversation was limited to the bare, professional minimum. That was not unexpected. But what was a little surprising was that, walking through a crew room about two weeks later, Kelly overheard Jack telling other fellows what a terrible pilot she was. Later, she told some of them that Jack had never let her fly, so he couldn't possibly judge her performance in the cockpit. They thought she was lying. But finally one of them said, "Hey, Jack! Hear you never let her fly. So how come you can say she's no good?" He stammered a bit, and then said, "I've heard a lot of fellows say so." "Oh, who?" Thus put on the spot, he changed the subject.

Kelly's competence is such that, to date, her career is not in danger. But she could still be badly hurt by the little tumble-weeds of gossip set in motion by a few of her male colleagues for their own inscrutable reasons. Only when severely provoked does she fight back, or tell her side of a story, and when she tries to explain to one male pilot why another one bad-mouths her, she meets a wall of disbelief. Even the engineer on her round-trip flight with the unfortunate Jack, knowing that she had indeed not flown, and having heard the rumors of her incompetence strewn around by the rejected one, found it hard to believe her story when she told him why captain and copilot had been cool on the return trip.

He was such a nice guy! He wouldn't do a thing like that! He's been flying for this line for fifteen years! He's got a lovely wife!

She showed him the bruises on her arm. He still could not believe her—or, at least, believed reluctantly.

The really nice guys just cannot believe these stories, which a number of women pilots readily recognize. The good guys know they couldn't do anything like that—either force themselves upon a woman, or lie about her flying. They identify: if they themselves couldn't do anything like that, how could their good buddy Jack? And it's not as if Jack is some geezer from a generation past, who hasn't grown up seeing women doing men's work. No, no—he's one of us!

That is a major part of the frustration for someone like Kelly: the unwillingness of fellow pilots to understand her plight and believe that male colleagues of their own age group could be such jerks. And it only takes one really determined mean mother to screw up the career of the finest female pilot.

Furthermore, what the jerks—few as they are—don't seem

to realize is that their actions may do damage extending far beyond individual careers. The engineer on Kelly's trip didn't know until much later what had gone wrong between the downflight and the return, but he did note that "there was tension in the cockpit that you could cut with a knife."

You don't want tension in the cockpit, unless it's of the razor-sharp professional kind that concentration and alertness bring to a situation requiring fast reaction and absolute control. Ill-feeling and resentment can be dangerous. Denise Blankenship once flew with a captain who spent three days deliberately trying to get a rise out of her. Coincidentally, there was an FAA inspector along for part of that trip, and he apparently found no fault with anything she did. But the captain kept riding her with a constant stream of criticisms, laced with derogatory sexual comments, until she finally began to feel rattled. She made a missed approach while talking on the radio and moving the flaps, which he should have been doing for her, and he was absolutely triumphant with abuse. After the landing he made a proud announcement in the crew room: "Hey, guys—I'm finally getting to her!"

She got over it. So did the passengers. No thanks to him.

Beverley Bass ran into a comparable situation. For three days she flew copilot with a captain who, although he permitted her to fly alternate legs, refused to introduce himself or speak to her. He wouldn't even answer when she read her checklist. The only way around that problem was to hand the checklist to the engineer and have him read it out.

It was an eerie sensation, feeling like an invisible person sitting next to this guy. With all sense of teamwork gone, Beverley began to feel that her flying was deteriorating. There was no way she could do her best work. Looking ahead at almost a month more of this potentially dangerous stupidity, she decided to take herself off the trip.

Sounds like an easy decision. It wasn't. She could read the reaction with her mind's eye: one of the girls can't hack it! *None* of the girls can hack it! Women fliers squeal and quit!

Choices must be made. If a guy decides a flight sequence has become intolerable and potentially dangerous for one reason or another, he quite correctly removes himself from that situation and expects—also correctly—to hear no more about it. If one of the girls does it, she has to think what effect her action will have on the other women.

Beverley made her choice. On landing in Dallas she was called into her chief pilot's office for commendation on quite another matter, which gave her the opportunity to say what she wanted to say: I can't fly the remainder of this trip—this guy's being impossible.

Up went the chief pilot's eyebrows. Very interesting. This captain is generally regarded as one of the best, but on his last trip he also made trouble with his copilot.

The upshot was that the chief pilot himself ended up flying the remainder of the trip and made the captain ride in the back of the airplane.

Women got a decent shake that time around. Sometimes, at least on some airlines, we get pretty good support treatment.

There was one exceptionally fine flier who did not get the honest treatment she deserved. Through her experience we discovered the drawback to being among the best in a man's business—you can make enemies that way. Like the rest of us, she felt that in being accepted by the airlines she was entering into a special world of enormously qualified people whose accomplishments far outshone hers. But when she got there she found that she had flown bigger and more sophisticated equipment than most of them had even heard about, and that in experience and proficiency she was way ahead of them.

She's far from dumb. She kept her accomplishments to herself and simply flew the best she knew. But somehow the men resented her particular combination of laid-back skill and good looks. The better she got, the worse they behaved. To us, she's a pilot's pilot, a natural, a born flier whose talents have been honed by challenge and practice the likes of which most of us have never known. But her fellow fliers on the line persisted in treating her like an untrained upstart. What goes on here? They simply thought they were superior because they were men, not because they were better at their jobs, and she didn't belong with them. For a colleague to be smart, exceptionally talented, pretty and nice is more than some guys can take.

She should have been, I suppose, harder-nosed and thicker-skinned. Sheer meanness and harassment got to her. Trip after trip was a torment. The job she loved turned ugly. It was no way to spend a life. How much can you and should you ignore? There's a limit. She reached it, and she quit. The struggle wasn't worth it. But it was only that one job she quit. She'll be back with us someday, one way or another.

There's another hazard for women in the cockpit: having an affectionate working relationship turn into something closer. It's generally agreed by the women in the industry that it is best to keep professional and personal lives totally separate. You *must* be objective about the people you're flying with, and keep your mind on your work.

So we all say.

One of the most vocal exponents of this philosophy is a young woman I will call Sarah. She is adamant about cockpit attitude. Whatever your position in the crew, you do not attempt to combine business with pleasure—other than the sheer, never-ending pleasure of flying and the simple camaraderie of the cockpit. Furthermore, says Sarah, you do not attempt to be the center of attention or the dominant force. If captain, you use your authority in such a way as to encourage the cooperation and initiative of your crew. If you're copilot or engineer, you assist the captain in the smooth performance of his work. Nobody solicits or encourages distracting arguments or sexual advances, however veiled. Nobody makes them. Ideal! Above all, male and female flight crew members do not get involved. So she says. In principle, she is absolutely right.

Another thing Sarah insists upon is privacy. "There's nobody at my company right now who knows anything about me and my guy. They really can't understand what I must be doing with my personal life, or what my personal life can be like. Nobody there knows of anybody that I date, or see or want to. All they ever see of me is at work, in the airplane or the office. I'm sure they're curious. But they can just stay curious! Oh, every once in a while they'll say, 'How's your love life?' I'll just say, 'It's fine,' or 'It's the pits' or however it happens to be at the time. But that's about it."

Her colleagues would be fascinated to know that Sarah has become unusually interested in one of her company's captains. They flew together for the first time several months ago. He and Sarah, equally cool, dispassionate and professional, found each other attractive. In the course of the month in which they were together they became, as Sarah puts it, "quite emotionally involved."

To have an affair with a professional colleague was a great risk for Sarah, far more than it was for him, and it was a risk she didn't want to take.

"You could ruin your professional reputation—throw it all away for a fling on a layover. For male pilots, it's different. It's almost expected of them. Not for us. We're not supposed to be emotional. Can't have flings. Can't fall in love. If you see a woman who's going to fall in love in the cockpit, you see a woman whose professionalism you're going to doubt. As soon as you become emotional, you're seen as unprofessional.

"And then there's that good old-fashioned thing called 'losing respect.' It's risky to date somebody you're working with, to have an affair. If—when—that affair ends, there's still something left. There's an echo of a relationship. You have that person to deal with, a person who has now become privy to your personal life and emotions. And maybe through him the entire company knows your most private affairs and feelings. Cheap talk gets about. A woman who's had an affair with another flight officer risks the possibility of becoming fair game for everyone else she works with. I could lose the respect I'd worked an entire career to earn."

But in spite of herself, Sarah was falling in love and finding it more and more difficult to handle the difficult task of separating her professional and personal lives.

As the month neared its end, Sarah and her captain figured it would be just as well they were to be parted before things got too hot to cool down. With bidding assignments the way they are, the chances were that they would never fly together again.

But fate took one of those strange turns, and the very next month they found themselves flying together again. It was the kind of pleasure-torment that neither of them wanted, and yet . . . And yet they nobly fought off temptation, like people of a much earlier generation.

For a while.

Sarah realized that she was looking forward to her work days more and more, that she was always worrying when the trip's last landing was over.

Some time during that second month they started spending as much time together as possible. She worried. What would be the result if the relationship didn't work? They talked about that, among other things. She wasn't hurting her job performance, but she could be jeopardizing her professional standing. There probably was some gossip. "Hey, you hear about Sarah? Easy mark!" That kind of stuff got to be less and less important.

But theirs was a considered kind of passion. "That month was filled with two- and three-day trips and plenty of time to get to know each other. On layovers, we'd talk while we jogged up and down beaches and around schoolyard tracks. The usual time spent with crews at restaurants and relaxing between flights gave us a chance to discover we liked the same sports, the same foods, music, books, humor, people and had the same hopes or expectations of life. And of course we shared the knowledge and love of flying. It was an important bond."

And then there was the simple closeness of a two-person cockpit. "Long flights at altitude with the autopilot gave us lots of time to talk. We were isolated in our own little room in the world, surrounded by the beautiful scenery of the sky. I'd always enjoyed the sights from thirty-five thousand feet—sunrises and sunsets, summer thunderstorms building in the distance, moonrises over the Atlantic and clear nights when you're caught between the stars above and the city lights below—but now it was as if each setting was for our pleasure. Everything that had been lovely before became even more beautiful and spectacular."

There was nothing about the dazzling stage settings or the intimacy of the cockpit to put a damper upon heightening feelings. Only common sense and a genuine dedication to their responsibilities kept these people concentrating on their work to the exclusion of their emotions. "We made our own personal rules to keep things professional. We'd have to wait until above eighteen thousand feet"—when traffic and radio communications are light, and the plane pretty much flies itself—"to talk to and about each other on a personal basis. And we talked about everything from geography to sentence construction, from aircraft systems to philosophies of life.

"Somewhere between the electrical system and Aristotle, he interrupted himself, turned to me abruptly and said, 'I'm in love with you.' " And her heart leapt.

That was the real beginning of something far more than an affair. The time spent together got to be more and more, longer and longer, and now these two pilots have plans to make a lifetime of it.

They're probably married by this time. But whatever the result of this situation, which is obviously not unknown in any walk of life, it's perfectly clear that there is one factor at work that cannot be pinned down by rules, regulations or even high ideals, and that is the human emotion. And there's no good reason why there shouldn't be a happy ending to sagas of love in the cockpit. Romance in the sky doesn't have to be a problem.

Better, perhaps, that the lovers should work different

shifts. Better yet, they should work different airlines. As noted, there have been some great demonstrations of pilot marriages. But I think one of the most joyous celebrations of love in the air is the union of Tangela and Rocky.

You know Tangela. She was the one with the Ph.D. and the Vidal Sassoon haircut. Of course, that was when her name was Angela.

Angela's story is that she was called out one cold and stormy night in Dallas to fill in for an absent flight engineer. She did her preflight walkaround in a downpour and entered the cockpit soaking wet. The captain, one Rocky Tricoli, a veteran of fifteen years with American Airlines, eyed her dripping hair and squelching feet and said, "Hey, a lady flight engineer! How about a kiss? I've always wanted to kiss my flight engineer!"

Weird, thought Angela. "First they call me out on a night like this, then I have to fly a three-day trip with a guy who wants to kiss a flight engineer." Well, it was only a matter of time before she ran into his type. Into each life some drips must fall.

But before the trip was over she realized that Rocky was no drip. He was a warm and friendly fellow who treated her in all ways as the professional she is except that, throughout the trip, he teased her gently about letting him kiss his flight engineer. So, as she left the airplane on the last leg of the flight, she let him plant a big kiss on her cheek. "We have," she notes austerely, "been friends ever since."

The wedding was far from austere. Angela never does anything by halves. She and Rocky chartered an American Boeing 707 jet, at a reputed fee of $3,500, dubbed it *Wedding Bells One,* equipped it with a volunteer company flight crew and invited something over a hundred relatives and friends—including me—to come along for the nuptial festivities. Bride, groom and volunteer crew wore Hawaiian costume in readiness for a luau to follow, adding an additional splash of color to already colorful proceedings.

Wedding muu-muu hitched up to her knees. Angela was at the controls on takeoff from Los Angeles International Airport. On gaining the desired altitude, she relinquished her post to the borrowed pilots and took a stately walk down the aisle with Rocky while the plane maintained a holding pattern over Santa Catalina. The ceremonies over, Rocky made his usual perfect landing.

Angela likes matching initials. Settling comfortably into wedded bliss, she proclaimed her new name: Tangela Tricoli.

Both she and Rocky still fly, and are living happily ever after.

Postscript. As for me, when I'm asked about sexual harassment on the job, I have to reply that I haven't had any. Affection, yes; brotherly-sisterly stuff, as noted; a very occasional leer. When other women talk of harassment, I silently ask myself, "Where's mine?"

Truth is, I have become part of the cockpit equipment to a degree that is almost irritating. Take the occasion on which we drew a particularly attractive selection of female flight attendants. The captain looked them over appreciatively and said, "Hmm . . . I see we have three terrific gals on board."

"Three?" I said. "*Three?* What about me?"

18

A New Day Has Begun

I couldn't believe what I was doing. Guilt and self-reproach kept gnawing away at the back of my mind. I ran the record of the past few hours through my head, and I could find hardly anything that I had done right. Oh, sure, I'd tried to leave earlier, but trying doesn't count. Not being insistent was the basic mistake. As pilot, I was responsible for everything that was going wrong. Nature sent the weather, but I should have avoided it. Bad luck compounded the problem, but we wouldn't have had the bad luck if I hadn't done something wrong in the first place. . . .

Useless to think along those lines, but the thoughts kept nagging me. Hour after hour, year after year, I had harped at my students: don't take risks. Don't give in to that Hurry-up, have-to-get-someplace-by-Monday-morning syndrome. Don't fly a single-engine airplane over mountains at night, and *especially* don't do it if you think you've got instrument conditions —*bad weather of any kind anywhere near*.

Well, there we were. It was after dark, the weather was a three-act drama of special effects, none of them favorable, I was piloting the Cessna 172 on instruments over the Adirondacks and we'd had an electrical malfunction. There were two of us. The guy in the right seat, who had cheerfully admitted he couldn't tell a Cessna from a sitting duck, was having a wonderful time, enchanted by the romantically dim light of the cockpit and nature's fireworks display building up ahead.

But we were in a very uncomfortable, potentially dangerous situation.

My companion, an individual of some romantic interest to me at the time, was doing a circuit of campaign politicking in New York State and had asked me to fly him around that Sunday so that he could make a few speeches and shake some hands.

What we should have done in the first place was to fly north and work our way south. We didn't. Leaving New York City early that morning, we gradually worked our way north to Lake Placid. The plan was to go on from there to Saranac Lake for a short stopover, and then fly directly back to Westchester Airport in the New York City area.

We had a great time heading north. At every stop I'd park my borrowed plane and read my book while a campaign staffer picked up my friend and whisked him off by car to do his campaign number. Then he would come back to the plane with maybe hamburgers from one place and maybe some wonderful Italian salami and provolone from the next, so we sort of picnicked our way through a bright, sunny wonderful day. The only little tiny, niggling concern was that the farther away we got from New York, the longer it would take to get back. And I had counted on doing the whole flight in daylight.

But it still wouldn't be a long trip. I had a flight plan, and I'd figured out that it would take us two hours to get from Saranac to Westchester. That was no problem in a Cessna 172, because it would have four hours of fuel aboard. And we had summer hours to fly in. I thought that, if we left at six o'clock in the evening, we'd get home at eight o'clock with two hours of fuel remaining and at least forty-five minutes of good solid daylight left.

Naturally, I kept paying attention to the weather as we racked up the mileage. The forecast was fine. It was a wonderful, warm, comforting day. However, that comforting feeling of an August day is probably due to the heavy moistness of the air, and the moist air on that particular day had all the ingredients of a dandy thunderstorm building up somewhere, sometime . . . a subtle, unsettling, churning quality, with a sort of lifting action. Pilots simply call it unstable air. We feel impending weather in our bones, no matter what the forecast.

But I didn't think it mattered. For one thing, it obviously wasn't imminent. For another, we'd still have full daylight for hours. We would only have to do about forty minutes of flying over any kind of mountainous area before getting to our approximate midway point of Albany, after which we'd take the scenic route right down over the Hudson River and a lot of small to large local airports with good radio communication contact. After that, a quick left turn, and over to Westchester. We'd also be in clear contact with Air Traffic Control in New York.

There was nothing to worry about as long as we had daylight. I looked at my charts and planned my checkpoints ahead of time: towns, villages, railroad tracks, rivers, landing fields, highways, the lot. It would be okay even if there were scattered thunderstorms. We'd be able to circumnavigate anything as long as we could see it. We had time.

Politicians . . . ! It got later and later. There was another hand to shake, another hello or goodbye, another tale of woe to listen to, another heated argument to rebut with carefully marshaled facts, all of which took time. Okay, he was smart, terrific in the way he talked to people, good-looking, pleasant company, but he was making me feel edgy. Mustn't get edgy. Still, gotta keep to that schedule. I was no longer sitting in the airplane, waiting. I was looking at my watch and pacing up and down the ramp. If only I'd gone with him this time, I could've been tugging at his sleeve. "Time to go. C'mon, wrap it up, let's go." But he was miles away.

When at last the staffer's car appeared, I dragged my passenger into the airplane and nailed him down. Time had been getting so short that I didn't even file a flight plan before leaving. I planned on filing VFR as soon as we took to the air—as soon as he was unquestionably aboard.

We finally got the wheels off the pavement at Saranac Lake at eight o'clock. My politician friend looked interestedly down at twilit treetops, and gave me one of his melting smiles.

I'd done one last weather check before leaving. There seemed to be no problem. The air was a little unsettled, the wind was out of the southwest, there was a haze layer, but nothing dramatic could be anticipated.

Time to file the VFR flight plan.

Within seconds, I knew we could be in for trouble. The haze layer was much thicker than it had appeared to be from the ground.

I kept on climbing up through it, climbing and climbing with the visibility close to nil, heading south with nothing but haze to look at. To the west, it was even worse. The setting sun had turned the haze into an opaque glare. There was no way I could fly visually, not if this kept up.

At about 7,500 feet, we got above the haze layer and started dodging clouds. They began to build. I called Flight Service and filed an instrument flight plan, then switched back to ATC. Since the airplane had the instrumentation, we might as well take advantage of the air traffic control system.

ATC cleared me up to nine thousand feet, and up we went.

The light was starting to go, and I didn't like that much.

We would have some sort of daylight as far as Albany, but from there on it was going to be *really* dark because of the cloud coverage. Gone were all the wonderful checkpoints I'd so carefully picked out when I'd planned to go by pilotage. Once in a while I caught the dull gleam of the Hudson River. That was all. I didn't even know where the airports were. I was going totally by radio navigation, cursing myself for behaving like an amateur on my day off from the 727.

Because of the haziness of the sky and the pollution around

the New York area, the sunset was magnificent. Through the billows of orange cloud we could see the sun sliding down. As it sank, a few stars blinked up overhead and spattered the evening sky.

My friend thought it was spectacular.

"Isn't this exciting!" he exclaimed. "That is really beautiful. How do you know where you're going? How do you track on the VOR? How about letting me fly a little?"

No problem about that. We were floating placidly as a leaf on a gentle stream. Just because we were flying IFR over darkening clouds didn't mean that we couldn't enjoy the exhilaration of the flight. Clearly he was getting a kick out of it.

In the dying light we skimmed over towns and airfields, invisible to us but not inaudible. I explained what the controls were for and how they were used. He held the yoke in front of him and touched the rudders with his feet, getting the feel of the airplane and that incredible sensation of being responsible for holding the craft in the air. Between making my various radio contacts, checking the map, watching the instruments and keeping us on course, I gave him a few pointers on navigation and the workings of the VOR.

He thought it was all terrific. And it was, for me, too, until my alternator circuit breaker popped.

It must be fate for me to have electrical problems in small planes. This time I had a flashlight and someone to hold it for me, fortunately a cool, unflappable fellow.

"What's happening?"

"Something's going wrong with the alternator. And in order to protect all the electrical and electronic circuits in the airplane, that circuit breaker pops out. So I'm turning off all my nonessential equipment, and I'm running off my twelve-volt battery."

He found that interesting, but by no means alarming.

Trouble was that, since I was flying on instruments and had to continue flying on instruments because I had no horizon and no reference to the ground, just about all my equipment was essential. I needed to keep the VOR going, just as much as I needed my background lights and my radios—basically all the electrical and electronic circuits. Sure, the battery should be able to do the job, but it was probably good for only about thirty minutes of flying time.

Well, I'd have to use the battery when absolutely necessary and push that circuit breaker back in. I pushed it in and we flew on wordlessly for a while, serene as any ordinary night flight with all systems operating. And then the alternator circuit breaker popped again.

The battery took over. As the minutes ticked by, lights began to dim and radio reception became scratchy and weak. Damn. Worst part of it was, I had no way of knowing what the electrical problem was or how to troubleshoot it. All I knew was that my time in the air was limited and I'd be lucky to get to Westchester with any kind of electricity operating. But way in the distance a vast blur of light was seeping up through the haze—Manhattan, with its spillover to the other boroughs. And I thought, Even if all electrical systems fail and I can't navigate, my engine's still going to keep going. If worse comes to worst I can just head right toward New York City and land at La Guardia or Kennedy. Sure, it's a little embarrassing to land there in a Cessna 172, but so what? Any port in a . . .

Storm. I was looking over to the right, about forty-five degrees from our course, to where the city would be in that smudge of filtered light. And right over it was the biggest, meanest-looking thunderstorm you ever saw.

I called the New York flight watch station and asked how the weather looked over La Guardia, Kennedy and Westchester airports. Approaching terrible at all three, they told me cheerfully, giving me a glowing report of a high energy thunderstorm presently over La Guardia moving at a rapid rate to the northeast.

Great. Just where I was going. Oh, God, if there's any way I can get this airplane to move faster and beat that storm! The lights were getting dimmer, the voices were getting thinner and my companion was having the time of his life. Oh, it was so romantic, so lovely, sitting in the soft light of the cockpit and looking over at a city that seen from the sky was a glow of orange smeared with black, like an enormous pile of autumn leaves on fire. And then those searing white bolts of lightning zigzagging from one black cloud to another—Halloween shapes and colors projected on a vast screen while we rode softly on a cushy layer of overcast and haze. Yeah, sensational.

Voices scratched thinly over the radio and the lights flickered.

"Most terrific, beautiful flight I've ever been on," said the guy next to me, turning away from the window with a pleased smile and using the flashlight to illuminate some documents he had decided to read in between thrilling incidents.

He seemed completely oblivious to the fact that we were in a dangerous situation.

But I was beating the storm. I was getting closer and closer to Westchester and I still had the use of the electrical system, erratic and threadbare as it was.

Westchester approach vectored me down for the final.

I had told ATC I had this slight radio problem, so they were aware of it. I pushed in my alternator circuit breaker one last time. The lights brightened, the radio volume intensified and I could not only see all the instruments with absolute clarity but also hear everybody on the air—no more of this please repeat stuff. I was all lined up on final approach, safe and sound, happy as a clam, feeling good. The air was still pretty smooth, I suppose the calm before the storm, as I switched over to Westchester tower and reported, "On final, outside the outer marker."

The tower said, "Cessna 9101 Hotel, would you mind making a three-sixty out there? We've got a Gulfstream II that's coming up behind you and we'd like to get him in front of you."

No problem, and I said so. He was probably cruising at 120 knots and I was puttering along at about 80 at that point.

"Sure, go ahead!"

I was just as secure as I could be. Weather okay, electricity okay, fuel okay, no reason why I shouldn't go around one time to let the speedier aircraft land first.

Cool as you like, I went into my 360-degree turn. I'd just come around to about 270 degrees when the air suddenly got extremely turbulent and heavy rain pellets, in the form of something very much like bullets of ice, started hitting the windshield.

At that point, I told the tower in no uncertain terms that I wasn't going to make another 360. The weather was catching up with me and I was going to intercept the final approach course and track it inbound.

Sensing my urgency, the tower responded instantly and with crisp professionalism. "Cessna 9101 Hotel, report the outer marker, cleared for the approach."

I reported the outer marker. The rain pellets dissipated as we got closer to the airport, because we'd cut in ahead of the coming storm, but the winds had picked up ferociously. They were a sort of mixed bag, coming from all directions, so there was quite a lot of wind-shear activity going on. Too much for a small plane. I knew that within minutes our airplane was going to be out of its environment—thrust into a situation beyond its limitations.

I kept the speed up on final with my flaps up. I didn't want to slow down; I wanted to outmaneuver the weather that was driving up behind me. What I had to do was get that plane down, and quickly. It was not a smooth approach.

"Gee whiz," said the fellow beside me, with his first slight trace of concern. "Can't you slow it down?"

I shot him a glacial look, sideways, saying nothing. We came in fast and thumped down in one of those hardworking, never-let-it-relax landings, very calculated and very firm. The moment we touched down, the alternator circuit breaker blew again. Our lights went out, and stayed out. I found out later that the voltage regulator was malfunctioning and that the fuses had melted into each other because of the extreme heat.

The rain was catching up with us again, splatting on the windshield and hitting the aluminum wings with a sort of pinging sound. Without taking time out to transfer me to ground control, Westchester tower directed me to the general aviation ramp. Speaking through a tinny drumroll of sound as the deluge hit us, I called Westchester Operations and asked them if they would please send a car over to the tie-down area to pick us up. A staticky voice answered, "Affirmative. Will send someone right over."

My passenger unloaded the airplane and stowed our few belongings in the courtesy car while I ran around tying down the plane. It was more than the usual tie-down job because I wanted to make sure that the airplane would be absolutely secure against the violent weather. Winds were picking up into near-hurricane gusts by the time I'd tied down the last wing and leapt into the car, soaked to the skin and wet hair plastered down my face.

We had landed at a dark, dirty ten o'clock instead of at a nice, clean, dry, summer-sunny eight. I was not in my merriest mood as we transferred to my car in the parking lot. Nor was I very chatty during the drive to Manhattan.

He drove while I pondered. My thoughts were filled with all the reasons why we shouldn't have taken off, why we shouldn't have come back that night. Okay, so there were Monday morning appointments. We could have spent the night upstate somewhere and come home early. And even postponed the appointments if necessary, instead of taking the chance of canceling them permanently. Flying home in the morning would have been the safest, most logical thing to do.

My own voice echoed hollowly in my head, laying down the law to my students. And I had just done all the things I'd told them not do to. I had broken all the rules of good judgment.

Not only that, I was letting people down. I could have let them down a whole lot worse if we hadn't had a bit of luck in sneaking in under the worst of the weather. I could see the headlines:

HOTSHOT FEMALE AIRLINE PILOT KILLS HERSELF
AND COMPANION IN CRASH OF SMALL AIRPLANE.

Some hot shot. Some example.

I preached silently to myself all the way home, telling myself that at least I'd learned a lesson and wouldn't make the same mistake again. It had been a pretty bad scene.

The man of the moment, on the other hand, thought it all very exciting and lots of fun. Going around all those wonderful puffy clouds and watching that beautiful display of fireworks had been an incomparable, memorable experience. I glowered at him. He gave me back a melting smile. Why shouldn't he? He hadn't understood a thing about what we'd been going through, and the worst discomfort he had suffered was getting a little wet while dashing from the airplane to the car.

One nice thing, though. He had kept his cool and trusted me to fly the airplane. Another nice thing: we'd come home safely.

I watched this imperturbable guy as we wound our way through the soggy streets of Manhattan. How could he keep buzzing with energy and still be so laid-back at the same time? Did he really not know what we'd been through? Strange!

But, for some reason, I kinda liked the guy.

The job had been getting slightly humdrum. Maybe that had had something to do with my sudden outbreak of unprofessionalism.

One can get stale, and one shouldn't permit it.

Staleness is no excuse for a mistake, and I was not about to use it as such, but the episode did pull me up short and make me think.

Was I bored with being flight engineer after so many years on the line?

Yes, a little. I didn't like the sense of being stagnant. I had thought that, by this time in my life, I might be close to getting in line for the left seat.

Captain Bonnie Tiburzi. . . . Still sounded good. I had been initiated into the International Order of Characters, which gives every member a nickname, as Captain Bonnie. I would have to face up to the fact that that might be the only way I'd ever make captain.

Or perhaps I was being unduly pessimistic. But, with the demise of Braniff, and the layoffs and cutbacks and economic upheavals throughout the majors, I might very well have to wait another ten or fifteen years. That seemed like forever. When I was first hired, I looked forward to an apprenticeship of about that long. What was I doing—standing still? Kidding myself? If I cared to switch to a smaller airline, I might yet speed up the process of advancement.

But I didn't want to. And the longer I thought about it, the less I wanted to. American was family now.

Being bumped back to flight engineer had given me a chance to see that there was a world outside the cockpit, and that maybe the cockpit wasn't even the center of the world. It represented, for me, a marvelous, enviable job in which I hoped to rise, but it wasn't the whole of life. I was glad that I had found myself to be an adequate representative for products and causes of various sorts. If something were to stall my career as a professional flier, I would nonetheless be capable not only of flying but of serving as a spokeswoman for women in aviation now and for those who wish to be. I could teach ground school, write articles, give lectures. Maybe even write a couple of books.

Of course, I would *love* to fly captain, and I have every hope that I'll still make it.

There is no question, though, that today we're at the end of an era. Airline flying isn't what it used to be, even to those of us who still get rhapsodic about rainbows and fabulous cloud formations. That swift and exciting progression from DC-6s to Constellations to 707s and 747s, and flying the transcons and hopping over the Atlantic to long layovers in Paris and Rome and establishing enduring links with many parts of the world . . . those days are almost gone. The captain doesn't stroll down the aisle anymore and chat with the people, an Olympian personage showing off his buttons and stripes and expertise. Passengers cannot come up to the cockpit and visit the way they used to, because they might turn out to be hijackers. On some flights you cannot even enjoy the sights anymore. "Ladies and gentlemen, we are now, as you know, crossing the Atlantic, and if you look down very quickly below you to the right you will see the *Q.E.2*—" and *voom,* you're supersonically gone, craning your neck and seeing nothing.

What happened to the thrill? There's a lot of jokes and laughter, but not much adventure. The romance and the glamour and the glory went out as progress came in, in the same way as the great overland railroads faded away. We still have cowboys in the sky, guys who think they have exclusives on the airplanes, but they are few and they don't seem to realize that the Indians, the sodbusters, the pioneer women in their bonnets and the vast herds of buffalo are gone. Technology has overlain history. It has gotten to the point where we are flying computers with wings. And it's almost irrelevant who's flying them.

Except if it's me . . .

Can't get around it. The magic lingers on.

There was an ISA meeting in Jamaica awhile back, at a time when the full complement of working women airline pilots, worldwide, was about 140. The number is lower right now, but we're convinced that the condition is temporary. Most furloughed women will be rehired, either by their own airlines or others, and young companies are already hiring female fliers.

We talked about our beginnings with the airlines, maybe a little more than usual because, within our time, a number of female astronauts have been hired by NASA. They were scientists rather than fliers, but we were nonetheless proud of them. We wondered what kind of hard days they'd been through to get accepted. And we were glad that another area of endeavor had opened to women.

As for ourselves, we did some reassessing. None of us, we agreed, had deliberately decided to become an airline pilot for the sake of pushing a cause or displaying militant feminism. Practical feminists do what they're good at, and if that runs a gamut that includes playing classical guitar, raising a family and flying an airplane, so much the better. I think, in time, some of us did get to the point of being a little more belligerent than we had expected ourselves to be.

Those of us who belong to the first generation of women airline pilots can see the difference between ourselves and the next generations. There *was* something a little quirky about us. As originals, we waded blindly into an area that was virtually closed to us, and found we had to compete more strenuously than our male colleagues to hold our own as *personalities*. So we did. We tried to be a little better than the job required us to be, and a little more aggressive than our private selves. Some of us put on an act of being thick-skinned; some came across as being arrogant and pushy. It was a way to sideswipe or ward off ridicule and putdowns, and hide the fact that we were hurt by insulting behavior. If we came out swinging, it was to avoid being swung at rather more than we felt was necessary.

But the next batch was different. For a while—a rather short while—when the airlines were very healthy, people who didn't care all that much about flying were picking up licenses because the airlines were hiring, the money was good and being a pilot was probably more fun than sitting at a desk.

Our new kids are different in yet another way. They've got something of everything except the mixed blessing of being unwitting trailblazers. They like to fly, they like the excitement, the money's okay and they don't have to fool around breaking down any barriers. I'm sure they get some flak, but the younger male pilots of today have grown up seeing and accepting women in every setting from coed college dormitories through D.A.s' and doctors' offices to the boardrooms of major companies, and they don't think it's cool to make cheap wisecracks at the competent women who occupy the cockpit with them.

Today's women have more anonymity than the first of us had. You can't see the chips on their shoulders and they don't bristle the way some of us used to. We old-timers in our early to mid-thirties tend to think that they're a little less colorful than we were, a little less dynamic. But then, there's no reason why they should be flamboyant—no reason why any airline pilot has to be.

After the serious discussions of that day in Jamaica, largely concerned with the future of women in the industry and the contribution that ISA can make to its members of today and tomorrow, we went on swapping stories well into the night . . . anecdotes about other fliers, cozy little stories about boyfriends, husbands, children, forthcoming marriages and the propensity of the guys on the airplane to run each boarding female through some kind of mental scanner. One of the highlights of the day had been Denise Blankenship's account of her recent rise to captain with Piedmont, concluding with a vow that girl-watching was going to be strictly rationed as long as she was in the left seat.

"I'm gettin' all the guys to go on a guy watch. All these years I've been up there, and it's been, Lookee here, Lookee there, and you look and it's some girl coming up. But now its gonna be, Okay, check out the men! We're gonna watch men today!"

Another of her stories had been about her very first trip,

the one on which almost everything in the world had gone wrong. During one of the innumerable delays, a woman passenger with a worried look had flagged down a flight attendant.

Said Denise: "This passenger said to the flight attendant, 'Ma'am, is that lady the captain?' And the flight attendant says, 'Yes, yes, she is.' And the passenger says, 'Well, that figures why we're having all this trouble.' "

The hotel had given our group a wing to ourselves on the third floor. Dinner over, night life sampled, we went off to our various rooms. Beverley and I were sharing, which meant that after all the goodnights were said we went on talking.

Yawning but still gossipy, we prepared for bed. Inevitably, the main topic was male-female relationships on the airlines and how the guys persist in making our womanhood an issue.

Once, Beverley told me, she'd flown copilot with a guy who was so apprehensive about flying with a female that he just stared at her the whole time, watching her every move. Ordinarily a pleasant and friendly fellow, he was just frozen by being paired with her.

"He flies *so* nicely, this guy," says Beverley, "but he made only an okay landing in Chicago. Just so-so. Coming into New York it was my leg. It was a bad night but I got real lucky and made a really nice landing in La Guardia. I mean, it really was a whole lot better than his.And he turns to me and says admiringly, 'You bitch!' And we both laughed."

Then there's the pregnancy issue, the big debate topic called Should Woman Pilots Have to Stop Flying the Moment They're Pregnant?

The Air Line Pilots Association once commissioned a study of that vital question, and the doctors came back and said, Definitely not, to be pregnant was a natural state for women. They could fly as long as they could get the controls back in their laps.

But the guys were making such a production about it! If you get pregnant, you have to stop flying right away.

Beverley thought this was pretty silly, and decided to have some fun with it.

"So I went to Al Brown, you know, Chief Pilot in Dallas, and I said, 'I just want to ask one question about our maternity clause.' He said, 'Yeah, well, what is it?' And I said, 'Well, I was just wondering, if it happened on a layover, do we get to deadhead home or do we have to work the trip?' He said, 'Beverley, get out of here! Just get out of my office!' "

We were laughing about this and getting ready to turn out the lights when there was a crisp knock-knock on the door. Like schoolkids in a dorm, we thought it was going to be someone complaining about us being too raucous so late at night. We opened the door and there was Denise—Captain Denise Blankenship—standing there filling the frame, all six feet of her, partially clad in skimpy little baby-doll pajamas, all pink and lacy, and her captain's hat.

"This is Captain Blankenship," she said sternly. "I've taken it upon myself to take charge of you all, and I'm making a bedcheck.

Whereupon she bounced away, laughing her head off, to rap smartly on the adjacent door.

Rank has its privileges.

And we laughed some more.

We may be a lot of things, but pompous we're not.

I don't have quite the presence that some of the taller, more striking women have, so I don't think I'll ever be able to top Denise's wonderfully triumphant arrival at the rank of captain.

Meanwhile, I may very well have the opportunity of checking out that maternity clause myself. I intend flying as long as I can, but there's no telling right now when I might have to take time off to attend to family matters.

I already attended to one of them.

I'm finding it possible to combine a flying career with a marriage to someone who is not a pilot and is only interested in flying to the degree that he is interested in everything in the world around him—especially me.

The guy who thought it was so beautiful and so much fun to fly around a thunderstorm . . . he is the one. We're husband and wife.

Could it be that I have it all? My career has opened a lot of doors for me, and flying has been supplemented by so many other things that some days I can hardly believe my luck.

I don't think I could be happier than I am today.

But tomorrow looks good, too!